DESCRIBING DISCOURSE

A PRACTICAL GUIDE TO DISCOURSE ANALYSIS

DESCRIBING DISCOURSE

A PRACTICAL GUIDE TO DISCOURSE ANALYSIS

Nicola Woods

HODDER
ARNOLD
AN HACHETTE UK COMPANY

First published in Great Britain in 2006 by
Hodder Education, an Hachette UK Company,
338 Euston Road, London NW1 3BH

www.hoddereducation.com

The advice and information in this book are believed to be true and
accurate at the date of going to press, but neither the authors nor the publisher
can accept any legal responsibility or liability for any errors or omissions.

British Library Cataloguing in Publication Data
A catalogue record for this book is available from the British Library

Library of Congress Cataloging-in-Publication Data
A catalog record for this book is available from the Library of Congress

ISBN-10: 0 340 809 612
ISBN-13: 978 0 340 809 617

Typeset in 10/12pt Berling Roman by Phoenix Photosetting, Chatham, Kent

What do you think about this book? Or any other Hodder
Education title? Please send your comments to the feedback
section on www.hoddereducation.com.

Contents

For Peter

Acknowledgements

Extra special thanks to Jonathan Wetton, who helped me to put this book together. I am extremely grateful for his meticulous and painstaking editing work that has been invaluable in making this text what it is. Thanks also to my colleagues in the Department of Linguistics and English Language at Sussex University for their support, collegiality and friendship. I am grateful to Bianca Knights at Hodder Arnold for her help and guidance. Finally, thanks to my students – particularly those who, over the years, have taken my courses *Discourse in Public Life* and *Discourse and Society*. This text grew out of those courses and owes much to the stimulating student discussions and debates that took place within them. Some of the real-life data included in the text was originally collected by my students, for which I am most grateful.

Every effort has been made to trace and acknowledge the owners of copyright. The publishers will be glad to make suitable arrangements with any copyright holders whom it has not been possible to contact.

The author and publisher would like to thank the following for the use of artwork in this volume.

p2 courtesy of The Advertising Archives; **p4** Apple logo reproduced with kind permission of Apple Computer, Inc.; Bic logo reproduced with kind permission of Société Bic; Citroën logo reproduced with kind permission of Citroën; Diners Club logo reproduced with kind permission of Diners Club International Ltd.; Ericsson logo reproduced with kind permission of Ericsson Ltd.; HSBC logo® is a registered trademark of HSCB Holdings plc. Hodder & Stoughton Ltd Licensee of the trademark; Johnnie Walker logo reproduced with kind permission of Diageo plc.; Mercedes-Benz three-pointed star logo reproduced with kind permission of DaimlerChrysler AG, Stuttgart, Germany; Michelin Tyreman logo reproduced with kind permission of Michelin North America Inc; MSN® Internet Services butterfly logo reproduced with permission of Microsoft Corporation; The Nestlé brand logo is reproduced with the kind permission of Société des Produits Nestlé S.A.; The Dog Trumpet Roundel Device® is a registered trademark of HMV Group plc through HMV (IP) Limited and is reproduced with the kind permission of HMV Group plc.; Renault logo reproduced with kind permission of Renault UK; Shell trade mark reproduced with permission of Shell Brand International AG; The 'Walking Fingers' logo is a registered trade mark owned by Yell Limited, and reproduced with permission; **p6** courtesy of The Advertising Archives; **p7** with kind permission of the Conservative Party/courtesy of The Advertising Archives; **p8** © Crown Copyright; **p10** courtesy of The Advertising Archives; **p11** © Photographer: Kevin Summers, Agent: Paula Claridge; **p21** reproduced with kind permission of Heinz; **p22** © Paul Lowe/ Greenpeace; **p30** supplied with the kind permission of the Labour Party, www.labour.org.uk; **p37** courtesy of The Advertising Archives; **p39** reproduced with kind permission of Suzuki; **p40** reproduced with kind permission of Ford; **pp42–44** courtesy of The Advertising Archives; **pp49–50** with kind permission of the Conservative Party/**p49** courtesy of The Advertising Archives; **p82** © Michal Mañas; **p102** reproduced with permission of Microsoft Corporation; **p109** © Time Inc./Time Life Pictures/Getty Images; **p119** reproduced with kind permission of Healthcare Events Ltd www.healthcare-events.co.uk; **p131** Topfoto/Ann Ronan; **pp133–134** © Crown Copyright; **p136** © Crown Copyright; **pp153–155** © Crown Copyright.

Introduction

Language

Language is integral to the fabric of our daily life: we talk, we listen, we read and we write. We learn – at school, at home, in our work and our leisure time – and this learning is achieved largely through language. In our jobs or professions and in our everyday experience we deal with people: we may have to manage them, teach them, heal them, defend them or bargain with them; we may have to convince them, counsel them, reassure them, dissuade them, break bad news to them or justify our actions to them. In our human relationships, invariably, we all need to explain things to people, tell them our stories, consult with them about a problem, make plans either with them or on their behalf, or complain to them of unfair or unjust treatment. We make friends, try to please them, entertain them and amuse them. Alternatively, we may want to exert power over people or grant power to them; we may want to negotiate our position with them or renegotiate it at some later stage. All these activities, these social relations of ours, involve language; most of them, in fact, are more or less wholly circumscribed by linguistic communication.

For language is a social practice – and many would want to say that it is the defining social practice. Our social relationships are almost wholly realized in language; language leads us to act and behave in certain ways, and it is a powerful shaping force in how we think about and construct the world we live in. It would certainly be a mistake to believe that our social practices consist of nothing but language; but it is equally certain that the way we use language is an essential part of our human experience. It may even be largely through the social practice of language that we actually 'construct' ourselves as we negotiate our way through life.

Our language has different levels of structure: sounds, words, grammar, and so forth. But just as language does not exist in a social void, so the elements of language do not exist in a vacuum either. Words do not 'contain' meaning in themselves and meaning is not 'discovered' in them: meaning is something we construct, as social beings, in our own minds. We all have different minds, personalities and individualities, and so we also construct different meanings, for ourselves and for each other, in our use of language. And if it is through our social and linguistic relationships with the rest of the world that we construct meaning, then without the context of those relationships our language is essentially meaningless.

Since meaning is constructed – negotiated, if you prefer – in our social practice of language, rather than simply contained in words, then it follows that the relationship between the forms and functions of our language is necessarily flexible. No linguistic form – be it a word, a phrase or a sentence – can simply be associated with one particular function or meaning. Our utterances mean what we intend them to mean, and the essentially cooperative practice of our social behaviour ensures that our linguistic intentions are, for the most part, understood by those with whom we interact – regardless of their syntactic form or their dictionary definitions. Thus, while the utterance, 'It's getting late', may be classified as *declarative* in its syntactic structure, it may not necessarily perform a simple *informing* function. If uttered by a speaker waiting for a lift at the end of a long night, it will quite reasonably be understood as a *request* to be taken home. The speaker is (syntactically) *declaring* something to be the case, yes, but the intention of this linguistic item of social behaviour – the meaning negotiated in this context – is to *ask for* something to be done.

By the same token, any particular communicative function, whether informing, questioning or commanding, may be fulfilled by a variety of linguistic forms. A teacher who wishes to maintain order in her class may exclaim, 'Who's talking?', using an *interrogative* form to perform the function of *ordering* someone to stop talking. Her intended meaning will be understood perfectly – in the context.

Indeed, the reason that this complex and fluid arrangement actually works in practice lies in the crucial concept of *context*. We understand that 'Who's talking?' functions as a command, but only when we know the context in which it is uttered: in this case, by a schoolteacher in a classroom. If the same expression is articulated (even by the same teacher) in a different context – perhaps apprehensively asking a friend in the kitchen if her dinner party guests are getting on with each other – then the function and meaning of the interrogative form, 'Who's talking?', will be correspondingly different, and yet will be understood just as readily. Similarly, if the same expression is used in a classroom, but not by a teacher, then different functions and meanings again will be associated with the utterance.

The ability to communicate competently requires us to learn and understand the dynamic and shifting system of communication in context, and we learn it by becoming familiar with patterns and routines of language usage. Without necessarily realizing it at a conscious level, we follow socially and culturally constructed communicative conventions. Even a simple task such as buying a newspaper will involve us in a complex and carefully observed routine of communicative etiquette; handling relationships with our intimates entails correspondingly more intricate patterns of interaction.

How easy is it, for example, to finish a conversation with a friend? There is often much more involved than a simple exchange of farewells. In order to close the conversation without giving offence we may have to make excuses: 'Anyhow, I have to run now, I'm late'; or make an excuse on our friend's behalf: 'I won't stop here chatting; I know you need to get on'. We may adopt the strategy of arranging the time for our next meeting: 'I've got to go now, but I'll see you at Sue's next week'; or choose to leave the arrangement merely implied, as in 'See you later' – a form of farewell that has now become so conventional that we sometimes say it to people we are unlikely ever to meet again, in spite of what the words suggest that it *ought* to mean.

Our use of language, then, depends on an ability to negotiate our way through a complex network of conventions, assumptions and expectations. If an interaction departs from the patterns that our expectations lead us to predict, it can be an uncomfortable experience. Our first instinct, in fact, is to try to find some explanation for this departure from usual custom; for example, we will wonder if we have misunderstood the context in some way, or whether perhaps the person we are speaking to is 'suggesting', in an indirect manner, something that we would normally expect them to express more directly. If no explanation can be found (that is to say, if nothing in the context of our assumptions and expectations can reasonably be shifted to accommodate the departure from conversational convention), we conclude that communication has broken down and we adopt whatever language strategy we consider appropriate to deal with this. The importance of context, and its effect on our interpretation of discourse, will be a central theme in this book.

Discourse

The relatively recent adoption by linguists of the term 'discourse' for the subject we study when we examine 'language in use' – the real language that real people use in the real world – is at least partly a recognition of the fact that language is very much more than just the sum of the linguistic elements that compose it. Discourse is, at the very least, language plus context – by which I mean the context that we bring with us when we use language; the context that includes our experience, assumptions and expectations; the context we change (and which is itself changed) in our relationships with others, as we both construct and negotiate our way through the social practices of the world we live in.

Even if you are approaching discourse analysis for the first time, it may be that you have come across definitions of discourse already: you may have brought your own meaning with you to this book. You may already have certain assumptions and expectations of what the study of discourse involves. But discourse analysis is practised and studied by people working in a variety of academic fields – including linguistics, philosophy, anthropology and sociology – as well as by many working within related professions. This wide diversity in both practice and practitioners has led to an equally wide diversity of aims and approaches to discourse analysis, and it is generally recognized that there is neither a single coherent theory nor a single definition of discourse.

Some would define discourse as language use above the level of the sentence. I have just characterized discourse, rather figuratively, as language plus context. In this book we will examine discourse in its broadest sense, as real language in use. Discourse analysts examine spoken, signed and written language, and may focus on any aspect of linguistic behaviour, from the study of particular patterns of pronunciation, through word choice, sentence structure and semantic representation, to the pragmatic analysis of how we organize speech encounters.

A wide array of linguistic 'texts' are explored in the study of discourse. These might consist of a conversation or a letter; a speech, a memo or a report; a broadcast, a newspaper article or an interview; a lesson, a consultation or a confrontational encounter; an advertisement, a flyer or a piece of gossip. Discourse analysts are as concerned (if not more so) to examine the way in which meaning is constructed *throughout* the text, as with the way this is achieved at any one point *in* the text. Intertextuality is important too: that is to say, how language is used not only throughout a single text, but also *across* a set of different but related texts. Texts have histories, and so discourses created at different times stand as reference points for each other; when, for example, a politician makes a promise, it will often be viewed in the light of pledges made in a former discourse.

But what is it that analysts are looking for when they analyse a piece of discourse? I have suggested that they are interested in the way that language is used, but what does this mean in practice? One answer is that it depends on which approach they are taking. The process of discourse analysis can be characterized (although I am simplifying now) in terms of two approaches, and we might think of these as the 'top-down' and 'bottom-up' aspects of analysis.

In the top-down approach, discourse analysts begin from an understanding or a conceptualization (their own) of the context in which the discourse is taking place. This understanding of the context informs and colours their analysis, and they look 'down' from this position into the utterances produced and rehearsed, in the expectation of finding evidence – linguistic evidence – of the assumptions, expectations and social constructs that create and define that context. A top-down approach to political discourse, for example, will be informed by the analyst's own characterization of the political realities against which the discourse is happening. If the analyst believes, or has reason to believe, that the electorate is being hoodwinked by a politician's manipulation of the meaning of certain political constructs, then it is evidence of this manipulation that the analyst will be seeking and endeavouring to make apparent.

A bottom-up approach, by contrast, will tend to begin with an analysis of the language – the sounds, words, utterances, interactional routines, and so forth – that are used in the discourse. Here the analyst will look for evidence that discourse is being constructed in a particular way. Rare words might be used especially frequently, for example, or words and phrases might apparently be chosen more for their sound than for their meaning; constructions might seem to be particularly complex; or certain phrases might appear to favour one set of 'specialized' meanings rather than another more 'everyday' set. An analysis of such distinctive language in the discourse will lead the analyst to speculate as to its motivation, and thereby to arrive at some understanding of a context that may account for it.

In reality, of course, the distinction between the two aspects, top-down and bottom-up, is not even remotely as clear-cut as I have dared to suggest. No analysis is ever entirely free of the analyst's own view of the context, and a totally bottom-up approach would certainly be an oddly formal and mechanical affair; equally, a top-down approach will almost always want to concern itself at some stage – and often in quite a detailed way – with the particular linguistic items that seem to stand as evidence of the manipulation or other device that the analyst has set out to expose.

In case you happen to be involved already in one of the methods of discourse analysis that already uses notions of 'top-down' and 'bottom-up' in another sense altogether, then I should point out that my characterization could just as easily have been framed as 'outside-in' and 'inside-out', respectively. The point I want to stress is that there is an intricate (and almost symbiotic) interplay between the approach that interprets utterances from the starting point of the context in which the discourse takes place, and the approach that takes as its starting point the linguistic level at which the utterances are produced. They are, more precisely, two essential aspects of discourse analysis; and not at all two different ways of doing it.

So, while the focus here is on the practical analysis of the language of certain professional discourses, at particular points we will naturally touch on a number of theoretical perspectives. Since we are most interested in real language in real use, the approaches that we will find most useful are those that focus on the dynamics of speech (and writing) as situated social practice.

Theoretical approaches to language use

As we have already seen, it is a fundamental principle that language is more than just sounds, words and sentences. In fact, when we speak (or write), not only do we say something, but we also do something, and not merely in the trivial sense that speaking and writing involve physical actions or movements. In using language we intend to convey particular meanings, and our utterances have a certain force that has consequential effects on our addressee(s). These ideas lie at the heart of **speech act theory**, an approach to the explanation of language pioneered by the philosophers Austin and Searle in the 1960s. The approach grew from original observations by Austin that there is a class of utterances for which the act of uttering them is genuinely the act of performing the process in question: 'I apologize', 'I promise' and 'I deny' are typical examples of such **performative** utterances. The exact form of words is not the issue here; it is simply that the process of apologizing, promising or denying is performed verbally, and it is the uttering of the words that constitutes performing the action. The words, in a real sense, are the deed.

In contrast to this use of language that does what is says, much of our linguistic interaction is implicit and indirect. What a speaker *means* may deviate from what is literally *said*, and in order to interpret indirect speech the addressee must draw upon a number of interrelated and interwoven factors, including the nature of the speech situation, the larger linguistic context of the utterance, the aims and goals of the conversation and the background 'knowledge' shared between participants in the interactional episode. The philosophical work of Paul Grice (1975) is often invoked in discussing conversation and indirectness. Grice argued that conversation does not (normally) consist of a succession of disconnected remarks, but rather is a cooperative endeavour in which conversationalists mutually acknowledge the direction and purpose (or purposes) of speech exchanges. In accepting the **cooperative principle**, we seek to make our conversational contributions appropriately truthful, informative, relevant and clear. These four aspects of conversational cooperation – which are descriptive rather than prescriptive, incidentally – are often set out as Grice's **maxims of conversation**. In simple terms, they can be summed up thus:

- *Maxim of quality: **speakers' contributions should be truthful and speakers should not make statements for which they do not have evidence.***

- *Maxim of quantity: **speakers should make their contributions as informative as required, but no more.***

- *Maxim of manner: **speakers should make their contributions in a brief and orderly manner and avoid obscurity and ambiguity.***

- *Maxim of relevance: **speakers' contributions should be relevant and relate to the purposes of the speech exchange.***

What is important for us here is that, because of the essentially cooperative nature of conversation, if one or more of these maxims appears to be flouted or broken, we nevertheless still endeavour to interpret some meaning from what is said: we will try to infer the **conversational implicature** of the speaker's utterance. So it is that when a doctor tells her unfortunate patient, 'There's only so much more that we can do,' the patient knows that the prospects for her future health are likely to be poor.

In settings such as medical consultations, indirect speech can be used to soften the impact of harsh news. But we all use indirect speech in our everyday interactions and it is a strategy that we rely on particularly when we wish to phrase our utterances in a polite form. As we mentioned earlier, 'It's getting late' is more indirect than 'Give me a lift home now'; it is also more polite.

Politeness theory, as developed by Brown and Levinson (1987), examines the way in which people conduct conversations and other types of interaction in a way that engages with what Goffman (1967) refers to as 'face-work'. In everyday speech encounters we often have to ask for favours, issue demands and make promises, as well as carry out an array of other communicative tasks which involve making 'face-threatening acts'. For example, the act of borrowing something from a friend may threaten both our own face (we do not wish to appear to be in need) and also that of our friend (who may not wish to part with the object we want to borrow). Brown and Levinson distinguish between two types of 'face-wants': **negative face**, relating to our need to act without impediment, and **positive face**, relating to our need to be approved of by (at least some) others. In order to soften the blow of face-threatening acts we employ particular linguistic strategies. For example, when making a request to a friend, we may use politeness strategies that pay attention to their positive face: 'Please can I borrow your beautiful red dress? You have such good taste in clothes.' Alternatively, we may employ negative politeness strategies by, for example, making a request in a deferential way that seeks to mitigate the threat that a request entails: 'I know it's an imposition, but could I possibly borrow your red dress?' And, as we have seen, indirect speech itself is also a useful politeness strategy: 'I'd love to go to the party, but I've got absolutely nothing to wear.'

As well as engaging with culturally constructed conventions in how we say something (being, for example, polite, indirect or relevant), we also have to manage carefully the sequential structure of our speech exchanges. Conversation is orderly, and so an utterance is interpreted by reference to its turn within a sequence. In everyday interactions we follow a particular etiquette of taking turns at speaking and, in these turns, we raise and rehearse certain topics. Patterns of turn-taking and topic management, along with many other aspects of the structuring and sequencing of social interaction, are studied in the approach of **conversation analysis**. This research tradition, which grew out of ethnomethodology (the study of how social order is constructed in the socially organized conduct of the members of a society), seeks to examine the competences that speakers rely on in participating in interaction: how do we construct our own conversational behaviour and how do we deal with and interpret that of others? Conversation analysis deals solely with 'naturally occurring' speech and, while recognizing that there is no value-free observation, is careful not to impose pre-established structures and definitions on how speakers talk in interaction. In this way, conversation analysis aims to study how conversational behaviour relates to the creation of social roles, social relationships and a sense of social order.

The importance of avoiding social and cultural bias in studying the language customs and conventions used in different contexts also underpins an approach to language called the **ethnography of speaking** (also referred to as ethnography of communication). Arguing against the dominant position of the time, in the 1960s and 1970s Dell Hymes claimed that linguistic theory should not only be involved with explaining a speaker-hearer's knowledge of grammaticality, but also with the examination of communicative behaviour in the context of culture. Those who take an ethnographic approach to language and discourse focus on the cultural values and social roles that operate in particular communities. They are particularly concerned not to impose their own cultural presuppositions on other societies, and use intricate methods of participant observation to study the language habits and customs of different cultures: for example, researchers may live among the community of speakers for lengthy periods of time in order to observe the minute, culturally defined details of language use.

In this book I have focused on the discourse constructed in the culture of which I am a member. Apart from the limitation that the analysis presented is naturally restricted to the culture being studied (if I had chosen to look at advertising discourse in Egypt, for example, or political rhetoric in Japan, then I would certainly have identified different discourse customs and conventions), the study of the language and discourse of one's own culture poses a particular methodological problem. As ethnographers point out, we are all so entrenched within our own culture that it is often difficult to achieve the (social) distance required to identify accurately its customary social practices (including socially conventionalized linguistic behaviour and discourse practices). To overcome this difficulty it is essential that the examination of language and discourse should be undertaken from an evaluative and critical position.

It is precisely such an examination that lies at the heart of work undertaken by discourse analysts such as Norman Fairclough, Tuen van Dijk and Ruth Wodak. The interdisciplinary analytical perspective known as **critical discourse analysis** seeks to examine language as a form of cultural and social practice, and it is an approach which allows the description and interpretation of social life as it is represented in talk and texts. Critical discourse analysis focuses particularly on the relationship between power and discourse, studying the way in which 'social power abuse, dominance, and inequality are enacted, reproduced, and resisted by text and talk in the social and political context' (van Dijk 2001: 352). The critical approach aims to challenge social orders and practices that we accept as 'natural', but which are, in fact, 'naturalized'; in other words, when one way of seeing and interpreting the world becomes so common (and so frequently constructed in discourses) that it is accepted as the *only* way. In casting light on this process, critical discourse analysts seek to make visible the 'common-sense' social and cultural assumptions (or ideologies) which, below the level of conscious awareness, are embedded in all forms of language that people use (Fairclough 2001).

Keeping this in mind, examine the following:

Corridor E2

Please vacate your rooms between 10 and 11 a.m. on Thursday mornings.

Your cleaner will need access to all rooms to carry out her duties at this time.

Thank you.

At a relatively superficial level we are able to make a number of immediate assumptions, I think, about the discourse transcribed above: for example, that the original form of the data was written, and quite possibly that it was presented as some type of notice. In examining its format, we might observe that the notice is composed in three parts, which we could characterize as heading, main body of text and closing. If we go into further detail, we see that the main body is itself composed of two sentences, which include an array of vocabulary from different word classes: nouns, verbs, adjectives, pronouns, and so on. Looking at it with a rather more 'comparative' eye, we might feel that the choice of the verb 'vacate' rather than, for example, 'leave', gives the notice a somewhat formal tone. The use of the polite forms 'please' and 'thank you' might even lead us to categorize the notice as a polite request.

Would this be a correct classification? The word 'polite' does seem to crop up in all manner of settings, and indeed often signals discourse that is neither particularly polite nor even, strictly, a request:

Polite notice: No smoking

Polite notice: No parking

Polite notice: Turn off all mobile phones

Leaving aside for the moment whether the notice addressed to Corridor E2 represents a request or, like the above examples, a command, there are still other assumptions that we make when reading and interpreting the communication. For example, our knowledge and experience allows us to be fairly confident that the notice was not posted in a hotel: hotel guests do not normally reside in corridors; and anyway, in seeking meaning from the notice, we apply our knowledge that, in hotels, cleaners tend to accommodate guests rather than the other way round.

The original location of the notice (as you will probably have worked out) was in a university hall of residence. One of my students became curious about, and critical of, the message, primarily because of the use of the pronoun selected by the producer of the discourse to refer to the cleaner. Note that the pronoun selected is 'her'. As it happened, the cleaner for Corridor E2 was male, and this is why the notice had caught my student's attention. As she said herself, had this not been so, the cultural suppositions and stereotypes betrayed in the notice might well have passed her by. However, while the influence of discourse, and the cultural assumptions that it constructs about our world, may sometimes work at a level below conscious awareness, this is not to say that they do not influence our perceptions of the social world in which we live – in this case, a world in which all cleaners are female.

Just as we construct ourselves and our world through the social practice of language, so the discourse presented to us also seeks to construct us in particular ways, to fulfil certain social roles – usually roles that are of benefit to the producer of the discourse. Advertising discourse, we might say, constructs us as consumers; the discourse strategies of police interviews construct us as suspects; and medical discourse constructs and maintains the relationships that define our social roles of being a doctor or a patient. Of course, this is to take a rather narrow view of advertising, legal and medical discourse; it ignores, for example, discourse between advertisers and their corporate clients, between solicitors and barristers or barristers and judges, and between doctors and hospital administrators (to name but a few examples). In this book, though, the focus is placed on the interface between institutions and 'ordinary people'; and so we restrict ourselves to those areas of professional discourse where the professional is dealing with 'members of the public'.

Professional discourse

Every profession has its own way of speaking and writing: its own particular styles of language (its *register*) and its own conventions for the construction of discourse – the professional discourse analyst, for example, uses language in a way that the vast majority of ordinary people would find more or less impenetrable. It is clear that when a professional speaks to a non-professional, their use of language can be a barrier: there is an asymmetry between the knowledge, experience and understanding of the participants in the field; and since the speech exchange (if it is a speech exchange) is so circumscribed by language, a differential of power and authority is created and maintained.

This is not to say, however, that we are always merely passive receivers of discourse. By taking part in discourses we are able to change them. In the chapters that follow, while we will often look at how the asymmetrical relationships that hold in discourse give some participants power over others, we must also bear in mind that dimensions such as power are not static and can shift in moment-by-moment negotiation. The inherent asymmetry can, and often needs to be, reduced if the non-professional participant is to acquire any kind of equity in the proceedings, and in some cases the non-professional can genuinely negotiate a shift in this differential. There are cases, however, where this is scarcely possible: in the context of the police interview, or sometimes of the classroom, the differential may be so institutionalized and engrained as to make negotiation more or less impossible for all but the most articulate or resourceful.

In this book we examine the discourse typical of five professional fields, and we begin in chapter 1 with an analysis of the discourse of advertising. This is arguably the most 'planned' form of discourse that we will consider; it is also (at the moment) a more or less totally one-way channel of communication, in which the producer and receiver are relatively distant – indeed, one of the central challenges for advertisers is create a relationship across this divide. How they rise to this challenge is the main theme of the chapter. The language of advertising is widely characterized as *persuasive* and *seductive*, and its discourse exploits linguistic devices that are cleverly designed to attract us to a lifestyle of aspirational consumerism; so successfully, indeed, that it both reflects cultural and social values and also contrives to create new attitudes and needs.

In chapter 2 we examine the discourse of politics and consider the ways in which politicians use *rhetorical* and *deceptive* linguistic devices – including many borrowed from the field of advertising – to lead us towards a particular view of political reality. We consider the increasing influence of the media on politics over the past decades and examine how we have all become the victims of 'spin'. Although much of the chapter is concerned with political speech-making – which is a discourse very nearly as planned as an advertisement – it also takes some account of the discourse that is characteristic of the political interview, where utterances are not able to be rehearsed so rigorously.

In chapter 3 we turn to the discourse of the law. Here we observe a sharp distinction between the language of written legalese – the *impenetrable* and *forbidding* language of contracts and deeds – and the spoken language of police interviews and courtroom interactions, both of which are widely seen as *coercive* and *manipulative*. We consider especially the implications of the complexity of the discourse for those caught up within the legal system; and, in focusing on spoken legal interviews, we explore specifically the ways in which discourse reflects and maintains asymmetrical power relationships. We note how spoken police interviews of suspects are 'reinvented' into written statements to be taken to court; and we conclude by examining the manipulative, linguistic cut and thrust that is characteristic of the courtroom.

In chapter 4 we examine the discourse of medicine and explore the gulf between the professional 'voice' of doctors and the personal speech of patients. A study of the written discourse of medical information materials reveals that, while they are presented as informative, they actually adopt many of the forms of persuasive social advertising and tend to be shaped within a paternalistic model of 'doctor knows best'. The patronizing attitude towards patients is also found to be a feature of the interactional discourse constructed in medical consultations: analysis of these face-to-face spoken exchanges also suggests that the fracture between the medical voice of the doctor and the 'lifeworld' voice of the patient results in a discourse in which miscommunication and misunderstanding thrive.

Finally, in chapter 5 we turn our attention to the discourse of education, where again we examine written as well as spoken interaction. We cast a critical eye on conventions for academic writing and find that the demand for an impersonal, detached style entails the removal of the writer's values, beliefs and opinions. Examination of classroom interactions reveals the extent to which teaching is talking and learning is largely linguistic: we look at the ways in which both teaching and learning are constructed in classroom discourse, and how ideas of legitimate knowledge and its representation are encapsulated in distinctive discourse.

About this book

I hope that the book will be accessible to people coming for the first time to the study of discourse, regardless of their age or background. I have therefore not assumed any prior knowledge of linguistics or terminology, nor any prior exposure to the various theories or rationales of discourse analysis. In restricting my examination of the professional fields to those areas where the professional is interacting with the non-professional, I have, I hope, also ensured that no specialist knowledge of these professions is needed on the reader's part.

I believe that it should be possible for a reader interested only in one of the five professional fields to pick up the thread of the book at the beginning of that particular chapter. Nevertheless, I feel it will be of much greater benefit to treat the book as a piece in itself, and consequently I should warn that anyone starting the book beyond the halfway point is likely to find the treatment a little brisk. I do not by any means attempt to cover every aspect of discourse in every chapter, and themes are developed as the book proceeds.

In each of the five fields we examine, we begin by characterizing the discourse of the profession more or less from the layman's point of view. We then proceed to analyse the linguistic elements of the discourse, with the aim of building up a picture of how these contribute to its characterization and form an image of the professional context of assumptions and expectations that the discourse creates and maintains. In this respect, the treatment of discourse in this book can be characterized as 'bottom-up'.

Each of the chapters takes a fairly enquiring tone. I have assumed that readers will see themselves as joining with me in a collaborative analysis of the various examples of data that we examine together. I have established several analyses in each chapter as semi-formal exercises, but have never ventured to suggest that there is a 'right' answer to any of the questions they contain – let alone that I might be able to supply it. These exercises are not accompanied by 'answers'; rather, the reader is invited to accompany me, in the text that follows each exercise, in looking at how we might go about finding interpretations of the data. At an early stage in each chapter I have tried to set up an exercise designed simply to suggest to the reader what some of these analytical techniques might look like, and to create a shared context in which our work might ground itself. I have also added some 'further exercises' at the end of each chapter; these tend to be more concerned with what an interested reader might do next, rather than with assessing any knowledge acquired.

One final note: context, as I have already emphasized, is crucial. Inevitably this book is grounded within my own personal context, which happens to be Britain in 2006. In examining some of the professional fields I have felt able to extend that context across the Atlantic; in others I have felt less confident of doing so. The chapter on political discourse, for example, reflects (and casts a critical eye on) the dominance in Britain of the centre-left project headed – as I write this, anyway – by Tony Blair.

All the same, British and North American politics owe so much (as we will see) to the linguistic devices contrived by the copywriter that we make the discourse of advertising our first port of call.

Come and get it

The discourse of advertising

Advertising is the rattling of a stick inside a swill bucket
George Orwell (1936)

Introduction

Well, how would you define advertising? And what exactly counts as an advertisement? Most dictionaries focus primarily on its function as a public notice or announcement, but the art of advertising clearly extends much further than this. In our everyday lives we meet advertising in many forms, from the well-known media of press promotions, television commercials or billboard posters, to the less obvious devices of advertorials, product placements, event sponsorships, junk mailings or carefully staged large-scale public relations exercises – all, incidentally, requiring very much more time and effort (and language) than is needed by Orwell's swine-herd calling his pigs to the trough.

Some advertisers choose to address us with direct or hard-sell techniques, while others send us messages which are far more indirect, subtle or even subliminal. There is a trend at the moment, for example, for record companies to pay buskers in busy underground stations to perform acoustic versions of the label's latest releases: the hope is that commuters will find themselves humming the tune on the way home and so be motivated to buy the record. Are the record companies really advertising here? There is some debate about this tactic: detractors call it *stealth marketing*; proponents liken it to the *viral buzz* of internet-led promotions, and indeed many are forecasting that the advertising industry is about to change dramatically along these very lines. Either way, the process certainly accords with Leacock's (1924) famous definition of advertising as 'the science of arresting the human intelligence long enough to get money from it'.

It goes without saying that the power of advertising is immense – as is the time, money and skill that goes into it. Producers of commercial goods and services routinely pour vast sums into promoting their wares through the advertising media, knowing that a successful campaign can win them vital market share and that failure to advertise effectively can have devastating results on the bottom line and the share price. The stakes are high: advertising agencies command steep fees and a successful brand manager is one of the hottest properties a business can have. Advertising is widely regarded as the driving force behind our consumerist culture;

so much so that it is plausibly credited with having kept Western economies growing and thriving over the last 50 years.

The function of advertising, of course, is promotional: to draw to our attention
and keep in our minds the availability and desirability of a product, service or brand.
In order to achieve this function it must first reach its target audience, then capture
that audience with a message that is both attractive and memorable. At its best it is
a stunningly powerful means of communication, every bit the equal of any popular
hit in modern music or film (indeed, advertising mixes with both these genres in a
highly interactive way), and truly classic advertisements rightfully take their place
at the cutting edge of modern art.

My own favourite advertisement never appeared on the TV or in the press and
would never have won any prizes as a work of art. Nevertheless, it had all the essential qualities of a great ad: it alerted the audience to the availability of the product
and emphasized its desirability and value. It was the call of a market trader in West
London, selling slightly overripe bananas at the end of the day: 'Come and get 'em!
The ones with the spots are the ones with flavour. Your money saver.'

Exercise 1a

Examine the following 1960s advertisement for Coca-Cola (© Coca-Cola) and
consider what makes it such a typical example of advertising discourse.

- What is the overall tone of the advertisement? If the campaign were running on TV, what sort of voice would you expect to be hearing?
- Examine the words used in the copy. How carefully do you think they have been chosen? How innovative are they?
- What do you notice about the grammatical structure of the sentences?
- Who is the advertisement addressed to?
- What is they key message of the advertisement?

Sound, words and sentence structures, together with the construction and manipulation of meaning will be key themes in our analysis of advertising discourse. Consider your answers to the above questions as the chapter develops.

Much – though by no means all – of the power of advertising derives from language. In no other field (apart from poetry, perhaps) is so much creative energy put into producing so few, carefully chosen words. Slogans, catchphrases, jingles and puns are crafted with such skill and cunning that, while deconstructing a piece of advertising copy can sometimes look embarrassingly like literary criticism at its worst, it is hard to overstate the forethought that will have gone into constructing it in the first place.

No one would pretend that advertising slogans or catchphrases will pass into everyday usage in the same way as phrases from the Authorized Version of the Bible or Shakespeare's plays have done. When they do, however, all the more credit is due to the copywriter, for we can safely assume that the inspiration will not have come from the contemplation of divinity or through the graces of the Muse; he or she has probably had to conjure a little gobbet of eternity from something far more mundane.

Be they ever so humble, phrases such as 'your flexible friend', 'naughty but nice' (coined by Salman Rushdie, no less), 'it's the real thing', 'stop me and buy one', 'hello, boys' and 'say it with flowers' have all passed into British vernacular from advertising copy. Thus, just as John Mortimer's civilized barrister Rumpole delights in quoting from the Bard and the Bible, so too in John Sullivan's *Only Fools and Horses* wheeler-dealer Derek 'Del Boy' Trotter delights in serving up advertising straplines: his 'you know it make sense' and 'a little dab'll do ya' were originally slogans for road safety and hair cream ads, respectively. Del Boy's most characteristic catchphrase, 'lubbly jubbly' (normally uttered when easy money is in sight) even includes the name of the product: Jubbly was an orange drink sold in the 1950s in a triangular carton. The original slogan, 'Lubbly Jubbly', for reasons we will see as this chapter proceeds, is a beautiful example of the technique of crafting a word-message for an advertisement.[1]

At this point we should note again that language is by no means the only tool in the advertiser's locker. Indeed, sometimes it is barely needed at all: ads for fashion houses, for example, will often feature only a carefully crafted visual, accompanied by a discreet name or logo. Occasionally a brand's logo becomes so well known that it enables us to identify the company without any linguistic clue. See, for instance, how many of the logos you can recognize in Figure 1.01 overleaf.

3

Fig. 1.01   Famous logos

How well did you do? If you recognized several, you might like to consider that it is still relatively rare for a successful logo to be entirely without any linguistic suggestion as to its reference. The Apple and Shell logos depicted are, most obviously, an apple and a shell themselves; the Diners Club and Ericsson devices are based (though fairly abstractly) on the initial letters of the companies concerned; as a clue at least to the product being advertised, the Michelin man is wheeling a tyre, the Bic boy is holding a pen, the HMV dog is puzzling over a gramophone; more abstruse, perhaps, but the Nestlé picture features a nest, and the Johnny Walker figure is striding and carrying a walking stick; finally, the Yellow Pages logo is normally printed yellow in colour. Nevertheless, Citroën, HSBC, Mercedes, MSN and Renault do have logos that are genuinely language-free. If you identified these correctly, then you are in part attesting to the talents of the brand managers involved.

Logos, pictures and visual displays are an integral part of almost all advertising above the level of the newspaper small ad; and of course music is a fundamental and often indispensable element in many broadcast advertisements. While this chapter will naturally focus on the language of advertising, it is nonetheless important to understand that advertisers use language in synchrony with many other forms of communication in conveying meaning in their messages. Often there is an extremely strong relationship between the pictures used and the language employed. In Figures 1.02 and 1.03, designed and distributed in Britain in 1971 and 1994 by one of the world's most prestigious advertising agencies (Saatchi and Saatchi), the impact of the message derives from and relies on the relationship between language and picture, and it would be more or less impossible to explain the significance of either in isolation.

This is a convenient point at which to remind ourselves that not all forms of advertising are aimed at simply selling commodities. The Saatchi ads are examples of 'social advertising' – campaigns that encourage us, for instance, to give up smoking, avoid speeding or donate money to charitable appeals. Saatchi was also responsible for Figure 1.04 on p. 7, a political ad from the late 1970s.

Advertising, in one form or another, has been a key weapon in the armoury of politicians for a considerable time, and not necessarily in its most obvious form.

Fig. 1.02   Anti-speeding campaign. © Saatchi & Saatchi

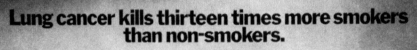

Fig. 1.03   Anti-smoking campaign. © Saatchi & Saatchi

Fig. 1.04   Conservative election campaign 1970s

Many branches of the press and broadcasting media, in spite of their protestations of independence, operate as mouthpieces for a particular political viewpoint – usually, as it happens, a viewpoint from which certain commercial interests (often their owners) are likely to benefit. The financial structure of almost all press and broadcasting enterprises, it should be remembered, is intricately and inextricably bound up in the advertising revenues they receive from national and multinational companies. Indirectly, then, political groups depend on these commercial interests for an important media channel, and the support of commercial media groups can be vital. John Major's Conservatives retained power in Britain at the 1992 general election, against all the pundits' predictions, benefiting enormously from a polling-day headline in *The Sun* attacking Labour. It was no handicap either that their advertising agency was Saatchi and Saatchi. Politics, commerce and advertising may be strange bedfellows, but they do seem to sleep together fairly regularly.

With so much at stake, government advertising, like commercial advertising, sometimes needs to be extremely subtle. After all, it is not always in the advertiser's interest to appear overly promotional – indeed there is a danger that people will be suspicious of such use of the advertising media (and we will see examples of this later in the book). The risk is especially high if a campaign is being funded from the public purse, or if the product or policy being promoted might seem to be at odds with the public good. In such circumstances an advertisement will invariably be better received if it gives the impression of merely imparting information.

Figure 1.05 overleaf was part of a 2004 campaign by the British government to encourage pensioners to claim credits that were due to them. In the leaflet form shown here, the casual observer might be reluctant to call it an advertisement at all. Nonetheless, it came squarely from the government's advertising

7

Pension Credit

The
Pension
Service

Part of the Department
for Work and Pensions

October 2004

Pick it up. It's yours.

- Will you qualify?
- How much could you get?
- How will you be able to apply?

Freephone 0800 99 1234 to apply

Fig. 1.05   Pension credit leaflet

budget, and at the time of its launch it caused something of a storm – not least for its high cost to the taxpayer's pocket. Above all, the campaign, which extended across several media (including peak-time national TV), attracted criticism because it looked suspiciously like a plug for the 'caring, sharing' Labour Party. Critics argued further that such a campaign was only required because Labour was being less than transparent in its tax-raising and relying on an opaque system to achieve revenue by stealth.

The example that follows overleaf (Figure 1.06) is obviously a commercial advertisement, but well worth examining in a similar light. It is not difficult to identify the era in which this advertisement was published. The marketing message for Bourn-Vita explicitly relies on wartime values to explain and justify the benefits of consuming the beverage: drinking Bourn-Vita, it is claimed, aids restful sleep, which in turn maintains your fitness and consequently facilitates your potential for the hard work that will be needed for the war effort. In buying the product, the ad implies, you are not indulging in luxury; you are doing your patriotic duty.

Many producers adopted similar advertising strategies in wartime. Companies supplying the 'needs' of the armed forces with chocolate, chewing gum and cigarettes were keen to let the public know of their patriotism, with Nestlé, for example, telling the public at large that 'supplies of chocolate products for those at home are limited...the needs of our armed forces come first'.

In the USA, where the economy was hugely stimulated by the war, an odd situation developed, with suddenly wealthy consumers experiencing shortages of many everyday commodities. This meant advertisers had to meet the challenge of keeping domestically scarce brands in the public eye, and in a favourable light too. Consequently, smokers were told that Lucky Strike Green had 'gone to war' (the metal in the green packaging colour was needed for aircraft production); and Americans missing their favourite breakfast drink were exhorted to consider that 'maybe your canned Florida Grapefruit Juice is over Nazi rooftops tonight'![2]

In these examples, informative and persuasive strategies are woven together, as the advertisements seek to fulfil the function of providing information as well as urging the consumer to buy, or at least keep trying to buy. This multifunctional and multifaceted nature of advertising discourse – like all other forms of discourse, in fact – is a feature that we will see regularly throughout this chapter.

Yet it is hard to resist the conclusion that it is really the function of persuasion that lies at the heart of advertising discourse. For whether the presentation is soberly informative, lyrically imaginative, weirdly abstract or just unashamedly price-busting, an advertisement's ultimate objective is always promotional. Put simply, ads are there to persuade us to think and, more importantly, to act in certain ways: to purchase a particular brand of perfume, to conquer an unhealthy addiction, to lend support to one political party rather than another. Consequently, the discourse of advertising is liberally peppered with persuasive devices at every level.

Persuasion, however, does not take place in a social or cultural vacuum. Consider the Bourn-Vita advertisement again. Would it work today? Or have our value systems changed in a way that makes the marketing message hopelessly obsolete?

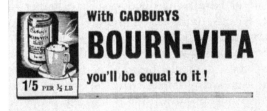

Fig. 1.06   Bourn-vita advert. © Cadburys Schweppes plc

www.fasterbeans.com

SAME BEANS ONLY FASTER

Fig. 1.07 Heinz 'faster' baked beans

Life moves on, and people's needs, desires and aspirations change – as advertisers are quick to note.

Clearly the focus in this recent ad, Figure 1.07, for one of Britain's favourite and most traditional teatime foods is on the 'speed' of the product. The food itself, we are told, has not changed, but it is now 'faster' (hence the representation of beans as cars). The marketing message is reflecting a change, not in the product itself, but in the consumer's lifestyle – a shift from the traditional concern that food should provide nourishment and sustenance, to a modern-day view that it needs to be prepared in a hurry. This up-to-date element is reinforced by the direction of readers to an internet website, called fasterbeans.com. The product, it is implied, is perfectly in tune with our high-tech, fast-living age.

Advertisements are highly dependent on context and inextricably linked to societal values and cultural conditions. While frequently seeking a single 'essence' that universally drives consumer motivation to buy a product, advertisers also tailor and target their messages to particular audiences (Brierley 2002). The Swedish car-maker Volvo's attempt to market its cars in the same way in different European countries was soon dropped in favour of adopting different sales strategies for different nations: Volvo cars were promoted in the UK with the focus on their safety, while in France the emphasis was on their design and in Germany on their performance. Any examination of mass communications will always need to take account of this dependency on audience, context and culture.

For advertisers, the concept of audience is particularly crucial. Considerable time and money is spent on researching the demographics of populations in order to achieve the best opportunities for marketing products or services: in television advertising, for example, careful predictions are made about likely viewers and attention is paid to the timing of commercial breaks as well as to the programming that surrounds them. A good deal of revealing work has been done by discourse analysts on the importance of tailoring messages to particular audiences: research on television advertising in New Zealand finds, for example, that advertisers tend to favour speakers with strong local dialects, in order to associate their products with Kiwi identity and values (Bell 1991). For broadly similar reasons, advertisers may employ speakers with foreign accents or deliberately use foreign words to evoke an impression of mystery or a sense of the exotic.

But we are straying into details now. Before we focus on the particular strategies that advertisers use in order to construct their messages, let us remind ourselves once more that in examining the discourse of advertising we are enquiring into the subtle mechanisms of a communicative form that genuinely pervades our lives – one which is employed with consummate skill by the most powerful commercial and political interests in our societies as they attempt to shape and control our thoughts and actions. Some observers may choose to see advertising as a pernicious form of brainwashing, and advertisements as responsible for creating artificial desires which in turn encourage the unnecessary consumerism that props up a capitalist political system. Later in the chapter, we will discuss in more detail the extent to which advertising may not simply reflect social values, but actually construct new social needs and desires.

Let us also remind ourselves that, as we mentioned at the outset, advertising discourse is painstakingly pre-planned and organized, to a degree scarcely encountered in any other field of communication – although, as we will see, political speechwriting comes close. Consequently the messages it constructs are forbiddingly intricate and do not readily permit formal analysis. Linguists like myself make distinctions between hierarchical levels of language – phonetics, phonology, morphology, syntax, semantics and pragmatics – but these represent fairly blunt instruments in this field. The boundaries between these levels are fuzzy and imprecise even in theory; when we come to investigate real language in everyday usage, the lines inevitably blur even further.

All the same, for our present purposes it will be practical, in the context of a bottom-up approach to discourse, to consider the construction of advertisements first in relation to sounds, words and structures – the characteristic sound patterns they tend to employ, the words they choose to feature and the way their sentences are most typically organized – and then to put a searchlight on some particular discourse devices that advertisers use in order to manage and manipulate meaning. Crucially, though, we must bear in mind that all these features are likely to be subtly and skilfully interwoven.

Freshly frozen, fruity flavours: the sounds of advertising discourse

This section will explore the sounds of advertising in two parts. First, we will look at speakers and consider which speakers' voices are selected to advertise which types of products. Second, we will investigate the use of specific sound patterns in advertising discourse, and consider how advertisers employ particular plays on sound, such as repetition, rhythm and rhyme.

Advertisers have always looked to particular personalities to market their goods: famous faces are widely acknowledged as lending prestige to the products they advertise. However, the selection of appealing voices is also an industry art form in itself – and not just for radio commercials. Television voice-over artists are stars in their own right and their casting is often reckoned to be just as important as the visual element of an advertisement. The timbre of the voice is a key factor: for example, voices may be perceived as seductive, smooth, friendly, cheerful, honest or authoritative.

Much of this, no doubt, is down to the personal characteristics of the artist or the character(s) famously played by the artist if he or she is an actor. But much will also depend on the speaker's accent. While other areas of the media, such as news broadcasting, still tend to select speakers from a relatively limited range of accents – and received pronunciation (RP), or an accent near to it, remains largely the norm in Britain – advertising is characterized by a greater degree of diversity in the voices reflected and represented. At the time of writing, I am aware of campaigns for a bank, a perfume and a theme park, employing a Geordie accent from north-east England, a French-accented English voice and a near-RP accent. Which campaign do you suppose features which accent?

The fact is, we associate different voices with different personality types and lifestyles. Of course, this is stereotyping, but we do connect RP with an air of authority and tend to believe that speakers of RP are likely to be intelligent, educated and knowledgeable. Equally, we consider speakers of certain regional accents (such as Geordie) to be friendly, trustworthy and sociable. Non-native accents can hold very particular associations: the British perception of French-accented English reflects a deeply entrenched view that the French lifestyle is one of sophistication, elegance and finesse.

Advertisers are aware of these associative reactions and make use of them in their selection of specific speakers for particular promotions. In the light of this, you would have been right to suppose that the RP-speaker was selected to advertise the bank, while the Geordie accent was chosen for the theme park; the association of the French accent with sophistication made it an ideal choice for persuading us to purchase the perfume. This is by no means to suggest that advertisers are hidebound by such associations; rather, they represent templates that can be departed from in order to create a different or unexpected response, or to appeal to a less-than-typical target audience. Still, you might like to ponder the ramifications of using a cockney or Liverpool accent to advertise a bank's new bond offer; or German-accented English to promote a luxury perfume.

The choice of specific speakers for particular advertising campaigns is thus far from random: voices are carefully chosen, reflecting typically held associations between ways of speaking, speakers and lifestyles. Writers of advertising discourse habitually play on the associations of these voices to help persuade us that their products or services are a ticket into a particular lifestyle – one that we perhaps hanker for, admire, aspire to or will feel at home with. We purchase a bottle of Chanel N°5 not in order to smell more pleasant: a bar of soap will achieve the same result at a fraction of the price (Camay used to advertise its soap as containing 'perfume worth nine guineas an ounce'). Rather, we are buying into a life of luxury, sophistication and elegance. As J. B. Priestley put it:

> There, if only we buy something, is the Blue Yonder. There is the enchanted life
> we have always felt we deserved to enjoy... Just a tin, a packet, the payment of
> a small deposit, and Successful Living, Gracious Living, Casual Living, the lot,
> are within our grasp... (1966:51)

The discourse of advertising, almost by definition, includes us too, the readers and listeners, the audience: we are, effectively, being engaged in a 'conversation', and our role is an important one. Some advertisements address us directly: the voices talk straight to us from the television screen or the magazine page. In other cases we are involved more as spectators, perhaps of a soap-style romantic drama (remember those coffee ads[3]) or of a comedy sketch. The marketing messages here are rather more subtle: if the drama stimulates you, then, by association, so will the coffee featured in it; if you are the kind of person that appreciates this brand of humour, then you will appreciate the brand of beer too. It is by no means a new technique.

Exercise 1b

Examine the following advertisement for Martini, which appeared in *Woman's Own* magazine in 1960.

'What'll you have?' he said.
'Martini', I said.
'Just by itself?' he said.
'Of course', I said
'With a twist of lemon,
if they have it'
'Wise girl,' he said,
'I can see we agree'.
'Yes', I said, and after that
we never looked back.

Better drink

MARTINI

Sweet or Dry
or Bianco

© Bacardi & Company Ltd

- How is the reader located in relation to the speaker?
- What is the message implicit in the advertisement?
- How is this message reinforced by the way the reader is located?
- Would the advertisement work today? If not, why not?

Here a dialogue is constructed between a man and a woman, and we, as readers, are invited to imagine ourselves 'overhearing' the conversation taking place. We hear the speakers agreeing on their choice of alcohol: it is so good they plan to drink it neat, with only a twist of lemon. As the dialogue develops, we find that agreement on their favourite drink has led to an arrangement for their future life: after all, they 'never looked back'. A message is implicitly being constructed and conveyed: drink Martini and find your soulmate. And we, the audience, are being invited to enjoy the frisson of eavesdropping on an intimate moment; cosily located in this role, it appears, we are most receptive to the advertiser's seductive message.

In addition to the careful choice of speakers and the selection of style of address, advertisers construct their messages by making particular plays on sound: aesthetic and poetic strategies of sound-play catch our attention and make the messages more memorable. There is little doubt that the sounds used in advertisements are distinct. In fact, it seems that even when we are unable actually to distinguish the words and phrases being used, we can nevertheless tell when programming shifts from regular features to commercial breaks: there is something uniquely characteristic about the overall sound of TV advertising (Crystal and Davy 1969).

Plays on sound are not limited to spoken advertising: written forms also make use of stylized sound strategies in an attempt to catch our attention, make messages memorable and persuade us of the value of products and services. In the same way that we recognize some products from simple visual logos, so too other products are uniquely characterized by the linguistic slogans or jingles that are used to market them. Some of the following will probably be familiar to you:

Let your fingers do the walking

Probably the best lager in the world

The ultimate driving machine

The mark of a man

It's the real thing

Because you're worth it

The world's favourite airline

Put a tiger in your tank

Any time any place anywhere

Splash it all over

Loves the jobs you hate

What do you want to watch?

Just do it

Créateur d'automobiles

(Yellow Pages, Carlsberg, BMW, Old Spice, Coca-Cola, L'Oréal, British Airways, Esso, Martini, Brut, Mr Muscle, Sky, Nike, Renault)

Sound-play is also employed with particular effect in the naming of commodities. Just as some commercials for expensive scents will use French-accented speakers, so some perfumes are given French-sounding names, like Anaïs Anaïs, Rive Gauche or L'Air Du Temps. The names conjure up a sense of the exotic and, like French-accented voices, we associate them with romance, elegance and sophistication. The examples above are perfumes for women, of course; fragrances for men tend to be marketed under different labels which we associate with masculinity – familiar brands have included Chrome, Boss and Aramis. (Masculinity, like many other concepts, is culture-specific; you might like to note that a male fragrance successfully marketed in Germany as 'Kevin' failed to achieve great popularity elsewhere.)

Such name-plays are not limited to beauty products. After relocating in 1879 to a greenfield location near Bournbrook Hall outside Birmingham, chocolate-maker Cadbury chose to give their new site the French-sounding name, Bournville – apparently selected because French chocolate was popular and fashionable at the time. Bournville remains a key Cadbury trademark to this day (as indeed does Bournvita, which we mentioned earlier).

It is not only labels that evoke certain connotations and associations. Sounds do too. **Sound symbolism** is the linguistic term given to the association of certain sounds with particular meanings, concepts, ideas or even emotions. **Onomatopoeic** words that represent non-linguistic noise with ordinary speech sounds are a simple example: buzz, swish, bang, zing. Onomatopoeia is regularly used in advertising:

Snap Crackle Pop (Rice Krispies)

Plink plink fizz fizz (Alka Seltzer)

Schhh…you know who (Schweppes)

Clunk click every trip (UK road safety)

But sound symbolism is more than just language imitating sounds. Take the following two words from Maori, the indigenous language of New Zealand (both words refer to creatures):

Pūrerehua (pu-ray-ray-hu-a)

Ngārara (nga-ra-ra)

Say the words out loud to yourself, using the pronunciation guide. If you were told that one of these creatures was more dangerous than the other, which would you identify as the more vicious? If you were informed that one was prettier than the other, which would you guess that to be? If you were advised, finally, that one is 'butterfly' and the other is 'snake', which do you think is which? If you decided, correctly, that *pūrerehua* is likely to translate as 'butterfly' and *ngārara* as 'snake', then it is likely that you were guided in your decision by sound symbolism.

Thus, just as we make stereotypical associations based on speakers' voices, so we also draw conclusions based on particular semantic associations of speech sounds. Sound symbolism takes many forms and is used by advertisers to lead us into making precisely such connections. It has been noted, for example, that the fricative sounds 'f', 'v' and 'sh' are often used for the naming of household cleaners in English: think of Flash, Frish, Vim and Cif (Vestergaard and Schröder 1985). Because of their characteristically harsh pronunciation, we are drawn to associate fricative sounds with abrasive qualities, and are thereby led to an impression of the effectiveness of the cleaning products being promoted. For obvious reasons, such sounds tend to be avoided in advertisements for moisturizing creams.

Advertisers recognize that sounds have power, and marketing companies use this power in creating brands, as the following extract shows.

StrawBerry Is No BlackBerry: Building Brands Using Sound

As soon as the naming gurus at Lexicon Branding Inc. saw the hand-held wireless prototype that Research In Motion Ltd. had produced, they were struck by the little keyboard buttons, which resembled nothing so much as seeds. 'Strawberry!' suggested one. No, straw- is a slowwwww syllable, said Stanford University linguist Will Leben, who also is director of linguistics at Lexicon, based in Palo Alto, Calif. That's just the opposite of the zippy connotation Research In Motion wanted. But -berry was good: Lexicon's research had shown that people associate the *b* sound with reliability, said David Placek, who founded the Palo Alto, Calif., firm and is its president, while the short e evokes speed. Another syllable with a b and a short vowel would nail it...and within seconds the Lexicon team had its fruit: BlackBerry.

(*Wall Street Journal*, 26 August 2002)

It is also common to find sound repetition employed as a device in advertising discourse: replication of both vowels and consonants helps to embed products in our memory. The repetition of consonant sounds, often in initial position, across a sequence of words, is known as **alliteration**. 'Freshly frozen fruity flavours' is an alliterative phrase which might be used to good effect in the marketing of an ice lolly, a 'Jubbly' perhaps. But what about 'freshly frozen peas' or 'freshly frozen chickens'? In these phrases alliteration might draw our attention away from the **oxymoron** in which two contradictory terms are combined: food can either be fresh or frozen, but not both. All of the following ads include alliteration. (Note again that sound-play is not restricted to the spoken medium: when we read, it seems that we 'hear' sounds in our heads, and sound-play of this type can work in written as well as in spoken advertisements.)

Fanatical About Furniture, Passionate About Prices (Courts furnishings)

Fragrance Control At Your Fingertips (Haze air spray)

Long-lasting hydration for softer, smoother skin (L'Oréal moisturizer)

Your Throat Feels Smoother When You Suck A Soother (Soothers lozenges)

The last slogan above is also an example of **rhyme**, a device which associates words in our mind and in so doing makes the messages they convey more memorable. Advertisers are keen to employ rhyme, particularly in the construction of slogans. The following ads all use sound-play based on rhyme.

TV You Want To See (UK Gold satellite TV)

A Mars A Day Helps You Work, Rest and Play (Mars chocolate)

You Can Do It, When You B&Q It (B&Q hardware store)

Work Smarter, Work Faster (Encarta CD-ROM)

In the final slogan above, note that 'Smarter' and 'Faster' constitute only a near-rhyme (a device sometimes referred to as **assonance**). However, in RP English at least, 'smarter' is a full rhyme for Encarta, the name of the CD-ROM encyclopaedia being advertised.

When an advertising slogan is set to music to form a jingle, **rhythm** becomes an important feature too. The Mars and B&Q slogans above were both made into jingles and the musical rhythm is apparent even when the words are spoken without music. The musical jingle for Murray Mints – 'Murray Mints, Murray Mints, Too Good To Hurry Mints' – was finally dropped from their advertising (after what seemed an eternity), but the 'hurry' element persisted in their slogans for years thereafter: the effects of rhythm and rhyme had contrived to embed the notion deep into the audience's psyche.

We see, then, that advertising discourse makes extensive use of a variety of sound-plays: advertisers select certain speakers to promote their products, choose to address us with voices which establish particular role relationships between producers and consumers, and play on sounds with aesthetic qualities that are pleasing to the ear. The addition of the musical-poetic devices of rhythm and rhyme, along with the exploitation of repetition and reiteration of key sounds, has the effect of making marketing messages even more memorable.

In the next section we will explore the vocabulary of advertising language and examine how words are carefully selected by advertisers in order to promote their products and persuade us to purchase them.

Good, better, best: word choice in advertising discourse

Advertisers continually seek novel words with which to promote their products. Persuasive discourse invariably becomes humdrum over time (we get tired of hearing the same old slogans); therefore, in a quest for novelty of expression, copywriters often look to create new words or forms of words to market their wares. Words formed in this way are known as **neologisms**, and the discourse of advertising is a particularly rich hunting ground for them. A campaign for a bubbly chocolate bar, for example, exploited the '-bubble' suffix to come up with words such as 'delectabubble'; and the similar creation, 'bubblicious', is now quite common in everyday use in the USA. An ad for Max Factor make-up boasts of 'New Lashfinity with Permawear' and asks: 'Like Lipfinity? You'll love Lashfinity.'

The '-finity' suffix, one must presume, is used in order to suggest that the make-up is long-lasting – an idea that is certainly reinforced by the 'perma-' prefix. In a similar way, Cadbury extended their brand name Bournvita with the suffix '-ality' to produce the alluring 'Bournvitality'. Another linguistic blending saw the first electric kettle to feature automatic switch-off marketed as the Forgettle.

Novelty of expression can also be achieved by changing the forms or spellings of conventional words. An archetypal example in Britain is 'Beanz Meanz Heinz'. The device of altering the spelling of 'beans' and 'means' to conform to the spelling of Heinz, first adopted some 40 years ago, has recently been partially revived: the label on the company's cans currently reads 'Heinz Baked Beanz'.

The UK Milk Marketing Board's slogan, 'Drinka Pinta Milka Day', brought into being a new word, 'pinta', as in pint of milk, which remained in use through a couple of decades of advertising, and today has an everyday status in Britain almost on a par with that of cuppa, as in cup of tea. The attention-grabbing device of spelling words as they sound can be seen in 'Betcha can't eat just one' (Lay's potato chips), 'Milk's gotta lotta bottle' (Milk Marketing Board again) and 'Wot a lot I got' (Smarties chocolates). The breakfast food Ricicles was marketed as 'twicicles as nicicles', and the Weetabix cereal people came up with two words never seen in print before: 'Withabix' and 'Withoutabix'. More recent examples of manipulated spelling are found in an ad for Nokia phones, which feature an X-press keypad, and in Dunhill's male fragrance X-centric.

Occasionally an advertiser will coin a new spelling to engineer a pun: the makers of Corona lemonade assured us that 'every bubble has passed its fizzical'. Advertisers especially like to play on words which are **polysemous** – a linguistic term used to explain the semantic process whereby a single word has multiple related meanings (foot, for example, can, in a related way, refer to the bottom of the leg, a unit of length and the bottom of a mountain).[4] The use of such terms creates **lexical ambiguity**, and the multiple meanings suggested by polysemes are employed to strategic effect by copywriters. Humorous plays on polysemic words, such as in puns, are particularly characteristic of marketing messages: a washing powder is claimed to take 'another load off your mind'. Puns can date, however, and be context-specific. Try to spot what is happening in Figure 1.08 opposite, a 1940s ad from Heinz.

Here the advertiser is exploiting the lexical ambiguity of 'serve', and punning on its two meanings of 'serve in the armed forces' and 'serve for dinner'. The pun is reinforced by the fact that 'ready to serve' had traditionally featured on Heinz cans anyway, and there may also be a pun on 'already about', as 'ready about' was a marching order meaning 'get ready to turn'.

Lexical ambiguity can also result from the use of **homonyms** – words with different meanings that are either pronounced the same (**homophones**, for example *threw* and *through*) or spelled the same (**homographs**, for example *lead*, the metal, and *lead*, a dog's leash). Some homonyms have the same pronunciation and spelling, but different and unrelated meanings: for example, *bear*, the animal, and *bear*, the verb meaning to tolerate. Effective puns can be created out of such ambiguities: Almay cleansing lotion claims to provide the user with 'no more pore excuses'. In the same way, Sonneti clothes are marketed under the slogan, 'wear you're at'.

Ambiguity is not restricted to the level of the word: it can be exploited nicely at phrase level too. Figure 1.09 on p. 22 is a piece of social advertising created by Saatchi and Saatchi in 1994 for Greenpeace. How is ambiguity being used here, and to what effect?

First, note the double meaning of nuclear power: a source of energy; and a country or nation which has this source of energy (or weapon) at its disposal. The interrelationship between these two meanings is clearly crucial to the impact of the marketing message. The advertisement also plays on our interpretation of the expression 'women and children first'. In this case it is not so much that the phrase has a dual meaning, but rather that the ad provokes us to construct a different interpretation of the expression: essentially, that it is the female and infant members of society who will suffer first in any nuclear warfare or disaster.

Advertisers have always relied heavily on the use of descriptive words to make the objects of their promotions stand out and appear unique. Verbs are rarely left unembellished by adverbs: it is noticeable how frequently 'smoothly', 'softly' and 'quickly' appear in advertising discourse. Advertisements also contain a high

Fig. 1.08   Heinz 'Always ready to serve'

percentage of adjectives, which allow advertisers to build multiple layers of description to promote their wares. Several studies have examined the use of adjectives in both American and British advertising discourse (see, for example, Bolinger 1980). In an analysis of 200 American television advertisements, the following ten adjectives were found to be the most frequently employed: *New, Beautiful, Better, Free, Extra, Good, Fresh, Great, Clean* and *Light*. In Britain, the following ten were the

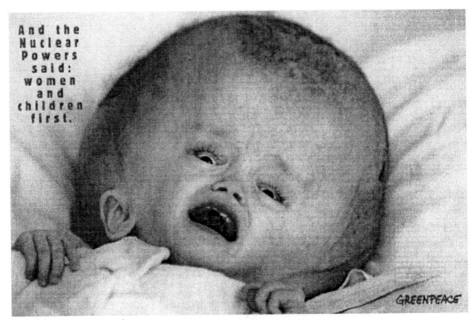

And the
Nuclear
Powers
said:
women
and
children
first.

GREENPEACE

Fig. 1.09   Greenpeace advert

most frequently used: *New, Full, Good-better-best, Sure, Free, Clean, Fresh, Wonderful, Delicious* and *Special*. In the light of our earlier comments concerning the influence of culture and context on advertising, it is rather revealing that the lists from the USA and Britain are so similar. As Norman Douglas (1917) pointed out, 'you can tell the ideals of a nation by its advertisements'.

Clearly some of these adjectives – beautiful, great, wonderful, delicious, special – look suspiciously like evidence of **hyperbole**: the rhetorical device of exaggerating a statement far beyond its literal meaning. This kind of language is meat and drink to the advertiser, although it has to be used subtly if it is not to be overwhelming: an audience can tire of hearing their toilet cleaner extolled as brilliant, fantastic or fabulous. Note that these terms are relatively **synonymous**: they have similar meanings and so may be used more or less interchangeably. Advertisers often list synonyms, especially those that are hyperbolic, in their marketing messages.

More interesting, perhaps, is the adjective at the top of both lists: new. This word lies at the heart of some of the most obvious and well-worn devices exploited by advertisers over the years, for it is the basis of that oldest of marketing tricks – the product relaunch. You will have noticed how often a sagging brand is suddenly livened up and presented as 'new'; it is less likely that you will have noticed any particular difference in the product itself.

Undoubtedly the most daring and high-profile relaunch of the last decade of the twentieth century in Britain was the makeover of the Labour Party. Miraculously transformed by the media-savvy spin doctors behind the project, New Labour emerged from a long period of unelectability to sweep into power in 1997 with a landslide majority of historic proportions. Unlike many relaunched soap powders, it actually was new (it was considerably more right-wing, for a start); but the phenomenon of New Labour serves as a further reminder, if we needed one, that the power of advertising can be harnessed just as effectively by political parties as by producers of consumer goods. We will have more to say on this subject in the next chapter, naturally.

The power of descriptive language to persuade us is evident. However, advertising language is frequently manipulated to suggest meanings far beyond the scope of the product or service being marketed. One popular device is the employment of colourful or figurative language that establishes comparisons and associations between objects or concepts which might otherwise appear unconnected. Figurative language is often used to make language more vivid than literal forms allow. Compare, for example, the literal expression, 'He shouted loudly', with the figurative, 'He roared like a lion'. This figure of speech is known as a **simile**, with one object (in this case, the shout of the man) being likened or compared to another (the roar of a lion). Consulate's menthol cigarettes were famously 'as cool as a mountain stream'; the US Coffee Bureau assured us that 'good coffee is like friendship: rich and warm and strong'; and, in a recent example, Nivea Soft (a shower gel) is claimed to be 'like gentle summer rain'.

A further example of figurative language is found in the use of **metaphor**. Metaphorical usage is also non-literal, but rather than drawing analogies by identifying likeness, metaphor expresses one object, event or action as actually being another, in order to highlight a perceived resemblance. Advertisers lean heavily on metaphor: at the time of writing, for example, Tropicana fruit juice is being advertised as '100% pure sunshine'; and in the early 1990s an ad for Jaguar cars described the XJ-S Convertible as 'a place in the sun that moves like the wind' – an example of a metaphor and a simile being used together.

Exercise 1c

Metaphor is a particularly familiar device in dating ads. Examine the following examples from the *Looking for Love* column of a local newspaper.

> **BRUCE WILLIS** looking for his Demi Moore, attractive, intelligent, professional, sporty guy 31, n/s, w.l.t.m. gorgeous brunette 25-35.

> **FILLY 34** n/s, seeks intelligent Stallion for stable relationship, interests include animals, cycling, badminton, art, live music, countryside, pubs, dancing

> **ANGEL WITH** halo & wings but in need of TLC, 43, WLTM male with lots of tinsel to make me shine for years to come. Don't let me be boxed again!

- What metaphors are being used, and why?
- Try to compose three 'lovelines' to which you think the advertisers above might be tempted to reply. Use metaphor.
- What do you think underlies the repeated use of abbreviations in these ads?

In the first example the metaphorical reference is to Hollywood and stardom, with the aim of conjuring connotations of fantasy and romance in the reader's mind. It is interesting to note that the young man writing the ad clearly has a high opinion of himself, and has a definite, if rather shallow, picture of the woman he wants to meet. The second example, with its metaphorical reference to horses and a pun on 'stable', is trying to exploit the persuasive power of humour. In the final example the writer portrays herself metaphorically, and topically, as a Christmas tree decoration, looking to evoke sympathy as she dreads being put back into her box for another year. The sympathetic aspect is also evident in her need for 'TLC' (tender loving care). Quite what the tinsel metaphor refers to, one can only speculate.

Note also the typical use here of initialisms: abbreviated forms that need to be spelled out one letter at a time. Apart from 'TLC', mentioned above, we also find 'n/s' (non-smoker) and 'WLTM' (would like to meet); other typical instances might be 'GSOH' (good sense of humour) and 'LTR' (long-term relationship).[5] While such forms are partly motivated by the need to save space, they also function to create a social link between those who use and understand the abbreviations – tacitly creating a shared personal link between the writer and the reader of the message.

Advertisements for other types of products and services also use abbreviated forms: Efamol Evening Primrose Oil is advertised as containing EFAs and GLAs, both of which, apparently, aid and support 'womanly well-being', whatever that may be. Renault's Mégane has a 150 bhp engine, and is marketed on its rating in the latest European NCAP safety tests. Advertisements for Samsung computers inform us that they include a YEPP MP3 player and provide an HDTV experience. It can be argued that such abbreviations are employed to impress us with the scientific status of the product being marketed: even if we do not know the meaning of GLA, bhp or YEPP, we are nevertheless persuaded of the benefits of the products because they sound well researched and technically advanced (Vestergaard and Schrøder 1985). There may also be an element of the tacit appeal found in the *Looking for Love* ads: consumers can be flattered by this 'in-the-know' use of abstruse jargon.

The marketing of beauty products often exploits such scientific (and pseudo-scientific) terminology, not only in abbreviated forms, but also in word choice generally. Shampoos are advertised as containing pro-vitamin complexes, and moisturizers have active ingredients such as liposomes, polyphenols and antioxidants. As we saw with scientific abbreviations, the fact that we may not understand the meanings of these terms does not stop us from being persuaded that their use is beneficial to our health and beauty.

In contrast to this use of 'technical' vocabulary, advertisements for beauty products are also notably characterized by the use of linguistically vague terminology. Beauty creams promise to include natural ingredients or to protect skin from premature ageing. What counts as a natural substance or constitutes premature ageing (let alone how the process can be protected against) is neither described nor explained. It is reported that in the USA in the 1970s more than 2800 medical products on the market were found to be useless in treating the conditions they claimed to cure (Bolinger 1980). Subsequently, pharmaceutical companies were forced to reword and rephrase their advertising in order to escape code-of-conduct restrictions and avoid charges of misleading the public. As a consequence, medicines which had claimed to cure such medical conditions as headaches, constipation and depression, were obliged to be marketed as cures for 'malaise', 'irregularity' and 'that run-down feeling'. The vague nature of the words used in these claims makes it impossible to gauge whether the medicine being marketed has provided any kind of cure.

Another example of advertisers finding safety in vague terms can be seen in their use of **euphemisms**. These are words and phrases that may, for example, be used to avoid explicit reference to taboo or distasteful topics. Rather than saying that someone has died, we may say that they have passed away. Similarly, we may refer to sex as making love or sleeping with someone; in certain contexts sex can even be implicit in the apparently hands-off form of 'seeing' someone. Advertisers use euphemistic terms when promoting products which might cause embarrassment or unease if referred to directly. In this way, products are promoted for 'feminine hygiene' and 'sanitary protection', or as a cure for 'intimate irritation'.

We see, then, that word choice in advertising is motivated by a number of different factors. Words are chosen for their persuasive value, and hyperbolic forms such as brilliant, unique and superb are used frequently. There is a heavy reliance on descriptive vocabulary, especially adjectives and adverbs, in seeking to add value to the commodities being marketed. New words can be coined, to reinforce a sense that the product itself is a great innovation; and technical vocabulary and abbreviations are also exploited, to persuade us of the advanced nature of the products being promoted. Figurative language, such as simile and metaphor, seeks to paint word-pictures that often go well beyond a simple description of the product or service on offer. Vague vocabulary allows advertisers to market products in a way which escapes code-of-conduct restrictions and avoids careful scrutiny. Euphemism allows products to be marketed that might not normally be spoken about in public.

In discussing the lexical selection and word manipulation that is characteristic of advertising discourse, we have necessarily included references to phrases as well as words. For example, we have seen that phrases, like words, can be polysemic, metaphorical or euphemistic. In the next section we move on to examine in more detail the specific ways in which the characteristic words and phrases of advertisements are sequenced and structured in advertising discourse.

Just do it: sentence structure in advertising discourse

The sequencing and organization of words and phrases in advertising language is characteristically simple. We do not find complex sentences or utterances containing many parts, but rather the use of short, snappy structures that facilitate fast and easy comprehension. It is not difficult to see why this should be so. Consider the following exhortation from the Soviet Union:

> Toilers in Agriculture! Strengthen the fodder basis of animal husbandry! Raise the production and sale to the state of meat, milk, eggs, wool and other products!

And compare that with the message put out by the British government at a time of arguably greater national crisis:

Dig For Victory

Frequently an advertisement will home in on a key quality of the product (good, fresh, etc.), without any intervening grammar such as 'our product is...', and simply add a few clever words to emphasize that quality further:

Fresh to the last slice (Sunblest bread)

Good to the last drop (Maxwell House coffee)

Sweet as the moment when the pod went pop (Bird's Eye frozen peas)

So creamy it's almost fattening (Burma Shave foam)

In other cases, the 'our product is...' construction emphasizes the uniqueness of the merchandise on offer: 'The *Sunday Times* is the Sunday papers', or 'Coke Is It' (Brierley 2002: 183). The following is also a much-favoured construction:

Happiness is a cigar called Hamlet (Benson & Hedges)

Happiness is egg-shaped (UK Egg Marketing Board)

Happiness is a quick-starting car (Volkswagen)

Slogans to promote a company's identity tend to be short and snappy too, typically in a 'we do this...' structure. A successful slogan of this sort allows a company's identity to be advertised across a number of different campaigns, and can prompt a sense of familiarity with the producer as well as the products being marketed.

We try harder (Avis car hire)

We never forget you have a choice (British Caledonian airline)

We won't make a drama out of a crisis (Commercial Union insurance)

We keep your promises (DHL courier)

We never sleep (Pinkertons detective agency)

We put the dot in dotcom (Sun Microsystems)

The central message behind the traditional commercial advertisement is, of course, *buy this product*. However, few advertisers actually resort to sending quite such blunt commands, and they seldom choose the verb 'buy' anyway (unless they want to contrast 'buy' with 'rent', for example; or, as in the current ad for Smart cars, to contrast 'buy me for my looks' with 'love me for my fuel economy'). Nevertheless, many advertisements do use **imperative** forms of syntax and urge us to 'try', 'choose' or 'use' the products or services they seek to sell.

Choose Your Style At Specsavers (Specsavers opticians)

Pick Up A Penguin (Penguin biscuits)

Switch To Powergen (Powergen electricity)

Use Ex-Lax Pills, The Overnight Wonder (Ex-Lax laxatives)

Don't Leave Home Without It (American Express card)

Imperatives of this type are an overwhelmingly pervasive feature of advertising discourse: it is hard to think of many other contexts, other than the military services or (perhaps) education, in which we would be prepared to accept being ordered about in this way. But the point is (and it is a key point in discourse analysis) that this language does not genuinely order us to do anything, any more than the utterance from the policeman in the interview room, 'Would you like to take a seat?' is seriously inviting us to make a choice. The imperative form simply suits the snappy style of the advertising slogan, and over time we have come to regard it as a perfectly acceptable form of address *in this context*.

Actually, the same snappy style – and indeed some of the other persuasive devices we have mentioned so far – sits quite happily in certain journalistic contexts too, particularly in those magazines whose main function is largely promotional. Many of the feature articles in such publications tend to be 'advertorial', and often their headlines are virtually indistinguishable from advertising copy. Can you predict, for example, which of the following phrases are advertising slogans and which are feature headlines? All are taken from a single issue of *Woman & Home* (May 2005). (You will find the answers in the notes at the end of the book.[6])

Get balance in your crazy life

Your shape, your way

Less is more

Relax on the perfect sofa

Big, bold and beautiful

Small is beautiful

Entertaining ideas

Get into the groove

Great hair, no effort

Real stock, real simple

The personal touch

Stay perfect

What's your favourite way to dance?

Everything you need for the great outdoors

The secret of youthful looks

Want to colour away the years?

27

Notice the final example above, which exemplifies another construction much favoured by advertisers: the **rhetorical question**. Such questions do not genuinely expect to receive an answer, but rather are posed to make a particular point or employed for specific effect.

In a credit card advertisement, the question about lack of credit is constructed into a problem, to which the acquisition of a Capital One credit card is the answer: 'Been turned down for credit? Look what just turned up'. Problem solving, or at least problem reduction, is a claim made in many advertising campaigns: advertisers aim to persuade us that our needs can be fulfilled and problems alleviated through patterns of purchase and consumption. It is in the advertiser's interest that we have as many problems as possible; in this respect, advertisements may not simply *reflect* our concerns, but also serve to *create* them.

How many products have you purchased recently that would not have been readily available ten years ago? Most purchases of this type will have been prompted by a marketing-driven creation of a new need. Consider shampoo for men: is men's hair really so different from women's to warrant the production and purchase of a different product? Is the product actually any different or is it just the packaging that is novel? Similar strategies undoubtedly underlie women's recently acquired need for 'feminine hygiene' products, not only during menstruation, but every day of the month.

However, advertisers notoriously fight shy of offering cast-iron solutions to the problems they invent. Vagueness is endemic here. Having caused you to suspect that you might be paying too much for a product or service, advertisers are happier to leave you with a question rather than an answer: 'Are you paying too much for your electricity?' Strategies of opaque comparison are often achieved through the use of **comparative** adjectives and adverbs claiming that one product is better than another: advertisements for washing powders notoriously say that their products wash whiter, but seldom tell us whiter than what. Advertisements for cars claim that their models are 60 per cent quieter, 70 per cent safer or 80 per cent more reliable, but it is extremely difficult to access the objects of the comparisons (Vestergaard and Schrøder 1985). When an insurance company rhetorically asks, 'How much could you save on your car insurance?', the answer will reside in a jungle of small print and will almost certainly depend on you being a man of 55 with a small hatchback, a hefty no-claims discount, a lockable garage, a postcode in some quiet suburban community and not having shopped around for a better quote for the last five years.

A certain amount of regulation has crept into this area recently, with the result that the small print gets smaller and denser, and more or less unreadable for anyone over 45 without having to change spectacles. This is a nuisance for advertisers too: clouds of tiny writing on TV tend to distract the viewer from the beauty of the images; and small print is notoriously difficult to do on the radio – the favoured tactic at the time of writing is to read it incomprehensibly quickly in a voice that sounds utterly bored. (Given what we have said about the importance of voices in advertising, ask yourself why that should be so.) Whiskas cat food used to be marketed under the slogan 'Eight out of ten cats prefer Whiskas', but the regulators finally took umbrage at this spurious claim and insisted on a change. The advertisers came back with a tongue-in-cheek 'Eight out of ten cat owners who expressed a preference said that their cats preferred Whiskas'. The new slogan may have lacked a certain snap, but its self-mocking clumsiness (and the very opposite of the typical advertising sentence structure, we note) made it a minor classic.

While comparative constructions are used in advertising discourse in a manner which is deliberately vague or ambiguous, other strategies of sentence structuring are employed to suggest wholeness, entirety and unity. Take my last sentence, for example. Note that I describe a strategy of sentence structuring by reference to three aspects of its character, using a **three-part list**. Why did I not choose just one descriptive term, or two, or even four? The answer is that lists constructed in three parts seem to have an air of completeness about them: just as we expect a story to have a beginning, a middle and an end, so we tend to expect a list to be constructed in three parts (Atkinson 1984).

In constructing essays and other pieces of writing you may have felt the need to compose ideas in this way. Often it is difficult, and we can get stuck for a third component. Nonetheless, we are more likely to add a third item to the list, even if it does not quite fit, rather than leave our list hanging with only two parts. Consider these:

The discourse of advertising is potent.

The discourse of advertising is potent and powerful.

The discourse of advertising is potent, powerful and persuasive.

If you prefer the third expression in the list above, you have been persuaded by the power of the three-part list.

The slogan for Mars chocolate bars, noted earlier to highlight the use of rhyme, is itself organized as a list of three: 'A Mars A Day Helps You Work, Rest and Play'. There are literally thousands of examples, as this has long been a favourite trick with advertisers. Jaguar cars were advertised with the slogan 'grace, space, pace'; Hoover's vacuum cleaner, we were told, 'beats as it sweeps as it cleans'; early Mackeson beer ads assured us that 'it looks good, it tastes good, and by golly it does you good'. The extra power of the third element in the list is most clearly evidenced in Martini's classic slogan, 'Any time, Any place, Anywhere', which is arranged quite gratuitously in a list of three: what, after all, is the meaningful difference between 'any place' and 'anywhere'?

In a more recent promotion, Wella shampoo (for women) is advertised as 'giving you shine when you want it, volume when you need it, attention when you feel like it'. Notice too how in this example the three-part structure leads us from the product's physical effects on the woman's hair (shine and volume) to its claimed benefits for her status and lifestyle (becoming an object of fascination). By a linguistic sleight of hand, the ad leads women to desire the product for the effect it promises to have on their everyday life – another example of advertisers leading us into consumerism by promoting more than just their products.

In the section on wording in advertising we saw how neologisms, or new word forms, are employed to persuade us of the newness and uniqueness of products. Similar novelty of expression is often seen in the way advertisers construct the sentences or utterances of their marketing messages. The 'grammatical rules' of sentence construction may be broken: we have already seen that slogans like 'fresh to the last slice' are not whole sentences. Verbs are frequently left out, in fact – sometimes for snappiness, but sometimes, perhaps, with a more obfuscatory purpose.

Exercise 1d

Look at the list of pledges below, advertising the Labour Party manifesto for the 2005 general election.

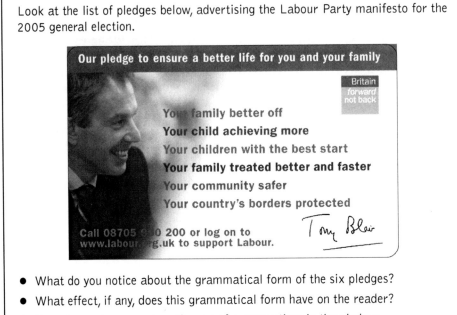

- What do you notice about the grammatical form of the six pledges?
- What effect, if any, does this grammatical form have on the reader?
- Examine and comment on the use of comparatives in the pledges.
- The pledges are clearly aimed at *you*. To what extent do you feel that you actually fit the bill for these pledges?

There has been a deliberate policy here to avoid the use of verbs altogether. The policy was widely commented on at the time, in fact, and there was a general suspicion that it was adopted in order to hide or disguise something. Specifically, what is the time reference of this promotion? Are Labour saying that your family *is* better off under their government? Or that it *will be*? (If so, when?) Or that it is *likely to be*? The point, of course, is that they are not actually saying any of these things: by avoiding the use of tense or modal markers, they contrive neatly to sidestep such questions altogether. (Indeed this whole election was characterized on all sides by the manipulative use of essentially empty language: Labour's manifesto was itself pegged on to the vacuous sound bite, *Britain forward not back.*)

It is interesting, too, that four of the six pledges are comparative in nature. As we have just noted, it is rare in advertising discourse to find the object of comparison given, and certainly there is no sign of it here. 'Better off' than when? Your community 'safer' than what? Given that Labour had already been in power for eight years at the time of the pledges, it is hard to imagine that we were being invited to make comparisons with the previous Conservative government. Again, this obfuscation is deepened by the lack of any time-referring grammar.

We might also note the constant use of 'your' – although it would appear only to ring true if you happen to have a family and children. A voter who happens not have a family is likely to feel somewhat ignored by these pledges, and the overall effect of the device is fairly artificial anyway. We will have more to say on this issue in the next section.

A further strategy of innovative syntax can sometimes be seen in the use of **count nouns** (nouns which can be counted: e.g. one car, two cars, more cars) as if they were **mass nouns** (nouns which are not typically open to counting in this way – you do not say 'two rices', and the addition of 'more' usually sees the noun remain in its singular form, 'more rice'). This little grammatical switch underpins (and adds a certain something to) Sekonda's claim to provide 'A lot more watch for your money', and the rhetorical question from Alliance & Leicester (a finance company): 'Want more car for your money?'

Just as we saw deliberate ambiguity being exploited at word and phrase level, so we also find plays on multiple meanings at the sentence level, with advertisers crafting sentence structures that can be read in more than one way. These have the effect of making you think twice about what is being said. The Conservatives' slogan, 'Labour isn't working', which we saw at the beginning of the chapter, is a typical example of the device.

The sentence and utterance structures of advertising, then, tend to be straightforward, simple and snappy. Readers and hearers are frequently addressed with direct commands (try, choose, use) or simple 'factual' slogans ('softness is a thing called Comfort'), which are often reiterated to produce a feeling of familiarity with the products or producers. Question sequences are employed, often rhetorically, and sometimes to suggest problems which the purchase of particular products will solve. Comparative forms are exploited, to suggest the superior quality of the commodities being marketed, though generally without the object of comparison being made clear. Advertisers frequently promote their products with three-part discourse structures that suggest wholeness, completeness and unity, and product innovation can be implied by the use of non-traditional syntactic structures. Finally, a new or unexpected viewpoint can be suggested by the use of sentences with multiple readings.

The levels of language use we have explored so far in this chapter – sound selection, word choice and sentence structuring – are all carefully interrelated in advertising discourse in order to achieve the construction of meaning. Indeed, we have seen that marketing messages are often deliberately constructed to suggest more than one single meaning: the use of metaphor, for example, allows literal language to be overridden by figurative forms that are designed to bring to mind associations which may persuade us to buy products not simply for what they are, but for the aspirational lifestyles that they evoke. Some of the tools in the advertiser's workshop, however, lie hidden at a rather deeper level. In the next section we will examine some of the specific semantic strategies that are employed to construct and manipulate meaning.

Just for you: the manipulation of meaning in advertising discourse

Beyond the choice of individual speakers, sounds, words, phrases and sentences or utterances, advertisers use particular strategies of semantic engineering to construct and manage meaning in the messages they deliver. In this section we will examine three semantic strategies which are highly characteristic of advertising discourse: **personalization**, **presupposition** and **personification**.

Personalization

In advertising, a primary aim is to reach the largest number of people possible and then to persuade these readers or listeners to purchase a product or a service. However, we are more likely to be persuaded to think and behave in a certain way if we feel that we are being spoken to personally. Advertisers thus face the problem of addressing large audiences while trying to make each audience member feel that the product is attractive on a personal level.

Advertising companies (in common with governments) have access to large databases, which not only include names and addresses, but also record demographic details of communities: for example, information of the likely age and social class of residents in particular neighbourhoods. They are therefore able both to personally address their promotional publications (Dear Mr Brown... Hello, Mrs Green...) and to identify the locations in which their products are most likely to reach their target audience. Put simply, if you live in an area with a high percentage of pensioners, you are more likely to receive mail advertising cruises, coach holidays and stairlifts. However, the conditions that characterize the production and interpretation of advertisements – not least the physical distance between advertisers and their potential customers – means that any personalization achieved in this way is likely to be more or less synthetic or artificial.[7]

A more potent strategy for the advertiser to create an illusion of personalized communication is to appear to have identified who you really are. This is often accomplished implicitly by the discourse device of using the pronoun 'you'. Look at how the following ads use 'you' so as to target a mass audience in a personal way:

There for you (Co-op supermarket)

Because you're worth it (L'Oréal cosmetics)

Puts beef into you (Bovril beef extract)

Guinness is good for you (Guinness beer)

We made it just for you (Samsung Digital electronics)

Note that in the final example not only is the potential customer individualized by the use of 'you', but the manufacturer is also personalized with the 'we'.[8] This

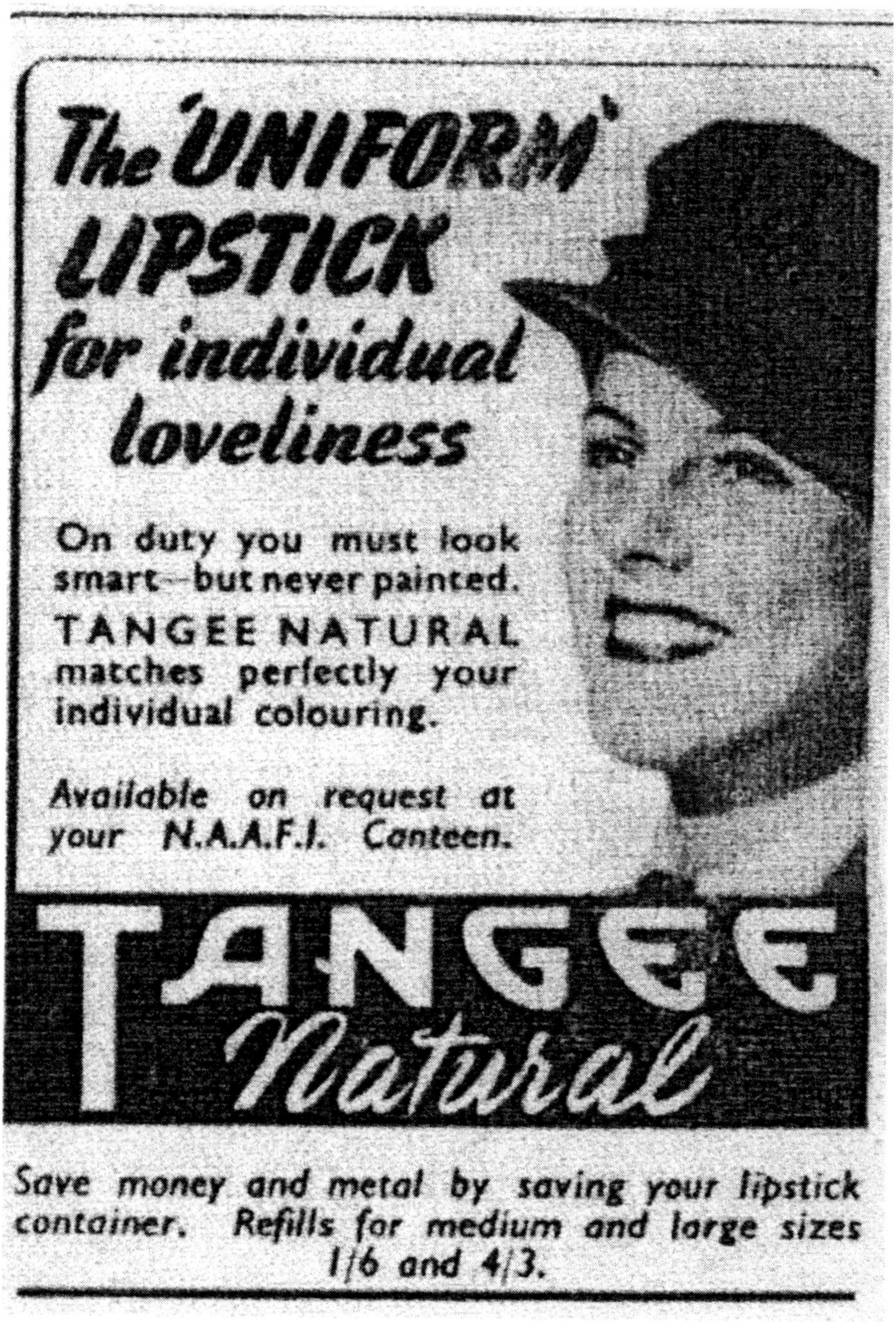

Fig. 1.10 Tangee lipstick advert

use of 'we' to personalize a faceless conglomerate or company is, naturally, found in many forms of advertising. It is not at all easy to imagine, however, quite who in the company this pronoun might genuinely be referring to.

Personalization is by no means a new ploy in advertising, as the wartime ad for Tangee lipstick (Figure 1.10), reveals. A number of personalization strategies can be identified in this advertisement. As in the examples earlier, the pronoun 'you' is used to speak directly to the recipient of the message – 'On duty *you* must look smart'. Further particularization is achieved in the claim that Tangee lipstick offers '*individual* loveliness'. Note also how the 'natural' nature of Tangee is claimed to perfectly match '*your individual* colouring'. This last claim, if it is to make any sense whatsoever, implicitly presupposes that the advertiser has some personal knowledge (presumably of the skin or hair colouring) of the reader. In this instance, then, personalization is being further achieved by the making of presuppositions.

Presupposition

Many forms of utterance allow the listener to infer semantically, as facts, propositions that are not mentioned explicitly in the utterance itself. A common (and rather trite) textbook example is, 'Have you stopped beating your wife?' Here the meaning of 'stopped' entitles us to suppose (or presuppose[9]) that the hearer has at some time been violent towards his spouse. In our everyday use of language we are constantly making such inferences: the simple statement, 'My son won the school prize', usually entails that the speaker has now, or once had, male offspring – this is at least part of the everyday meaning of 'my' and 'son'. Of course, different inferences and presuppositions may be made in different societies ('my' may not, for example, be restricted to birth children) or different eras (not so long ago, we might have felt entitled to presuppose that the speaker was married). The deep and rather hidden nature of such semantic relationships is further meat and drink to the advertiser. Consider the question: 'Which of our wallpapers would suit your bedroom the best?' Here the advertisers are deliberately presupposing that one of their wallpapers will be purchased (Vestergaard and Schrøder 1985). The consumer's choice, it is implied, is not whether to make the purchase, but simply *which* purchase to make. A similar strategy is seen at work in an ad for Grain Golden Wheat Bars, in which readers are asked, 'Where will you eat your fruit and flakes for breakfast?' Again, purchase of the product is presupposed; consumer choice is relegated to where the purchased goods should be eaten.

We saw in the advertisement for Tangee lipstick that personalization and presupposition can be related in advertising discourse: semantic implications can be framed in such a way as to suggest that the advertiser has some personal knowledge of the reader or hearer, and, in this way, a relationship of familiarity is implied between producer and consumer.[10] Recent advertising campaigns employing subtle variations on this strategy include a marketing message for Lacoste, whose clothes will allow you to 'Become what you are'; and for Manifesto perfume, which claims to provide 'A celebration of what you are'.

The claim can be gender-specific too: driving a Buick, we are told, 'makes you feel like the man you are'. A further variation of the strategy underpins a promotion for Estée Lauder make-up, in which the reader is urged: 'promise your skin a new future'.

Personification

While noting the use of personalized 'your' in the Estée Lauder slogan, we might also remark on the implicit suggestion that human skin has qualities we were not previously aware of. Apparently it has a future of its own, and it would also appear to be able to engage in the fairly high-level human interaction that is the making and receiving of promises. A similar device is at work in Nivea's advertisement for their Q10 cream: 'wrinkles hate it'.

The term 'personification' refers to the process of attributing human or animate characteristics to inanimate objects or an abstract entity. These characteristics may include sensations, emotions, desires, physical gestures and expressions, and even the power of speech. A typical example might be 'the pencil flew out of my hand'. In our everyday language, cars are often given such treatment (usually by men, it has to be said) in expressions like 'she's a good runner'; and nations are also given female or male characteristics in the expressions 'mother-country' and 'fatherland'. In the language of advertising, all sorts of products are invested with human characteristics: 'Washing Machines Live Longer With Calgon'.

Personification can also be a way of allowing the consumer to interact more naturally with a rather faceless organization. A classic device is to associate the organization with a particularly friendly face; or even with an animal that has similar attributes. The British insurer Churchill, for instance, is currently personified by a nodding rear-window bulldog figure (with all the associations for the British contained in that name and that animal): he is able to answer all our tricky questions about car insurance, usually just by nodding his head and saying yes (a curiously un-Churchillian characteristic, in fact).

For advertisers, the process of personification offers further opportunities to embellish the properties of the products they are marketing. An extreme case of attributing personal characteristics to lifeless products can be seen in a late 1990s promotion for Tampax tampons.

Exercise 1e

Look at the advertisement below and consider its use of personification.

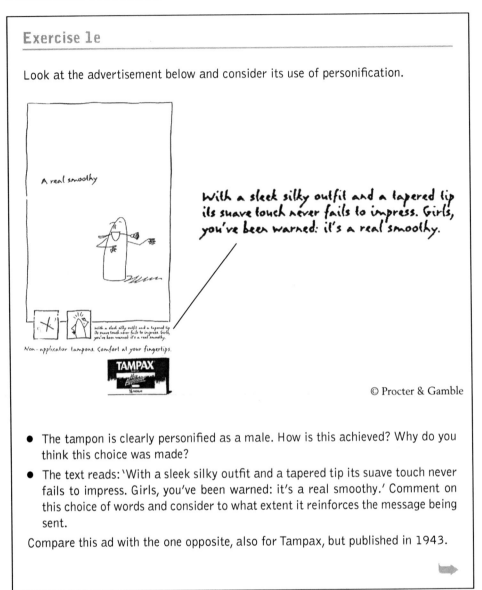

A real smoothy

With a sleek silky outfit and a tapered tip its suave touch never fails to impress. Girls, you've been warned: it's a real smoothy.

Non-applicator tampons. Comfort at your fingertips.

TAMPAX

© Procter & Gamble

- The tampon is clearly personified as a male. How is this achieved? Why do you think this choice was made?
- The text reads: 'With a sleek silky outfit and a tapered tip its suave touch never fails to impress. Girls, you've been warned: it's a real smoothy.' Comment on this choice of words and consider to what extent it reinforces the message being sent.

Compare this ad with the one opposite, also for Tampax, but published in 1943.

It is clear at first glance that the tampon is being represented as a person: it is depicted with a human face, arms and hands. More than this, the tampon is also given a specific gender: in Western culture and society, it is stereotypically men who give roses to women, and carrying a rose in the mouth is a traditional image of male romance. The language accompanying the picture confirms the process of personification: despite referring to the tampon as 'it', the headline tells us that the tampon is 'a real smoothy', and the text underneath advises us that the tampon comes with 'a sleek silky outfit' and a 'suave touch' which 'never fails to impress'. In this way the written text adds detail to the visual representation of the tampon as not only male,

SEALED IN ITS OWN SPECIAL APPLICATOR

Tampax, with its patented central stitching and its individual applicator, is the safe, simple and convenient internal sanitary protection for fastidious women. Invented by a doctor and produced by specialists it offers practical advantages available in no other form.

TAMPAX

Sanitary Protection

WORN INTERNALLY

Prices 7d. and 1/9. From all chemists, Boots, Timothy Whites & Taylors, departmental stores, drapers, Woolworth's, Marks & Spencer Ltd. and the N.A.A.F.I.

TAMPAX LTD, NORTHOLT, MIDDX
Distributors: SPLENDOR LTD., NOTTINGHAM

62

© Procter & Gamble

- What is the central message of the 1943 advert?
- The advertising concept for tampons has clearly changed in the 50-odd years between the two ads. What do you think has driven this shift?

but a male of a certain type, namely the smooth type, about whom girls (rather than women, presumably) have to be forewarned.

The question crying out to be answered is, of course, why an advertiser should choose to personify tampons in this way. One answer may lie in the relatively taboo nature of products concerned with 'feminine hygiene' – we have mentioned the device of euphemism in this context already – and it may be that the job of marketing them is made easier or more accessible by changing the nature of such goods from object to person. There is, too, a faintly humorous element to this treatment, which could have the effect of making the subject less forbidding.

The tone of the 1943 advertisement is very different from the 1990s example. Far greater attention is given to the description of the product: the tampon has 'patented central stitching' and an 'individual applicator'. The reader is also persuaded of the safety of the product: it is, after all, invented by a 'doctor' and manufactured by 'specialists'. Between the 1940s and the 1990s we thus see a change in focus from the provision of practical information about the product to persuasion through personification. While this shift may be explained by the fact that the product was relatively new in the 1940s and so in greater need of description, nevertheless a similar shift in focus, from informing to persuading, has taken place in all types of advertising (Dyer 1982). Indeed it can be argued that advertising has, over time, become less concerned with the communication of information about commodities and more concerned with the manipulation of social values and attitudes in a way that persuades us into patterns of consumption and consumerism.

We have explored three particular semantic strategies used in the construction and manipulation of meaning in advertising discourse. We have examined the discourse device of *personalization*, which functions to individualize recipients of mass marketing messages; the strategy of *presupposition*, which advertisers frequently employ to suggest a familiarity with their readers and hearers; and the tactic of *personification*, which promotes products, and occasionally producers, by giving them a life of their own.

Above all, in our discussion of the semantics of advertising, as well as in our examinations of sound selection, word choice and sentence structuring, we have seen how advertisers seek to establish relationships with potential consumers. As we have noted, they may use voices which speak to us directly or construct dialogues which cast us in the role of eavesdroppers; comparative sentence structures are also employed, along with question-and-answer sequences, all of which are aimed at establishing problem–solution relationships between consumers and products. The importance of these relationships cannot be overstated. The advertiser's central aim is to find a way of promoting products or services in line with the nature of the intended audience. It will be practical, then, to complete our analysis of advertising discourse with a brief study – a worked example, if you like – allowing us to focus in some detail on the importance of audience in the construction of advertising language.

We can examine the attention to audience by looking at the construction of two advertisements for cars, Figures 1.11 and 1.12, p. 39 and p. 40. Note that the cars advertised are of a similar type: both are SUV models, so we are comparing like with like. Comparison of advertisements for similar objects allows us to interpret any differences in the make-up of the marketing messages as a consequence of predicted audience, rather than as a result of the promotion of different products.

Figure 1.11 opposite is an advertisement for the Suzuki Grand Vitara XL-7 that appeared in *Auto Express*, a magazine which concentrates on cars and motoring. The advertisement for the Mercury Mountaineer (Figure 1.12) was published in *Elle*, which carries articles on a range of topics, including fashion, beauty and romance. Who, then, are the two adverts aimed at? And how are the marketing messages directed towards the particular audiences being targeted?

Fig. 1.11   Suzuki advert. The text top right reads: 7 seats, real 4×4 technology, 2.7 litre V6 engine. Everything about the new Grand Vitara XL-7 is impressive. It can take you, and six others, to locations near and far, on or off-road. XL-7, the perfect way to transport seven, by 4×4. To confirm your first impressions, call for an information pack on 01892 707007 or visit www.suzuki.co.uk.

Look at the two ads and try to identify how the advertisers tailor their message for two different target audiences. Try to locate any devices that are being used – especially at the levels of sound, words, structure and meaning, and consider how such devices are interrelated.

Clearly these messages are aimed at different genders. Consequently, despite the similarity of the cars being advertised, the language and the visuals are markedly different. We have already noted how linguistic and visual media are interwoven in the construction of marketing messages: we have seen especially how the visual element works together with language in order to evoke particular ideas, feelings or beliefs about the products being advertised.

The illustrations used here give us our first impression of the target audience. Both ads picture the car advertised, but the contexts are entirely different: the Suzuki is depicted with seven pairs of large muddy hiking boots in the foreground; the Mercury is placed in a city location that is clean, contemporary, modern and artistic. The fact that the associations may be stereotypical is important: in targeting particular audiences, advertisers have to rely on conventional ideas about the intended recipients of marketing messages. This results in generalized and clichéd assumptions being made about the interests and values of certain social groups (for example, age, gender and social class).

The language employed in the two advertisements works together with the visuals to address the intended audience. The Suzuki text opens with some numbers for our stereotypical male, relating to the technology of the vehicle and the number of the seats. Note the use of 'real' to describe the 4×4 aspect: does this not presuppose that 'unreal' 4×4 technologies exist – the 'reality' of the engineering

Fig. 1.12   Mercury advert

being implicitly compared to 'unrealistic', lesser models? There are also explicit linguistic contrasts being drawn: the vehicle can go both 'near' and 'far', and is suitable for 'on-road' as well as 'off-road' conditions. Note, too, the invitation to 'confirm our first impressions', which presupposes that those first impressions were positive. If they were, then they may owe something to a few of the advertiser's word choices – 'new', 'impressive' and 'perfect'.

What about the Mercury? No information (numerical or otherwise) is given about the technology of the vehicle: not even whether the vehicle is two- or four-wheel drive. Rather, the ad concentrates on describing the relationship between the car and the environment. And note the word choices for the designers: 'thoughtful', 'responsive' and 'acknowledging'. The manufacturers are being presented (to female readers) as considerate, kind and caring individuals. The thoughtful nature of the designers, in fact, makes the car itself an environment in which 'Grace' can live. The ambiguity of meaning here is deliberate: as well as being a feminine name, grace as a quality is a stereotypically feminine characteristic. Far more attention is paid to the passengers and the possessions which will be transported: we are told that the vehicle is designed 'to reflect not only where we live and drive most – but who and what we drive with'. The 'not only...but also' sentence structure suggests the multiple positive qualities of the vehicle. And as in the Suzuki ad, the text closes by making a presupposition: in this case, that this is a vehicle we have been waiting for.

In fact, looking at the texts as a whole, there are many more differences than similarities. True, both ads contain the adjective 'new', and both include web addresses, but neither of these is surprising. The differences are a consequence of the influence of the target audience. We can clearly see that the advertisers are shaping their messages (both visual and linguistic) to appeal to specific consumers.

We have just briefly explored the influence of gender on the making of marketing messages. However, gender is only one of many social or demographic factors which advertisers consider in designing messages for specific targets: statistics on age, social class, ethnicity and occupation are also used in order to appeal to particular groups. The focus on target audience is significant in all forms of advertising, and in order to fully understand the language of this mass media we need always to examine the relationship between the producers and the consumers of advertising discourse.

The linguistic strategies used within the discourse of advertising are multilayered and multifaceted, and are employed in a craftsmanlike way to construct the meaning of advertisements. The primary aim of advertising discourse is persuasion, and this is as true of social advertising as it is of commercial marketing. However, it is commercial ads which are most prolific in our culture, and it is commercial ads which seek specifically to lead us into a life of consumerism. This form of advertising, and the discourse which characterizes it, is a crucial factor in the organization and structure of our society – not least because it contrives to pervade many areas of our social practice in ways that can be invidious and controlling.

This is a convenient moment, then, to turn our attention to the discourse of politics.

Further exercises

1 Look back at all the examples of advertisements and slogans in this chapter. The bottom-up approach taken in this book inevitably means that certain examples are noted for the use of one particular device rather than another. Consider how many of the examples could easily have been selected as evidence of the use of several other linguistic devices.

2 Examine the following three Coca-Cola advertisements:

© Coca-Cola

Get cracking, pal...Have a Coke
(DO YOUR STUFF)

...or it's fun to make friends

It's an international event that always comes off smoothly when fighting men of Canada, Britain and the U. S. A. get together for a bit of sociability. Especially when there's Coca-Cola around to add friendliness to new acquaintance. *Have a Coke* is an invitation that everybody understands, whether it's spoken with a Canadian, British or American accent —or any accent in the world. It means *I'm for you, chum; we can get along*—from Los Angeles to London, from Macon to Montreal. At most any stop on the globe, *the pause that refreshes* with ice-cold Coca-Cola is a familiar symbol of good will.

* * *

Our fighting men meet up with Coca-Cola many places overseas, where it's bottled on the spot. Coca-Cola has been a globe-trotter "since way back when".

Coca-Cola
-the global
high-sign

"Coke"=Coca-Cola
You naturally hear Coca-Cola called by its friendly abbreviation "Coke". Both mean the quality product of The Coca-Cola Company.

COPYRIGHT 1943, THE COCA-COLA COMPANY

43

The first ad is from the immediate pre-war era, the second from wartime and the third from shortly after the end of the war. Look at all three ads for instances of the persuasive devices outlined in the chapter. Consider carefully whether these derive from the level of sounds, words or sentence structure, and ask yourself how these devices (and any others you might identify) contribute to the creation of meaning in the discourse. What evidence do you find of the adverts targeting particular audiences? Given that the drink itself, and its familiar refreshing and reinvigorating properties, could scarcely have changed much in the period between the three ads, try to isolate further the way that the advertisements appeal to the different value systems of wartime and peacetime. Would any of these advertisements work effectively today? You might like to look out for some current examples of Coca-Cola advertisements and try to identify critical similarities and differences between the advertising discourse of the present day and the period covered by the three older ads.

Finally, go back to Exercise 1a and look again at the answers you gave about the Coca-Cola advertisement there. Having read the chapter, would you answer any of the questions differently?

3 Try to assemble a reasonably wide selection of magazine advertisements for products that are essentially similar in nature, but aimed at different audiences: one example might be promotions for beauty creams, aimed at younger and older women. Analyse how the advertisers use different discourse strategies to target their audiences effectively. Are there any particular word choices that occur significantly often in appealing to one or other of the target audiences? Do you find any evidence of sound-play being used? How are the readers located in relation to the speakers of the ads? In what ways are meanings manipulated, for instance, by the devices of personalization or presupposition?

Claptrap

The discourse of politics

'If anybody wants to clap,' said Eeyore...'now is the time to do it.' They all clapped.
'Thank you,' said Eeyore. 'Unexpected and gratifying.'
AA Milne (1928)

Introduction

The intense mediatization of modern-day politics, and its increasing reliance on the techniques of professional advertisers and media-savvy PR experts, means that it is frequently unclear where to draw the line between the discourses of politics, media and advertising. Political discourse has been profoundly affected by the rapid media expansion of the twentieth and twenty-first centuries, and mass communication systems have resulted in a huge proliferation of the forms it can take. No longer are we restricted to listening to speeches in face-to-face encounters with politicians: we now also have access to parliamentary debates, radio phone-ins, party political broadcasts, TV-staged debates and press conferences, as well as highly polished multimedia election campaigns. The texts of political speeches and interviews are now widely available to us in electronic form.

On the face of it, this may appear to be giving us a greater opportunity to examine the language used by politicians, but in fact the opposite is probably the case. The truth is that more and more of the genuine business of politics is taking place behind closed doors – a phenomenon dubbed 'sofa politics' in the UK – and if we are able to observe it at all, it is generally only through the carefully managed filters of the media. Add this to the growing trend, in Britain at least, towards the employment of unelected policy-making advisers and consultants, and you have all the makings of a political system that is highly secretive about its communications as well as increasingly unaccountable to the electorate.

Consequently, most of the political discourse that we do get to observe is more or less stage-managed. Public statements are, whenever possible, delivered within the safe haven of a pre-arranged press conference or a friendly political chat show, where they can be prepared by professional speech-writers and rigorously rehearsed in advance. It is an open secret that politicians will look to grant 'in-depth' interviews exclusively to one broadcaster, in return for guarantees that certain issues will not appear on the agenda, and it is now commonplace for the UK government to decline to send a representative to a less-than-friendly news station to discuss a controversial issue, especially at short notice. Traditional door-to-door canvassing by prospective Members of Parliament has been reduced largely to a photo opportunity, with politicians literally scampering from house to house for the benefit of the cameras.

Even apparently spontaneous statements can turn out to be well-rehearsed performances: UK prime minister Tony Blair's short, and seemingly very personal, public statement after Princess Diana's death in 1997, for example, was later attributed to Alistair Campbell, his powerful communications adviser at the time. Blair's formidable skills as an actor and a showman have been more widely recognized since then, engendering considerable doubt as to how you tell whose words he is speaking.

As with advertising, then, we must be vigilant when we look at the discourse of politics to seek evidence of this stage management, especially in the form of rehearsed rhetorical devices – often called 'claptrap' since they are carefully designed to signal the right moment for the audience to break into 'spontaneous' applause.

Exercise 2a

Examine the data below, taken from a speech by Tony Blair to the Labour centenary conference on 10 February 2006. What is it that makes this so typically a piece of political discourse?

So what is the agenda that we are carrying through?

It is to modernize our country, so that, in the face of future challenges, intense and profound for us and like nations, we are able to provide opportunity and security for all; not for an elite; not for the privileged few; but for all our people, whatever their class, colour or creed.

It is to build on the platform of economic stability, the modern knowledge economy with the skills, dynamism, technological and scientific progress a country like Britain needs.

It is to put on top of the major investment in schools and the NHS, the quality and standards of service people expect today and on the basis of equity not wealth.

It is to set the goal of eradicating child poverty and march steadily over time to achieving it as we have begun to do.

It is why we understand that providing security is our duty and realize that to try to fight the new security threats of the twenty-first century without the laws and the resources that are needed, would be an abrogation of that duty.

It is why, albeit in ways often deeply controversial, we have sought to place Britain at the centre of world events from fighting terrorism to fighting global poverty and climate change, because, in an interdependent world, that is the place for Britain to be, to safeguard its own interests.

- Does the language of this speech strike you as formal or informal? Why? Are there any individual words that appear particularly formal or informal in this context?

47

- Consider how the speech is structured. How does this structure enhance the message that Blair is trying to convey?
- Examine Blair's use of 'we', 'our' and 'us'. In each case, who do these pronouns refer to?
- Are there any devices in the speech that seem to you to be obviously rhetorical? At which points (if any) do you suppose that Blair might be expecting the audience to applaud?
- In what sense can this discourse be said to have 'history', and how does it rely on former texts?

Bear in mind your answers to the above exercise as we proceed through our analysis of political discourse. You may well find it instructive to return to the exercise again at the end of the chapter and reappraise your answers.

It will, I imagine, be no great surprise if we find that the persuasive linguistic techniques used in advertising discourse are also commonplace in the language of politics, whether it be the exploitation of alliteration (an early twenty-first-century government paper on immigration bears the title *Fairer, Faster and Firmer*) or even rhyme (particularly in the press) as a form of sound-play: 'Blair's babes', 'Tony's cronies'. It might be the use of hyperbole and metaphor at word and phrase level: 'beacons of excellence', 'axis of evil', 'cascade of change'; or the employment of clever personalization and smart, snappy syntax: 'your family better off under Labour'.

It should not be a great surprise because there is nothing especially new about this crafting of language: political sloganizing has been with us since time immemorial. Political entities have long sought to encapsulate themselves in words and mottos, painstakingly whittled down to capture the central message that underpins their affiliation.

In God We Trust (USA)

Liberté, Egalité, Fraternité (France)

Never Again (Jewish Defense League)

The Union Makes Us Strong (Trades Union Congress)

The sound bite is not a uniquely modern phenomenon. Not much has changed in this respect from Cato the Elder's constant insistence that *Carthago delenda est* (Carthage must be destroyed) to George W. Bush's incessant mantra that the USA is at 'war on terror'. Repeated often enough, these catchphrases do seem to lodge in the brain, and can even acquire a friendly familiarity, rather like some of the successful advertising jingles we examined in the last chapter.

As with advertising straplines, so too political slogans and catchphrases vary widely. They can, for example, be potent and memorable: *Workers of the world, unite*; *Power to the people*. Or pointed and clever: *Are you better off than you were four years ago?*; *New Labour, new danger* (see Figure 2.01).

Fig. 2.01   Conservative election poster 1997

Like some advertising copy, they may be destined to be absorbed into everyday language: *Tax and spend; There's no such thing as a free lunch*. They can occasionally be strikingly stark: *Whoever is anti Chairman Mao we will have his head; Vote early, and vote often*. The majority, though, tend to be vapid and woolly: *Changing Britain, improving lives; Britain forward not back*. Even to the point of being semantically hollow or empty: *Are you thinking what we're thinking?* (see Figure 2.02); *Together we can*. While at least one, we might want to say, was just tempting fate: *Things can only get better*.

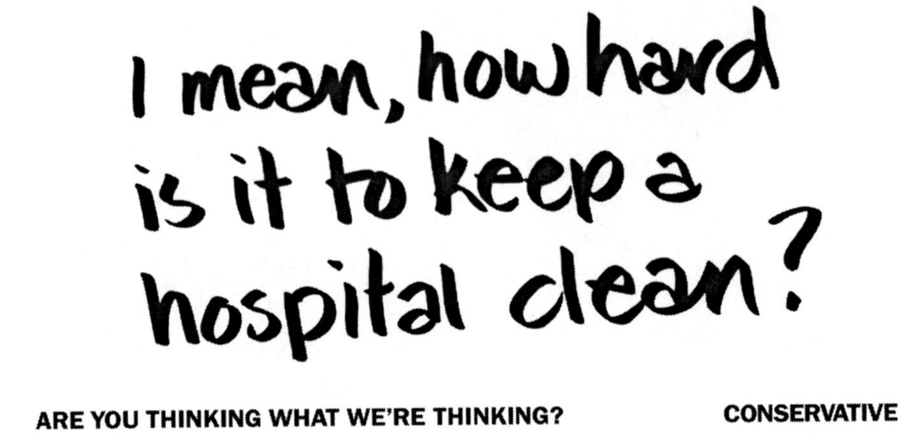

I mean, how hard is it to keep a hospital clean?

ARE YOU THINKING WHAT WE'RE THINKING? **CONSERVATIVE**

Fig. 2.02   Conservative election slogan 2005

Slogans are an important and familiar aspect of political language, but they are only a tiny fraction of political discourse, just as journalistic headlines and advertising straplines represent merely the tips of their industries' own particular icebergs. As with the language of advertising, political discourse is also multifunctional: it may be used, for example, to perform a variety of speech acts: to protest, to legitimize, to intimidate, as well as to persuade, of course. Indeed, in much the same way as the discourse of advertising seeks to persuade us to purchase a product or service, the language used by politicians is designed to lead us to a particular view of political reality, and to act in a way that is consistent with this view – by voting for a particular party, for example.

So the discourse of politics is by no means confined to rabble-rousing slogans and gimmicky phrases. Indeed, since politics has as its central aim the acquisition and retention of power for certain groups and individuals – and most particularly the authority to control the accumulation and distribution of a society's economic wealth and goods – the stakes of the commercial advertiser's game are raised here by a very significant amount. The linguistic devices that the political world employs can end up having far-reaching and even devastating effects: war, after all, is ultimately a political construct. The discourse of politics undoubtedly warrants a detailed and critical examination all of its own.

Such examination lies at the heart of **critical discourse analysis**. As discussed in the introduction to this book, this interdisciplinary analytical perspective seeks to examine the relationship between power and discourse, and particularly to look at the way in which authority, dominance and social inequality are constructed, sustained, reproduced and resisted in the discourse of written texts and spoken words. Critical discourse analysis aims to unpack the 'common-sense' social and cultural assumptions (or ideologies) which, below the level of conscious awareness, are embedded in all the forms of language that we use. By making hidden assumptions visible, critical analysis challenges the practice by which the words of powerful members of society are taken as 'self-evident truths', while the words of others are dismissed as irrelevant or without substance.

Critical approaches to discourse have been used to study many different discourses and it has been particularly influential in relation to the study of politics and politics-related discourses. It is an approach to language and discourse which, unusually, takes an overtly political position and, by bringing to light the workings of established social and political structures, seeks to challenge accepted patterns of inequality, oppression and repression. Fairclough, in particular, works from the thesis that the discourse presented by politicians constructs the principles governing our daily lives.[1]

Differences in political policy can indeed often be boiled down to different ways of using language, and a government or party that wants to manage public perceptions of political issues will need to make the management of language a high priority. In the highly mediatized political climate of the early twenty-first century, anyone speaking on the government's behalf, whether it be the prime minister or a junior Treasury adviser, will consciously strive to be 'on-message', in both the content and the style of their language. As Fairclough points out: 'the New Labour way of governing...is in part a way of using language' (2000: 12).

This need for 'political correctness' is an especially important feature in a democracy, where consent and consensus have to be achieved, and be seen to be achieved. It becomes even more urgent in the case of a politically apathetic Western democracy, such as Britain or the USA, where the carefully managed courting and motivating of a specific (and often quite small) target group of voters is elevated to prime importance.

The close association between politics and language is, as we have said, nothing new. Aristotle saw that human beings are naturally political animals who require and use language to pursue political ends. The construction of political systems and states, where individuals need to be persuaded to act cooperatively for the welfare of all, appears to rely on the use of a symbolic communication system, and it is quite conceivable that these two peculiarly human characteristics have evolved simultaneously. The village chief who needs to convince his villagers to cooperate in constructing a defensive wall, for example, relies on the unique ability of humans to use language for planning future action not motivated by immediate concerns.[2]

Certainly the power of rhetoric, the oratorical art of manipulating language for persuasive ends, was well understood in classical times. It is often claimed that Pericles governed the great Athenian democracy for 30 years by virtue of his rhetoric alone, for despite his huge influence he himself had no governmental policy-making power – only the democratic right to address the Assembly and persuade its members if he could. Curiously, he frequently found it necessary to convince them to build a defensive wall or two.

Cicero later went further, declaring the art of rhetoric to be the most valuable skill a Roman citizen could have – though naturally as the greatest orator of his day he had a vested interest in saying so. In classical times, however, there was a moral dimension to oratory and rhetoric that has not necessarily persisted: the ideal classical orator was both morally and politically virtuous, and the ability to use persuasive speech was subtly interlinked and correlated with issues of truthfulness, fairness and honesty.

As Lincoln said in 1864, 'you can't fool all of the people all of the time'.

Rhetorical language simply is not always honest: it may equally well be used to obscure or twist the truth. Consequently, political discourse, like that of advertising, needs to develop quickly and cleverly if its manipulative aspect is not to become too obvious. The public can easily tire of hearing or reading the same old tricks, and present-day administrations are finding themselves accused more and more often of indulging in 'spin', the black art of shaping the output of political discourse. Spin techniques include the careful manipulation of the press, the selective use of facts, cherry-picking (exclusively presenting evidence that supports a biased position), phrasing of language in a way that presents unproven information as fact, and the insidious use of metaphor and euphemism to influence and colour our perception of political events and actions. But, as anyone knows who has witnessed the rehearsed patter and devious dodges of a minister being interviewed, the overall effect of overtly manipulative linguistic devices can, often quite literally, be a turn-off: not at all what the spin doctor ordered.

George Orwell foresees some of this in his prophetic novel *1984* (first published, we should remember, in 1949), which looks forward bleakly to a time when government totally controls language – around 2050, he envisages. Even by 1984 the process is well advanced, and the effect, as described by Winston Smith, will be all too familiar to anyone who has seen a politician being interviewed on the evening news: 'The stuff that was coming out of him consisted of words, but it was not speech in the true sense: it was a noise uttered in unconsciousness, like the quacking of a duck' (Orwell 1952: 47). What's more, this style of speaking ('duckspeak') is actually regarded by the Party as a valuable oratorical skill: 'When the *Times* referred to one of the orators of the Party as a "doubleplusgood duckspeaker" it was paying a warm and valued compliment' (Orwell 1952: 249).

The challenge for present-day practitioners of the art of spin, then, is that, if it is to be effective, it must be subtle. If it is obtrusive, it can actually be counterproductive. The more that governments and political parties are seen to be devoting their time and effort to style and presentation, rather than to substantive policies, the greater the danger that the political process will be perceived to be falling into the hands of PR experts, focusing on form rather than substance, on appearance rather than reality. The word 'rhetoric' itself has begun to acquire a definite negative connotation. Tellingly, at a critical time for the New Labour government in Britain in 1998, deputy prime minister John Prescott was moved to declare that the party needed 'to get away from rhetoric and back on to the substance of government' (*The Independent*, 30 December 1998). The increased political focus on highly controlled media presentation, along with politicians' reluctance to engage in honest and open debate on specific issues, is widely seen as a major contributory factor in the high level of apathy among Western electorates in the early twenty-first century.

Fairclough sums up the current concern about rhetoric when he asks us to consider: 'Is New Labour's "new politics for a new Britain" just rhetoric, just empty words? Does the government's notorious taste for "media spin" mean that presentation becomes more important than policy, rhetoric more important than substance?' (2000: vii). Former Conservative prime minister John Major presented a personal view in the *Daily Telegraph* (22 February 2005): 'Politicians have always used spin to put a favourable gloss on events... But the difference now is that, as New Labour uses it, truth is too often turned on its head... Words mean what they wish them to mean. Bad news is good. Up is down. Black is white. Fiction is fact.'

Political discourse, then, is not by any means a neutral medium of communication. Like the discourse of advertising, it is one designed to lead its audience in the direction of particular thoughts, beliefs and, ultimately, actions. Therefore it needs to be examined in the context of communicative settings and political functions, and by reference to the political realities which are actually constructed in the discourse itself.

In conducting our examination, we will focus – as we did with advertising – on the levels of language that constitute political discourse. We will begin with the level of sound, which includes the representation of voices in politics as well as the devices of sound-play characteristically used in its discourse. We will also pay attention to the level of vocabulary, as we look at the ways in which political reality can be constructed by careful selection and presentation of lexical elements. We will then take account of syntactic structure, which, as we will see, is a key element in arranging political messages for maximum desired effect. And again, as with advertising, we will conclude by attempting to cast light on how all these elements (and others) are interwoven and layered to manipulate the meanings of political messages, whether rehearsed and stage-managed for media consumption or produced apparently off the cuff in the arenas of the debate or the face-to-face interview.

Sound policies: voices and sounds in politics

Just as politics is a linguistic subject, so language is a political issue. Which languages do we hear represented in the political arena? The UK, for example, is a multilingual nation, but how many tongues are spoken in the business of government? Official, standard languages tend to dominate in all political contexts, and in the UK and the USA this official language is English. But what of countries that have more than one official language? The example of New Zealand is instructive: since 1987, English and Maori have both had official language status, but the truth is that political affairs are conducted primarily in English. In Singapore there are four official languages – Tamil, Mandarin Chinese, Malay and English – but, as in the UK, the USA and New Zealand, English is the dominant language of the Singaporean political arena. In fact, English still rules the roost in many countries where the majority of the population does not even speak English or has only very limited knowledge of the language.

As well as being dominated by official and standard languages, politics has traditionally been a domain in which formal or conventional language is required, and, historically, the tone of political speaking has been reserved and, in many aspects, ritualistic and ceremonial. Look at the way in which politicians address each other in the UK House of Commons (interestingly, in the example that follows, the subject matter is 'spin'), and note the formality involved:

> Mr Gerald Howarth (Aldershot) (Con): On a point of order, Mr. Speaker. We have been expecting delivery later this week of the National Audit Office's annual report on the 20 largest defence projects——a report that always

commands widespread public interest. To my surprise, this afternoon the Press Association carries a story that the Minister responsible for defence procurement has held a press briefing providing a partial interpretation of the forthcoming NAO report. I have checked with the Public Accounts Committee, which tells me that the report is embargoed until one minute past midnight on Friday... Is it not a grave discourtesy to us and, indeed, to all Members with an interest in these matters, that the Ministry of Defence has sought to use its privileged position to taint and pre-empt public reaction to the forthcoming NAO report? If you agree with me, Mr. Speaker, can you advise me on what we might do about it?

Mr Speaker: Order. Perhaps I can reply to the honourable Member for Aldershot first... Obviously I am not aware of the circumstances surrounding the matter raised by the honourable Member for Aldershot. This is the first time that it has come to my attention. However, I would be very angry indeed if information required for the House went first to journalists. I am not happy with that, and I condemn such an action. The best advice that I can give the honourable Gentleman is that he should allow me to investigate the matter. My officials will look into it this afternoon and will get in touch with the appropriate Minister.

(*Hansard*, 22 November 2005)

Note the ritualistic use of formal titles rather than names: 'the honourable Member for Aldershot', 'the honourable Gentleman', 'Mr Speaker', as well as the strong focus on courtesy and order, and note too the formal debating chamber convention that every exchange should have an interrogative form and be directed to the Speaker of the House. It is a matter of some wonder that all these requirements and conventions are being solemnly observed at a moment of heated (and eventually headline-worthy) debate.

Some of the linguistic conventions actually border on the ludicrous: MPs are forbidden, for example, to refer to the House of Lords (the upper chamber) by name, and are expected to refer to it only as 'another place'; visitors, preposterously, may only be referred to as 'strangers'. While these are clearly vocabulary considerations, they nevertheless contribute strongly to an overall 'sound' of political discourse that marks it out as different from 'ordinary' discourse. Some modern politicians make political capital from expressing distaste for such ritual and ceremony, and in the late twentieth and early twenty-first centuries there has been a general and noticeable shift towards a greater degree of informality in British political speaking and political life.

This shift towards more informal ways of speaking may itself be an effect of the increased mediatization of politics that we have mentioned already. The BBC's digital 'Parliament' channel certainly demonstrates to the nation the arcane, ritualistic and unremittingly tedious nature of the political discourse conducted there. But at the same time other branches of the media have begun to embrace political personalities in an entirely new (and occasionally deeply embarrassing) way: politicians now appear regularly on TV game shows, talk shows and 'reality' spectacles – often seemingly blind or careless as to the risks these programmes may pose to their political reputations.

Hand in hand with this increased media exposure has come a significant shift towards the presentation of personalities in politics, perhaps at the expense of political principles. Politicians in key posts now need to look and sound like 'the real thing': the 2005 battle for the leadership of the Conservative Party in Britain was largely (and more or less self-admittedly) decided on rhetorical skill and presentation, and it was surely no accident that the winner, David Cameron, came from a background in public relations.

Of course, TV personalities have to have the right names. Tony Blair is the first British prime minister to be known officially by his nickname, Tony, rather than his full name, Anthony. Consider how unlikely it would have been for Winston Churchill to call himself Winnie, or Neville Chamberlain to adopt the style Nev. While the popular press often shortened the forenames of later prime ministers Heath, Callaghan and Thatcher to Ted, Jim and Maggie, respectively, these names were rarely, if ever, used publicly or officially. Indeed, it is possible to see Blair's use of Tony as deliberately misleading, and the media's acceptance of it as gullible. It is curious to note that one of the few public uses of the name Anthony Blair was by Blair's wife, Cherie Booth, when she stood for election as Labour candidate for North Thanet (this was before Blair himself became an MP). As an international statesman, however, Blair frequently finds himself billed – like it or not – with his full title: The Right Honourable Anthony Charles Lynton Blair, MP.

It is quite possible that the deliberate use of an informal tone or style of address, adopted in order to suggest a more personalized relationship between politicians and the public, will fall foul of the problem that advertisers face when attempting the same trick: the effect may well be merely synthetic, or even perceived as deliberate artifice. Such artificial informality seems to be a device that politicians are eager to attack if they spot it in others. Apparently oblivious to the fact that his own leader is so regularly mocked for his 'call me Tony' style, deputy leader John Prescott was nonetheless provoked to take a swipe at Cameron's efforts to build himself a similar image as a 'man of the people':

> It's no wonder they're still in opposition. No wonder they're on their fifth leader in eight years. Major, Hague, Duncan-Smith, Howard. And now Cameron. Dave Cameron. Blimey, every day of the week Dave's ditching something, and changing his beliefs... Let me give Dave a little bit of advice: politics is not, despite what he thinks, all about image... Cameron's all rhetoric, not record; image, not substance.
>
> (Labour Party conference, 11 February 2006)

If modern British politics is increasingly characterized by an informal tone (note Prescott's use of 'blimey'), then, in the case of Tony Blair at least, the informal way he chooses to be addressed is also reflected in a certain informality of speech style:

> Britain should also remain the strongest ally of the United States. I know there's a bit of us that would like me to do a Hugh Grant in *Love Actually* and tell America where to get off. But the difference between a good film and real life is that in real life there's the next day, the next year, the next lifetime to contemplate the ruinous consequences of easy applause.
>
> (Labour Party conference, 27 September 2005)

55

This was, we should remember, a carefully scripted and rehearsed performance. But by referring to the topical and popular British movie, Blair contrives to present himself as sharing tastes with the ordinary man or woman in the street, and his use of colloquial terms such as 'do a Hugh Grant' and 'tell America where to get off' looks to establish his status as 'just one of us'. Blair's use of these vernacular phrases is, strictly, a matter for lexical analysis, but it does also allow him to slide into a slightly more 'man of the people' accent: Blair, like anyone else, is happy to vary his accent a little to suit the audience he is speaking to, or the effect he is looking to create.[3]

Just as we saw with advertising, accent can be a key consideration in the sending of a political message. Interesting work has been done on identifying politicians' adoption of certain accents for what appear to be political reasons. It has been reported, for example, that Sinn Fein's leader Gerry Adams has absorbed certain southern Irish dialect forms into his own Belfast accent; and, similarly, that some members of the opposing Democratic Unionist Party have modified elements of their phonology in the direction of an Ulster Scots dialect. Politicians can therefore choose to 'sound' ideologically attractive, by adopting elements of an accent that demonstrably mean something to the public: specific sounds are clearly perceived to be, say, more Catholic, Irish and Republican than Protestant, British and Unionist.[4]

It will not have escaped your notice, I am sure, that virtually all the politicians mentioned thus far, from Pericles to Gerry Adams, have been male; this reflects the fact that, with a few notable exceptions, politics in Western democracies has tended to be largely a male-dominated domain. Traditionally, male voices have prevailed in the political arena. However, top political positions have become more accessible and open to women: in the early twenty-first century Germany and Liberia provide evidence of this, as does the appointment of Condoleezza Rice as Secretary of State in the USA.

The election of Margaret Thatcher as prime minister in 1979 was a landmark in the admission of women to British public and political life. As a woman entering a male-dominated arena, Thatcher was required to construct a particular public image and to speak with a voice of authority. It has been well documented that she went to considerable lengths to meet this challenge, training her voice both to become lower in pitch and to vary less in pitch pattern: in other words, to sound more like a man.[5] It is worth noting here that she also developed particular speech strategies to control the order and flow of political debates: for example, speaking through the natural pauses in discussions where changes of speaker-turn would usually take place, and employing a tone of voice that made it difficult for others to interrupt her statements. She also became a dab hand at the rousing set-piece political speech.

Speech-making is, as we have already said, a highly stage-managed performance. Political speech-writing is typically in the hands of cunning and practised professionals, experts at exploiting precisely the devices we have already seen used by advertising copywriters. It is no surprise, then, at the level of sound, to find that major political speeches are spiced up with similar linguistic devices, such as repetition, rhythm and alliteration, to ensure that their messages are as potent and memorable as possible.

Exercise 2b

Look at this excerpt from Tony Blair's speech at the launch of Labour's general election manifesto on 13 April 2005. You may even find it helpful to read it aloud, as we are going to concentrate most particularly on its 'sound'.

> There is a big vision behind today's Manifesto. It is that everyone, not just a few, should get the chance to succeed and make the most of the talent they have. It is to build in Britain the genuine opportunity society, where what matters is hard work, merit, playing by the rules – not class or privilege or background.
>
> But today I want to focus on the straightforward, practical ways to achieve it. Every line in this Manifesto has this driving mission behind it: to support and help hard-working families to cope and prosper in the face of the stresses, strains and struggles of modern life. Their interests come first. Their priorities are our priorities.

- Imagine you are writing a short journalistic piece about the speech. Can you identify any 'sound bites' that you might be tempted to pick out for a headline here?
- Do you notice anything about the rhythm of the speech, particularly in any sections where Blair is repeating or listing items?
- Does anything about this speech remind you of advertising discourse?

There are some real elements here of what politics 'sounds like'. There's a sound bite, a little hook conveniently placed for the election campaign to hang its hat on: *Britain – the genuine opportunity society*. Then there's a list of 'what matters', presented as three key qualities that together define the values of the audience that the campaign is aiming at – 'hard work, merit, playing by the rules'.

Of course, those three elements do all go together, don't they? Or do they? Our examination of advertising discourse has already shown us that a list of three suggests unity and completeness, whether justified or not. It also creates the familiar 'claptrap' rhythm that audiences recognize as both persuasive and properly political. No surprise, then, to find the inclusion of three contrasting elements: 'not class or privilege or background'. We are invited, by virtue of that contrast, to assume that these are qualities valued by rival parties, though of course this cannot be said explicitly, not least because it patently is not true.

The New Labour mantra of 'hard work' is picked up almost immediately, introduced this time by a dynamic metaphor: Labour's 'driving mission' is to 'help hard-working families to cope'. To cope with what? The 'stresses, strains and struggles' of modern life – another satisfying three-part list, this time loaded with sibilant alliteration. No time to ponder on what exactly the meaningful difference might be between stresses and strains, though, because the big strapline is about to be delivered: 'their interests come first'. And then, in case you did not catch it the first time, it is reiterated, in a slightly different form: 'their priorities are our priorities'.

We will return to more of this speech later in the chapter, to look at how these linguistic strategies interrelate with others to weave a discourse that creates a number of political meanings and presuppositions. But we should note for now that the rhythm of repetition rolls like a drum throughout the speech (as it does through much political rhetoric), and in so doing creates a noise that authentically 'sounds like' politics: the modern equivalent of tub-thumping. However, much of the repetition in this speech occurs at the level of sentence structure, and we will therefore pick up the thread again when we reach our analysis of syntax. For the moment, we will keep our focus on sound and, if only to avoid a premature charge of political bias, turn our attention to the discourse of the political party in opposition to Labour in the UK at the time of writing.[6]

On the Conservative side of the debate, unsurprisingly, the same sounds are being made. Again we find the rhythm of three, though David Cameron's style favours the setting of *it's not that, it's not that, it's this*. Here are a few examples from a speech given in 2006:

> Plainly we aren't in favour of anarchy
>
> And we aren't in favour of monolithic state provision
>
> We are in favour of striking a balance
>
> (Launch of Democracy Task Force, 6 February 2006)

The same style and rhythm is echoed later in the speech:

> It was not the same sort of problem that Old Labour had faced
>
> It was not a problem that arose from the failure of our ideas
>
> It was, on the contrary, a problem that arose from the triumph of our ideas

Again alliteration proves irresistible:

> Social mobility, safer streets, a strong economy, are good Conservative aims.

In fact, alliteration seems almost to function as the harmonic, or perhaps the counterpoint, of political discourse. Whether it is loaded on to a list, a contrast or a slogan, it is a feature of many examples of political language admired as notably memorable and potent:

> Judge my children not by the colour of their skin, but by the content of their character...
>
> (Martin Luther King, 28 July 1963)

> We will have no truce or parley with you, or the grisly gang who work your wicked will.
>
> (Winston Churchill, 14 July 1941)

Even George W. Bush (not a noted orator, it has to be said) exploited the device in his 2003 Address to the Nation when he vowed to help the Middle East become a 'place of progress and peace'. And Tony Blair, discussing global terrorism in a speech in his Sedgefield constituency on 5 March 2004, claimed that: 'no decision I have ever made in politics has been as divisive as the decision to go to war in Iraq... It was divisive because it was difficult'.

It may be that alliteration of this type is particularly useful in lending unity to two or more concepts that are not obviously connected in any other way. Divisive decisions do not always have to be difficult – unless, of course, your aim is to be 'all things to all people', a criticism that is frequently levelled at Tony Blair.

Our new, happy life: the vocabulary of politics

What a difference a word makes. Consider again Tony Blair's difficult decision: 'to go to war in Iraq'. What if he had said: 'go to war *on* Iraq'?

Careful and selective use of words is a crucial aspect of the construction of political discourse. In the above example, the difference between the prepositions 'in' and 'on' is critical to our perception of political events and situations: 'in Iraq' manages to convey the impression that Iraq just happens to be where the war is taking place. The UK, after all, is not technically at war with Iraq at all; the UK, we should remind ourselves, is simply supporting its ally the USA, which is at 'war on terror'. (I am reminded of Anthony Eden's insistence in 1956 that 'we are not at war with Egypt – we are in an armed conflict'.)

It would be wrong to imagine, though, that in political discourse a single word can generally make so much difference. As Wilson points out: 'in most cases it is the context, or reflected form of words, which carries the political message' (2001: 408). With this in mind, we should note that in political discourse constructed for public consumption the selection of words tends to be strategic or tactical. Norman Fairclough's recent corpus of New Labour political speeches finds the following words to be particularly frequent: 'new', 'we', 'welfare', 'Britain', 'partnership', 'schools', 'people', 'reform', 'promote', 'deal', 'young', 'crime', 'deliver', 'business', 'tough' (2000: 17–18). Most common of all is the word 'new': it had been used 609 times in 53 of Tony Blair's speeches up to that point. We will recall that 'new' is also abundant in advertising discourse, especially to convince consumers that a brand is 'the same but different': 'It's still Sudso, but now it washes even whiter'. The use of the adjective 'new' in political discourse seems to serve broadly similar functions, and appears in characteristic collocations such as *New Labour*, *New Britain* and *New Deal*.[7]

The process of rebranding a soap powder involves Old Sudso getting taken off the shelves and New Sudso taking its place. It may take a few weeks, but once the supermarkets have done their stuff, New Sudso is the only game in town. If you happened to prefer the old formulation, well...tough, really.

Old Labour, however, did not simply disappear in the wake of the new version. It sat on the backbenches and fumed, and from time to time it even made a proper nuisance of itself. Nevertheless, the rebranding of Labour as New Labour was a conspicuous success, as evidenced at three consecutive general elections, and it is hard not to agree with Fairclough's analysis that 'changing the name wasn't just reflecting a shift in political ideology, it was manipulating language to control public perception' (2000: vii).

The manipulation of language at the level of words and phrases generally needs to be achieved with some subtlety if it is to be achieved at all. True, the deliberate selection of emotionally charged vocabulary to label people or processes involved in politically sensitive issues is still evident in the press, particularly when political opinions are sharply divided – as in the case of a shift in immigration policy, for example, or an unpopular war. An article published in *The Guardian* (23 January 1991) discussed how jingoism was reflected in a single week's media coverage of the first Gulf War. Among its observations were:

We have	**They have**
Army, Navy and Air Force	A war machine
Press briefings	Propaganda
Our boys are	**Their boys are**
Professional	Brainwashed
Young knights of the sky	Bastards of Baghdad
George Bush is	**Saddam Hussein is**
At peace with himself	Demented
Statesmanlike	An evil tyrant

It has to be said that this kind of analysis is fairly unscientific, and the examples above were published, I suspect, as much for their entertainment value as for any serious discussion they might provoke. Extreme reporting bias is pretty soon exposed these days: there are plenty of pressure groups out there ready to blow the whistle on any evidence of media bias, especially if it affects them. This is not to suggest that media bias does not happen – it does. But even quite subtle bias at the party political level tends to be jumped on quickly, especially by governments whose spin doctors necessarily have finely tuned antennae for any suggestion of media slant.

The most serious media bias these days is probably engineered at government policy-making level anyway, either through carefully staged press briefings or pressure on editors to toe particular political lines. According to a report in *The Guardian* (22 April 2003), for example, the BBC cautioned senior management, in a memo dated 6 February, the week before the biggest protests against the Iraq war, to 'be careful' about broadcasting antiwar actions. As we have been suggesting, modern-day spin at the level of vocabulary is less about the deliberate use (or abuse) of emotionally charged lexical items, and more about the careful *promotion* of words and concepts designed to construct a network of presupposed political realities.

Look again at the list of words most frequently found in Fairclough's corpus of New Labour speeches: 'new', 'we', 'welfare', 'Britain', 'partnership', 'schools', 'people', 'reform', 'promote', 'deal', 'young', 'crime', 'deliver', 'business', 'tough' (2000: 17–18). Given that the party's decisive grab for the political centre ground was achieved largely on the basis of the 'Third Way' – specifically, a move to create partnerships between the state and the free market – it is unsurprising that we should find 'partnership', 'reform', 'promote', 'deal', 'deliver' and 'business' in the list. 'Schools', 'young' and 'people' are pretty straightforward too, considering that education was a key manifesto pledge. It is interesting, though, to see 'crime' and 'tough' up there. New Labour clearly saw crime (traditionally a Conservative trump card) as an issue they needed to bring further up their agenda; and toughness to be a feature of the Blair persona that they needed to reinforce.

It is worth recalling that it was Blair (as shadow Home Secretary in 1994) who had first promoted the slogan, *tough on crime, tough on the causes of crime* (an advertising copywriter's dream, surprisingly later attributed to Gordon Brown). Nevertheless, toughness was not obviously a key feature of the Blair style: it took a very careful and professional spin campaign of press briefings in advance of an authoritarian Welfare Reform Bill in 1999 to fully consolidate his image as a leader tough enough to 'crack down' on benefit abuse, for example. (Blair has always shunned the word 'crackdown', but it is remarkable how often it appears in headlines about him (Fairclough 2000: 42).) His willingness to embrace and foster the image of a leader able to make tough decisions continues to this day, as a party conference speech in 2006 shows:

> The point is that being on the side of the people means making change, and making change is hard, managing it difficult, dispelling the scare stories about it almost impossible. Yet without it, being on the side of the people is just an empty phrase. This is a moment to stand firm.
>
> (Labour Party conference, 10 February 2006)

The following, in a more typically informal style, is from a press conference in which he was asked about local crime:

> I don't think our laws there are nearly tough enough. I think we have got people who are engaged in organized crime who are able to just flout the law and do what they want. Well we should try and put a stop to it if we possibly can... if you go and talk to people who live with this type of menace, it is incredibly distressing and it makes their lives hell and it is not right and we should stop it.
>
> (11 October 2005)

The news media have played a strong role in this process, as no doubt they were intended to do. Blair's tough determination, his appetite for tackling controversial issues and difficult decisions, as well as his perceived predilection for cracking down, remains a constant theme in the press he receives at home and abroad. Notice how often the language of 'toughness' appears in the following news items:

UK's Blair says Tough Nuclear Power Decision Looms

LONDON – The British government must make tough decisions over whether to invest in a new generation of nuclear power, Prime Minister Tony Blair said on Tuesday as he prepared to launch a new review of Britain's energy needs. 'With some of the issues to do with climate change, and you can see it with the debate about nuclear power, there are going to be difficult and controversial decisions the government has got to take,' Blair told a committee of senior parliamentarians.

> (Reuters, 23 November 2005)

Blair pledges new drugs crackdown

Tony Blair has pledged to crack down on those who 'peddle the misery of drugs' as he launched a set of new measures.

> (BBC News Online, 25 November 2004)

No let up in terror fight – Blair

Tony Blair has vowed not to soften his crackdown on terrorism and its supporters either at home or abroad. Speaking during his visit to India, Mr Blair said he was determined to press ahead with moves in both the UN and the Commons to tackle the issue head-on.

(BBC News Online, 7 September 2005)

Certainly the September 2001 attacks in the USA, the probability of terrorist attacks in the UK, Britain's participation in the invasion of Iraq – along with a sharp increase in applications for asylum and economic migration – have all led to New Labour taking positions in policy areas where their political forefathers would have been very much further to the left. This, coupled with a Blairite tendency to seek consensual solutions whenever possible, has increasingly led them into debates and disputes about meanings and about the precise usages of names and labels.

On immigration, for example, we see dividing lines being drawn over labels and status. Traditionally, people seeking refuge in a foreign country have been referred to as 'refugees'; in early twenty-first-century Britain, the label 'asylum seeker' has been favoured instead. The two terms carry different **connotations** – associations and suggestions of meaning not explicit in the actual definitions of the words (their **denotations**). A refugee is usually defined as a person taking refuge from persecution, war or natural disaster. Asylum refers to the sanctuary, protection or shelter offered to those who are persecuted or dispossessed in this way. But it can be argued that 'refugee' predisposes us to believe that individuals so named are already receiving protection (a refugee is a person *taking* refuge), while the use of 'asylum seeker' makes it clear that the person is *seeking* refuge, which has not yet necessarily been granted. A government keen to control this type of immigration will naturally favour speaking of a policy on asylum, though an acknowledgement of the existence of refugees is still in order, naturally:

Because we need to ensure that only those we need and want to come to our country can do so, we will introduce strict controls on immigration and carry on reducing asylum numbers. But because the British people are also decent, tolerant people, we will continue to give asylum to genuine refugees and never play politics with immigration.

(Speech to launch Labour election manifesto, 13 April 2005)

Asylum, then, is what the government will *control* and *reduce*. Refugees, or at least *genuine* refugees, are still welcome, and always have been, since the government will *continue* to grant them sanctuary. Immigration, we note, is confined to 'only those we need and want': were you aware of that criterion? And who are 'we' in this case? This is an issue we will look at shortly.

The deliberate use of a label can have far-reaching and subtle effects. While not on the scale of the examples mentioned above in the context of the first Gulf War, nevertheless there is a selective use of labels in the political press and in the broadcasting media that can change the tone, flavour and dimension of the political reality being reported. When we hear or read of 'insurgents', what connotations does this word have? Different, surely, from freedom fighters. What about militants? Or activists? Or demonstrators? Or protesters? What are the differences in connotation between *liberating, occupying* and *invading*?

And what exactly is meant by a 'pocket of resistance'? By and large, if memory serves, what happens to pockets of resistance is that they get 'flushed out'. What other kinds of things get flushed out? And what is involved in flushing out a pocket of resistance? As I understand it, water is very seldom employed – unless it is a hail of bullets. There is a definite 'cleaning out' theme here, reinforced in the clinical connotations of 'taking out' enemy soldiers in a 'surgical strike'. By the same token, what is implied or presupposed when people are *killed, murdered, destroyed, executed, annihilated* or even *slaughtered*?

Words, as we see, are seldom value-free, and no description is ever entirely neutral. Linguists might categorize some of the terms above (perhaps 'slaughtered' and 'annihilated') under the heading of **dysphemism** – the use of a negative or depreciating word rather than one which is (relatively) neutral, like 'killed'. But the context here is crucial: 'killed' will still be regarded as excessively harsh if applied to a vet ending a sick pet's life. Indeed, in peaceful contexts like this veterinary example, it is common to go further and employ a **euphemism** – a mild or inoffensive term, such as 'put to sleep' or 'put out of its misery'. We have met the device of euphemism already in the context of advertising, of course.

Governments can find it expedient to use euphemisms. George Orwell's factual account of the use of the English language in political life recorded the following examples:

> *Pacification*: the bombardment of defenceless villages from the air, the inhabitants driven out into the countryside, the cattle machine-gunned, the huts set on fire with incendiary bullets.
>
> *Rectification of frontiers*: millions of rural dwellers robbed of their farms and expelled from their lands with no more than they can carry.
>
> *Elimination of unreliable elements*: the imprisonment of people without trial, and unlawful shootings.
>
> (Adapted from Orwell 1946)

According to Orwell, such phraseology is required when politicians wish to name things or events without calling up mental pictures of them. With careful phrasing, politicians can reinvent negative acts or atrocities in a neutral or even positive light. You might like to consider the exactness of his argument in pondering the meanings of 'friendly fire' and 'collateral damage'. Could you define the terms?[8]

Dysphemism is also abundant in political discourse, being used in a variety of ways, from discrediting the opposition in exaggeratedly harsh terms (New Labour criticized the outgoing Conservative government for allowing the 'disintegration' and 'degeneration' of inner cities), to disgracing an opposing army (media descriptions of Iraqi soldiers in the first Gulf War included 'blindly obedient', 'blundering' and 'brainwashed'). **Cacophemism** (the use of deliberately offensive terms) is less easy to get away with in politics, although Alistair Campbell (later to be Blair's communications chief) did once memorably describe the Conservative prime minister John Major, in print, as a 'second-rate, shallow, lying little toad of a man'.[9]

Context dependency, however, does apply to the positive or negative status of the vast majority of words and expressions, and over time this status can shift. Dysphemistic words and expressions may lose their negative associations and become more 'neutral'. In certain cases, and especially in those that represent a political struggle with regard to labelling, this process can involve the deliberate 'reclaiming' of words with negative associations: dysphemistic words for women (e.g. chick and babe), for homosexuals (e.g. queer and queen) and for people of particular ethnic origins (e.g. nigger) are currently being repossessed by members of the social groups once defamed by the use of such terms.

More commonly, and by contrast, terms that are 'neutral' and terms that are euphemistic may begin to take on negative associations over time (this process is referred to as **pejoration** – although some writers prefer 'pejorization'). An example from everyday US discourse would be the replacement of the word 'toilet' with the once euphemistic 'bathroom', which in its turn has become pejorated and replaced by a new euphemism, 'rest room', or, for female 'facilities' (itself an euphemism), by 'ladies' room' or 'powder room'. The process may well have moved on again since the time of writing; the linguist Stephen Pinker has dubbed this seemingly endless cycle 'the euphemism treadmill' (2002: 213).

An example of the treadmill in action can be seen in the process by which many British state-owned utilities and enterprises have been transferred into private ownership. The procedure was once known as *denationalization*. Under Thatcher, the Conservatives' appetite for the process proved highly inflammatory (nationalization had been a defining policy of the Labour movement) and the term *privatization* was consequently adopted. This, however, quickly became a pejorative term too, and although New Labour carried on the policy when they took office, they felt obliged to coin yet another, less negatively charged expression: *public-private partnership* (a classic example of New Labour's reconciliatory tendencies, incidentally, this time achieved by the simple addition of a hyphen).

This constant shifting of a word's connotations, and the fact that words tend to acquire different shades of meaning over time as the context within which their function changes, will often lead to a word becoming a contested concept.

At the time of writing (February 2006) a political storm was brewing over the meaning of the word 'torture'. A British High Court judge had ruled, with reference to the imprisonment without trial of 'detainees' at Guantanamo Bay, that 'America's idea of what is torture is not the same as ours and does not appear to coincide with that of most civilised nations'. Specifically, the Bush administration was accused of defining the term too narrowly, using it to refer only to 'intense physical injury and violent treatment leading to organ failure'. This definition would seem to allow the type of treatment said by the United Nations to be occurring at Guantanamo (excessive violence used to force-feed prisoners, gouging of the eyes and sensory deprivation, including that designed to induce a perception of suffocation) to be glossed over as somehow less than torture. The response to international criticism, by the way, is: 'remember these are *terrorists*' (Scott McClellan, White House press secretary, reported in *The Guardian*, 17 March 2006). As we said earlier, what a difference a word makes. Stamping someone with the label of *terrorist*, even in the absence of due process and fair trial, is apparently sufficient to justify the violation of that person's basic, and internationally endorsed, human rights.

It is a storm that may not blow itself out too quickly. The British government acknowledges only that Guantanamo is an 'anomaly' that will be dealt with 'sooner or later' (*The Guardian*, 18 March 2006). Meanwhile they themselves may be on shaky legal ground if it can be shown that they have assisted in any way with the associated process euphemistically known as 'extraordinary rendition' – the practice of transporting detainees to interrogation centres in countries where torture is known to occur. A more everyday wording might be 'transfer to sites of torture'. Language, as we pointed out at the beginning of the chapter, is very much a political issue.

Political and legal concepts that are heavily dependent on context in a shifting field of reference can often become contested in this way, though in some cases they are not left undefined for long. The 1980s Russian edition of the Oxford Students' Dictionary of Current English famously redefined some important entries: *capitalism*, for example, much to Oxford's surprise, was redefined as 'an economic system based on private ownership of the means of production operated for private profit and on the exploitation of man by man'. Other redefined terms included *communism, imperialism, Marxism, fascism, bolshevism* and *internationalism* (*The Observer*, 9 April 1985). It may well be that *democracy* is on the way to becoming a contested concept too. It is now more or less impossible to locate any meaning of it that can be defined independently of the context in which it is being used.

Words whose original meanings have been lost or eroded in this process of context-shift – whether it be a shift occasioned by progress, fashion or culture – are often left washed up on the shore of metaphor, clinging to existence only through their usage in a figurative sense. 'Witch-hunt', 'stalking horse', 'straw man', 'melting pot' and 'scapegoat' are all examples of this linguistic drift: the words have all but lost their original meaning, but still retain significant currency in the discourse of politics by virtue of their metaphorical power.

Others, such as 'gateway' or 'beacon' may not have lost their original meanings to the same extent, but their usage in metaphorical contexts now far outnumbers their literal use. They are, in all probability, well on the way to becoming clichés (like *rafts of proposals*), but have not quite got there yet. Such terms are much loved by politicians. In the early twenty-first century, the Labour government in the UK has initiatives for the unemployed involving 'gateway interviews'; and 'beacons of excellence' are found throughout the USA (where they are usually colleges) and the UK (where they can be almost anything that local government feels like bestowing the honour on).

We have already seen that metaphor is exploited readily in the discourse of advertising for persuasive ends. In much the same way the discourse of politics leans eagerly towards metaphorical usage, not least because it naturally enables the politician to reformulate a concept from a nebulous 'schematic' domain into a concept from a better understood and more concrete 'source' domain.[10]

One of the source domains for metaphors most commonly found in political discourse is the body and, specifically, disease of the body. Examine these examples from speeches given in 1987 by Neil Kinnock, leader of the Labour Party from 1983 to 1992: 'Unemployment is a *contagious* disease... It *infects* the whole of the economic *body*. If *limbs* are severely damaged the whole *body* is *disabled*' (cited in Wilson 2001: 409).

We have already identified debates on immigration as a prime location for linguistic manipulation, and it is notable that they are also characteristically loaded with metaphors relating to water. An analysis of political discourse in the 2005 UK general election – including evidence from party manifestos, press comment and legislation – identifies several metaphorical usages along these lines:

> an almost limitless *flow* of immigration
>
> mighty *tidal wave* of asylum seekers
>
> the *trickle* of applicants has become a *flood*[11]

Of particular interest is the way these patterns of migration tend to be represented as unstoppable or inexorable. Politicians often use metaphors of *containment* to suggest that Britain is 'full up' or 'at bursting point', and proposed solutions frequently invoke the idea of *reversing the tide of migration*.

In fact, political rhetoric features metaphors connected with *movements* of various kinds – not just the movement of water – and these lend themselves to being manipulated in a similar way to suggest unstoppability. This is particularly apparent in the treatment of abstract notions such as *change, progress* or *globalization* – constructs that it is not always in the politician's interest to present as anything other than inevitable. For instance, presenting globalization – essentially a function of the increased power of multinational companies – as an inevitable and natural phenomenon, can be a way of ensuring that the process is perceived as a given fact, rather than as a trend that could be controlled by government intervention or policy change. This is of particular interest in the case of New Labour, coming as they do from a background in which state control of the economy was generally seen as essential (Fairclough 2000: 26).

Exercise 2c

In the following (edited) extract from his speech to Labour's 2005 conference on 27 September, Tony Blair is talking about globalization. In the light of what we have just been saying, examine carefully how he represents this abstract concept.

> I hear people say we have to stop and debate globalization. You might as well debate whether autumn should follow summer… The character of this changing world is indifferent to tradition… It is replete with opportunities, but they only go to those swift to adapt, slow to complain, open, willing and able to change… unless our values are matched by a completely honest understanding of the reality now upon us and the next about to hit us, we will fail…
>
> The temptation is to use Government to try to protect ourselves against the onslaught of globalization by shutting it out; to think we protect a workforce by regulation; a company by Government subsidy; an industry by tariffs. It doesn't work today. Because the dam holding back the global economy burst years ago. The competition can't be shut out, it can only be beaten.

- How does Blair use metaphor to communicate his views about globalization?
- What effect does this achieve?

In this speech, Blair represents change, and particularly globalization, as both inevitable and natural, like autumn following summer. The world is changing (apparently by itself) and we must change in tune with it. Only by changing will we be able to cope with the next (unavoidable) onslaught. Globalization is presented as a natural process that is occurring beyond any political or human control: it has its own energy, force and momentum – especially since 'the dam burst years ago'.

Undoubtedly much of the persuasive force of Blair's argument comes from the figurative representation of abstract notions and the careful choice of 'natural' vocabulary. But there are other elements involved here too (just as there were in our examination of advertising discourse). We might note the use of short, snappy syntax: 'It doesn't work today.' We might look at the way he sets up contrasts: 'The competition can't be shut out, it can only be beaten.' We might consider also Blair's rhetorical use of lists: 'swift to adapt, slow to complain, open, willing and able to change' – incidentally, there is rhythm here, and perhaps even a suspicion of rhyme. But lists, contrasts and syntax all lead us into the linguistic level of sentence structuring, and it is to this level that we will turn our attention now.

Parallel lines: the sentence structures of political discourse

We have noted several times already that the mediatization of politics has been a driving force in shaping the political discourse constructed for public consumption. In an age of mass information and communication, the news media put a premium on language that is brief, topical and easy to express. Political speech-writers keep this requirement at the front of their minds when they write speeches: in the vast majority of cases, the target audience of the speech is not just the assembled multitude in the conference hall; it is also (many would say, far more importantly) the viewer at home.

By and large, the viewer at home does not want to see the whole speech (though some will, of course), and a political speech-writer will take good account of the fact that the media will need to edit the speech down to its key highlights, whether on air or in print. The writer will therefore be as concerned about the form of the message as with its substance, and will look to provide both in a format that the media will find easy to pick up, cover and communicate to the audience.

Modern political discourse is widely characterized by the prolific use of **sound bites**: concise, snappy messages that are clear and memorable. As straplines, these are also key items in an advertiser's brief, and throughout this chapter we have seen that devices employed in the discourse of advertising are found by political writers to be highly appropriate for their own use. But, perhaps with the advantage of more airtime on their side, political writers can afford to pay considerable attention to the way these sound bites are organized and sequenced in the structure of a speech.

Some of the structuring devices will be familiar to us from the discourse of advertising. Consider the following excerpt from Tony Blair's speech to the Labour Party conference in 2005:

> When we campaign for justice in Africa, that is a progressive cause.
>
> When we push for peace in Palestine, it is a progressive cause.
>
> When we act against global warming, it is a progressive cause.

What kind of cause is it? A progressive cause. Not much danger of that message being misunderstood: it is repeated three times. One cannot help but be reminded of *The Hunting of the Snark*: 'Just the place for a snark! I have said it thrice; / What I tell you three times is true' (Carroll 1876). And what about this excerpt, from the 2000 Labour Party conference?

> Today I make a further commitment. Line one of the contract in the next manifesto will be a promise to increase the share of our national wealth spent on education in the next parliament. Education, education, education. Then, now, and in the future.

We have noted the 'power of three' many times already, and we have noted too the potency of repetition. It is sad but true that *education, education, education* remains to date Blair's most memorable political sound bite. But let us look again at Blair's final use of the three-part device: 'Then, now, and in the future'. As the second of two consecutive lists of three, this is really the equivalent of the comedian milking his audience. Most likely, I would guess, it was included in the speech for Blair to add, passionately, tub-thumpingly, over the top of the applause predictably engendered by the first list – 'education, education, education'.

Just think about it for a moment. 'Then, now, and in the future.' What times exactly do these terms refer to? Blair might appear to be saying, in the past, the present and the future – which, in a way, might be rather neat. But 'then' cannot refer to the past here, not meaningfully anyway; it can only refer to *in the next parliament* – it is being used in its other accepted meaning of *at the time I have just specified*, which is plainly in the future. As a time indicator, 'now' can only have one meaning: *at the present*. But hold on: the increase in the share of wealth earmarked for education is a future increase – that is the very nature of the pledge that Blair is making. So what exactly does the reference to 'now' mean? And 'in the future' can surely only be referring to the same time as the first 'then' – that is, in the next parliament.

In fact there is a totally false linguistic opposition being created here. If Blair's words are analysed meaningfully, they actually scan out as *in the next parliament, in the future, and er...now, although obviously not right now*. But do you think anyone noticed this linguistic sleight of hand at the time? No, I dare say they were all too busy clapping.[12] The meaning of the utterance (or actually its meaninglessness) has been swept into the background by its form.

Exercise 2d

I promised that we would return to Tony Blair's speech to launch the Labour Party's 2005 general election manifesto on 13 April, and now we will look at it in full. Read it aloud to yourself at least a couple of times.

There is a big vision behind today's Manifesto. It is that everyone, not just a few, should get the chance to succeed and make the most of the talent they have. It is to build in Britain the genuine opportunity society, where what matters is hard work, merit, playing by the rules, not class or privilege or background.

But today I want to focus on the straightforward, practical ways to achieve it. Every line in this Manifesto has this driving mission behind it: to support and help hard-working families to cope and prosper in the face of the stresses, strains, and struggles of modern life. Their interests come first. Their priorities are our priorities. At the heart of it, is a strong economy.

Because hard-working families need a stable economy, we will keep inflation and interest rates as low as possible. We will never return to the stop go of the past. With growth, jobs and low mortgages in place, we can ensure rising living standards for all. The minimum wage will rise to £5.05 and then £5.35 from October 2006. We will keep or increase tax credits and extend the New Deal so that everyone gets the chance of a decent living wage.

Because hard-working families depend on the NHS, we will keep the NHS free at the point of use with rising investment but thoroughly modernized to put power in the hands of the patient, to get the treatment they need at the time they want, with a radical reduction in waiting times and further improvements in cancer and cardiac care.

Because hard-working families depend on state schools, we will keep investment rising year on year in our schools so that in time every primary, every secondary school is either rebuilt or has the classrooms, sports halls and computer facilities they need. But again, this will be combined with continuing modernization so that schools get the independence and freedom they want, to develop as they wish – guaranteed three-year budgets over which they have control, and where we insist on the basics of school sport, school discipline and good school meals being part of every school's daily life.

Because we can only compete in the future on the basis of our skills and talent, we will give every young person aged sixteen the ability to stay on at school or if they leave to go into proper quality training. We will provide three hundred thousand apprenticeships a year.

Because hard-working families need to know the law is on their side, we will create a criminal justice system which puts the victim first, punishes properly the criminal and we will put a uniformed presence, police and community support officers, in every neighbourhood in Britain so that we do not just cut crime but the fear of crime too.

Because we need to ensure that only those we need and want to come to our country can do so, we will introduce strict controls on immigration and carry on reducing asylum numbers. But because the British people ➡

> are also decent, tolerant people, we will continue to give asylum to genuine refugees and never play politics with immigration.
>
> And because the world we live in today means that problems in one part of the world can impact on all of us, and because the British people are a compassionate people, we will have a foreign policy that is strong on defence, fights the scandal of world poverty, especially in Africa, and takes radical action on climate change and the environment.
>
> This manifesto has specific, costed, detailed policy. It represents, on the basis of a strong economy and investment in public services, a radical acceleration of change. I believe this country is better, stronger and fairer than the one we inherited in 1997. But we can do so much more.
>
> This manifesto is also quintessentially new Labour. It has at its core the traditional value that we should stand up for the many not the few, breaking down the barriers that hold people back, allowing everyone, not just those at the top, to fulfil their potential. But it also deals in modern reality, in a fast changing world. Opportunity and security for all in this world of change. That is our purpose.

- Find every occasion in this speech where Blair uses the rhetorical device of three-part listing. What is the desired effect of each instance of its use?

- How is the main body of the speech structured? What effect does this have? If you were to use this structure in a more everyday setting (for example, in writing an essay or a letter), would it generally be received in a positive light?

- Examine Blair's use of the pronoun 'we' (and its associated forms). Does each instance always have the same point of reference? Does it matter if they do not?

We have already noted, earlier in the chapter, that this speech contained an example of an alliterated three-part list: 'stresses, strains and struggles'. There are naturally several other instances of the three-part list in the speech; the device is more or less irresistible to speech-writers. On the matter of economic stability, for example, Blair chooses to present three pillars:

> With growth, jobs and low mortgages in place, we can ensure rising living standards for all.

There are also three vital elements in his demands for schools:

> We insist on the basics of school sport, school discipline and good school meals...

The manifesto, Blair claims, has:

> Specific, costed, detailed policy...

And Britain is:

> Better, stronger and fairer than the one we inherited.

70

The last two examples seem a little suspect. What is the difference between 'specific' and 'detailed'? And 'better' is especially vague: presumably being 'stronger' and 'fairer' makes Britain 'better', but the three-part listing suggests that these are three improvements, not two. One would hope that Labour's much-trumpeted 'costed policy' is not similarly guilty of double counting.

Linguistically, the three-part listing is one of a number of devices, well-known to orators and poets throughout history, which fall under the heading of **parallelism**. Parallel structures can be drawn across sentences, inside sentences or even inside clauses and phrases (as in the two examples above that we have just analysed). John F. Kennedy's inaugural address in 1961 features a famous parallel across sentences:

> Ask not what your country can do for you – ask what you can do for your country.

Churchill's defiant warning to the Luftwaffe in 1941 is a similar parallel, though connected with 'and':

> You do your worst and we will do our best.

George W. Bush's inaugural address contains parallels nesting inside clauses, when he refers to US history as:

> ...the story of a power that went into the world to protect but not possess, to defend but not to conquer...

Ominous stuff, reading it now. The examples here are mainly of **antithetic** parallelism, in which a contrast is drawn between the elements that are paralleled: 'what your country can do' is contrasted with 'what you can do'; similarly, 'your worst' is contrasted with 'our best'; and 'protect' and 'defend' are contrasted with 'possess' and 'conquer'.

However, the Bush example, at the next clause-level up, also features a **synonymous** parallel: 'protect but not possess' is paralleled with 'to defend but not to conquer'. Here the parallel is not contrastive; rather the elements in the paralleled structures echo and reinforce each other. Prescott's 'Dave' speech of 2006, which we looked at earlier in the chapter, features a similar device: 'Cameron's all rhetoric not record, image not substance'. And Blair's 2005 manifesto speech features a combination of synonymous and antithetic parallelism in a passage we have mentioned before, contrasting one three-part list, 'hard work, merit, playing by the rules', with another, 'not class, or privilege or background'.

Repetition of sentence structure is a frequent unifying device in political discourse. 'New' Conservative beliefs are set out by David Cameron in a *we believe this, but not that* form, to point up differences from beliefs that Conservatives might be perceived to hold:

> We believe in personal responsibility. But not in selfish individualism.
>
> We believe in lower taxes. But not in fostering greed or favouring the rich.
>
> We believe in national sovereignty. But not in isolation and xenophobia.
>
> (Conservative Party website, 13 March 2006)

Blair's 2005 manifesto speech – a classic of its kind – is actually built on six repetitions of a particular structural form. Having established that *hard-working families* are the priority, he introduces each separate pledge of the manifesto on a *because this is what's needed, this is what we'll do* structure, with four of them having *hard-working families* as the subject:

> Because hard-working families need a stable economy, we will keep inflation and interest rates as low as possible…
>
> Because hard-working families depend on the NHS, we will keep the NHS free at the point of use…
>
> Because hard-working families depend on state schools, we will keep investment rising year on year…
>
> Because hard-working families need to know the law is on their side, we will create a criminal justice system which puts the victim first…

Parallels need not always be repetitious to this degree. A political mantra can be couched in a number of different verbal formulations, while still retaining its central antithesis (if that is what is wanted). In the early days of New Labour, when the political aim was to promote the idea of the 'Third Way', Fairclough observes that much of their discourse took a not only…but also form – providing examples such as 'enterprise yet also fairness', 'enterprise and fairness' and 'enterprise with fairness'. The syntactic form of these expressions, he argues, allowed Labour politicians both to draw attention to assumed incompatibilities between concepts (in this case, *enterprise* and *fairness*) and, at the same time, to deny any incongruity between them (2000: 45).

Grouping items together, then, whether in a list or in parallel structures, has the effect of unifying them – either to convey the impression that they are in some way related, or, as in the example above, to deliberately invite comparative inspection of them. The device can also serve to blur the act of agency (that is, who actually did something):

> Yes, several hundred people stoned British troops in Basra. Yes, several thousand run the terrorist insurgency around Baghdad. And yes, as a result of the fighting, innocent people tragically die.
>
> (Labour Party conference, 27 September 2005)

Here Blair groups together, with a three-part *yes* listing, the people stoning British troops in Basra, the rebels proliferating in Baghdad and the tragic deaths of innocent people. Who do we infer is responsible for the deaths? If our natural tendency is to associate the items in the grouping, then we will be led to blame the deaths on the stone-throwers and the rebels. Meanwhile, anyone else's possible role in the affair is relegated to the background.

Obscuring the act of agency is classically achieved by use of the **passive voice**. Look at the difference between the following three statements:

> Government introduces detention centres in asylum crisis
>
> Detention centres introduced by government in asylum crisis
>
> Detention centres introduced in asylum crisis

In the first, presented in the **active voice**, the agent, or actor, is clear (*the government*). In the second, presented in the passive voice, the agent is relegated to a secondary position. The third statement shows how the passive voice gives the speaker or writer the option to remove the agent altogether – this is known as an **agentless passive** construction.

However, not all such obfuscatory devices are so simple to spot. We have already considered how processes such as globalization are metaphorized in the language of New Labour in a manner that suggests they are inevitable and inescapable. A similar concealment can be achieved by the use of a kind of syntactic metaphorizing, and particularly by means of **nominalization** – the process whereby verbs, for example, are transformed into nouns. Look at the following statements to see how the verb forms (*increasing* and *causing*) can be nominalized to produce nouns (*increase* and *cause*):

> Increasing levels of binge drinking are causing concern

> The increase in levels of binge drinking is a cause for concern

Nominalization has the effect of making the second expression sound more impersonal or remote than the first: our attention is diverted from the process that is actually occurring and directed instead to the product of the process. Discourse analysts would say that the process is 'backgrounded' and the effects 'foregrounded' (see, for example, Fairclough 2000: 26). We can see the device of nominalization at work in Blair's 2005 conference speech, when he speaks about *change*:

> We were simply being tested by the forces of change.

> The pace of change can either overtake us, or make our lives better and our country stronger.

> So what is the challenge? It is that change is marching on again.

Change here is a nominalization; it has the syntactic form of a noun, and the force of this form diverts our attention from such questions as: *What is changing? Why is it changing?*, and indeed, *Who is responsible for it changing?* Equally, as with *globalization* earlier, *change* is represented here as inevitable: it is a 'force', it moves at 'pace' and it 'marches on'. This nominalization also supports the idea presented here that *change* is somehow separate from human agency: change can *overtake* us. It is, in fact, something that happens to us, rather than something that we can control.

Curiously, when it comes to changes in policy that the government can take credit for, the agency of change is made perfectly explicit. Blair's speech concludes with the words:

> That's what we have been in New Labour. The change-makers.

We should remember that this was a speech made to the Labour Party conference: the audience (at least the immediate audience) were the Labour Party faithful. Consequently, the 'we' of this final remark could refer to everyone in the hall, rather than just the government. It is an oddity of the English language, not shared by all others, that the pronoun 'we' does not distinguish between three possible shades of meaning. It can refer to 'me and you', to 'me and the people I represent, but not you' or 'me and the people I represent and you too'.[13]

In the discourse of politics, the strategic use of the 'we' pronoun not only functions to create a (synthetic) personalized relationship between politicians and the public; it can also, by virtue of its implicit vagueness, serve to depersonalize or to obscure the agents of political actions. Sometimes the exact referents of 'we' are difficult to identify. Consider the following examples:

> As a result of the rise in antisocial behaviour I intend to increase the powers of our police force.

> As a result of the rise in antisocial behaviour we intend to increase the powers of our police force.

In the first example it is clear that the speaker is responsible for increasing the authority of the police. In the second, the referent of 'we' is much more ambiguous: the person or agent responsible for increasing police powers is partially concealed.

Consider this excerpt from a speech by Margaret Thatcher:

> Mr. Chairman, *we* are determined that Britain should not tread that path. We shall fight to defend those qualities of tolerance and fairness and courage which have sustained us for so long. We shall fight for our freedom in time of peace as fiercely as *we* have fought in time of war.

> > (Cited in Wilson 1990)

Who is the 'we' referring to here? As Wilson (1990) explains, the first use is certainly unclear; given her dominant position in Cabinet and her occasional use of the royal 'we' anyway, it could refer to Thatcher alone (on the birth of a grandchild, she is reported to have announced, 'We are a grandmother'). Still, the second usage makes it more likely that both refer to the government. However, in the third, Thatcher seems to shift the referent of the pronoun to include not only herself and her government, but also the British people, and this is confirmed in the final usage: 'as we have fought in times of war'. Indeed, 'we' here includes not only the present-day population, but also, presumably, past generations of Britons. Probably intentionally, of course, Thatcher is also echoing Churchill's great wartime oration of 4 June 1940:

> We shall fight in France, we shall fight on the seas and oceans, we shall fight with growing confidence and growing strength in the air, we shall defend our island, whatever the cost may be, we shall fight on the beaches, we shall fight on the landing grounds, we shall fight in the fields and in the streets, we shall fight in the hills; we shall never surrender.

Thatcher's use of 'we', almost invisibly, and under the added cover of the *we shall fight* associations, serves to link her own values (and those of the Conservative Party) with those of the British population, both past and present: she and her party speak, in effect, for Britain.

This section has focused on the syntactic characteristics of political discourse constructed for a public audience. We have seen how such discourse is carefully crafted to lead us to certain views and interpretations of situations, events and actions, and we have examined how the language used by politicians leads us to particular views of political reality. In the following section we will briefly shift our focus to the analysis of more interactive political discourse, and particularly to the characteristic features of political interviews, discussions and debates.

That is just not true: the pragmatics of political discourse

If political events have become mediatized, then correspondingly media institutions have become political: media events have seen a significant upsurge in the representation of political figures. Politicians are now undoubtedly media personalities and, as we mentioned earlier, are featured in a widening range of current affairs and entertainment broadcasts, in Britain at least.

This is not to say that media focus is primarily on the substance of political argument at such events. It is largely for their perceived wit and speed of thought that politicians are invited to appear on TV quiz shows and talk shows, and many commentators suspect that for politicians the attraction lies more in the opportunity to build a political image than in the chance to push policy (Sauer 1997).

However, political debates and interviews – usually conducted under the aegis of serious news and current affairs departments – are widely seen as opportunities to focus on political substance. These can often be regarded (and marketed) as battles, and interviews in particular can be quite confrontational. While an interview is normally conducted on a one-to-one basis, nevertheless discourse analysts are keen to point out that three participants are always represented at the speech event: the interviewer, the politician and the public (see, for example, Ensink 1997). Members of the public, of course, may be physically present in the studio at certain events anyway (and can actually be involved in the questioning in the context of a staged debate).

Political interviewing is a highly regarded journalistic art. Pragmatic analysis, which focuses on the way we produce and understand language in the context of a speech situation, reveals, for example, that interviewers construct their questions carefully to place politicians in particular positions. Their questions are rarely neutral, and are often leading. In responding to tough questions, politicians will often be obliged to use evasive strategies, providing vague responses or contriving not to give straight answers. Claims and counterclaims follow one after another in quick succession, and argument will typically develop over what has or has not been said or meant (Chilton 2003).

Just before the invasion of Iraq by US and British forces in 2003, UK prime minister Tony Blair took part in a televised debate, chaired by the interviewer Jeremy Paxman, in front of a live studio audience. The subject of the debate was whether Britain should support the USA in invading Iraq, and members of the audience were selected deliberately for their scepticism over British involvement. A brief analysis of this political media event will serve to highlight not only some of the features of interactive debate mentioned above, but also some of the devices we have looked at earlier in the chapter.

This was a critical period for Blair in his political career, and early in the debate we get a chance to see the public face that he is choosing to put forward. Here he is referring to the evidence for, and the dangers relating to, weapons of mass destruction in Iraq:

> I just think these, these dangers are there and I think that it's difficult sometimes for people to see how they all come together, but it's my honest belief that they do come together and I think it's my job as Prime Minister, even if frankly I might be more popular if I didn't say this to you or said I'm having nothing to do with George Bush, I think it's my duty to tell it to you if I really believe it and I do really believe it. I may be wrong in believing it but I do believe it.

Consider how Blair seeks to pre-empt the threat of losing public popularity by identifying the possibility himself, emphasizing that he is being 'honest', 'frank' and determined to carry out his 'duty'. Blair frequently uses I and my, as in 'I think...', 'I really believe...', 'my honest belief...', 'my job as Prime Minister'. We see, in fact, that in contrast to other forms of political discourse in which pronouns may be used to cloud agency and personal responsibility, Blair's use of I and my here focuses attention directly on himself as an individual political figure or 'personality': he invites us to pay particular attention to his own personal beliefs and attributes, and he uses this moment in the debate to concentrate on the presentation of his public image – as an honest broker – rather than of any substantive political policies.

To try to prevent politicians from evading issues of political importance, interviewers tend to frame and construct their questions in a way designed to put interviewees on the spot. Examine the following moment, where Paxman questions Blair on the importance of the UN inspection team. Consider the syntax especially:

> **JP:** Has not Colin Powell demonstrated yesterday, quite conclusively, that a regime in which those weapons inspectors are back in Iraq is one in which it is impossible for Saddam Hussein to continue developing weapons of mass destruction?

Observe how the structure of Paxman's question predisposes a particular response: the question contains a complete proposition (i.e. the presence of inspectors will halt any development of weapons), effectively restricting Blair to either agreeing or disagreeing with the statement. Also, the negative construction of the question is highly conducive to a positive answer (compare 'Has *not* Colin Powell demonstrated...?' with the alternative, 'Has Colin Powell demonstrated...?'); the syntactic construction of questions is one key element in their potency in discourse, as we will see in the next chapter when we examine the discourse characteristic of courtroom testimony. Finally, note how Paxman's use of 'quite conclusively' gives further force to his question, effectively defying Blair to contradict the assertion framed.

Use of such syntactic techniques is not confined to television interviewers. The following question came from a member of public in the audience:

> **MOP:** Do you not agree that most of Britain don't want us to act alone without the United Nations, and do you not agree that it's important to get France, Germany and Russia on board with support to help us?

In order to deflect the force of powerful questions, especially ones designed to produce a firm commitment or promise, politicians often avoid giving direct answers, or choose to provide responses that are indirect, vague and ambiguous – as in this example:

> JP: OK, so they report back next week. Will you give an undertaking to this audience, and indeed to the British people, that before any military action you will seek another UN Resolution, specifically authorizing the use of force?
>
> TB: We've said that that's what we want to do.

Clearly, saying that you *want to do* something does not amount to giving the *undertaking* that Paxman requests. Note also that Blair shifts from the use of *I* to the use of *we*, which, as we have discussed above, frequently functions to obfuscate agency and responsibility.

Exercise 2e

We will look now at a longer extract from the interview, in which Paxman and Blair are debating the effectiveness of sanctions against Iraq and the treatment of the inspectors sent to investigate the alleged production of weapons of mass destruction.

JP: Well you said of those UN resolutions and the sanctions which followed them in the year 2000, you said that they had contained him. What's happened since?

TB: I didn't actually, I said they'd contained him up to a point and the fact is—

JP: I'm sorry Prime Minister: 'we believe that the sanctions regime has effectively contained Saddam Hussein in the last ten years', you said that in November 2000.

TB: Well I can assure you I've said every time I'm asked about this, they have contained him up to a point and the fact is the sanctions regime was beginning to crumble, it's why it's subsequent in fact to that quote we had a whole series of negotiations about tightening the sanctions regime but the truth is the inspectors were put out of Iraq so—

JP: They were not put out of Iraq, Prime Minister, that is just not true. The weapons inspectors left Iraq after being told by the American government that bombs will be dropped on the country.

TB: I'm sorry, that is simply not right. What happened is that the inspectors told us that they were unable to carry out their work, they couldn't do their work because they weren't being allowed access to the sites. They detailed that in the reports to the Security Council. On that basis, we said they should come out because they couldn't do their job properly.

JP: That wasn't what you said, you said they were thrown out of Iraq—

> **TB:** Well they were effectively because they couldn't do the work they were supposed to do.
>
> **JP:** No, effectively they were not thrown out of Iraq, they withdrew.
>
> **TB:** No I'm sorry Jeremy, I'm not allowing you to get away with that, that is completely wrong. Let me just explain to you what happened.
>
> - Paxman only asks one question in the whole of this extract. Why do you think this is?
> - How are interruptions and topic shifts used as a means of controlling the speech exchange?
> - How formal does this interview appear to you?

While political interviews often follow a question-and-answer format, here Paxman only poses a single question: in his first turn, he asks, 'What's happened since?' The rest of the exchange is characterized by statements from Paxman that Blair seeks to deny.

Consider also how the single question posed by Paxman is framed by claims about what the prime minister had already said about the effectiveness of sanctions: 'you said that they had contained him'. Paxman's question is therefore not neutral, but loaded: it places Blair in danger of being forced to deny or retreat from an assertion already made in another context. This type of situation is of particular interest to analysts, who see political discourse as constructed within a historical framework, with the discourse of one event being intertwined with other texts.

Blair makes two attempts at finding an answer to the question, but both times he is interrupted, as Paxman exercises his control over the speech exchange and places Blair in a defensive position. The second interruption of Blair's turn also allows Paxman to force a change of topic, from the issue regarding sanctions to the question of whether inspectors 'withdrew' or were 'thrown out' of Iraq.[14] The shift of topic here is deliberate, and leads to a further exchange of allegations and counter-allegations: 'that is just not true'; 'that is simply not right'; 'that wasn't what you said'; 'that is completely wrong'.

Finally, we might note (just as we did at the beginning of the chapter) that in spite of the confrontational nature of the debate between Paxman and Blair, the event is conducted with due regard to courtesy and politeness, partly echoing the conventionality of the debating chamber in the House of Commons. No 'call me Tony' here: Blair is addressed by a formal title, *Prime Minister*, and interruptions (by both Paxman and Blair) are typically prefaced by, 'I'm sorry'. Claims and counterclaims are frequently introduced by 'softening' expressions, such as, 'let me just explain' and (elsewhere in the interview) 'with respect'.

We see that, as with other types of political discourse, media interviews and debates are characterized by specific discourse strategies. Such political discussions are marked by confrontation and conflict: the political interview is the site of a power struggle between politicians, interviewers and members of the public.

Questions do not function simply as information-seeking devices, but are constructed specifically to place politicians 'on the spot', particularly with regard to what has been said before, either in the present context or elsewhere – great emphasis is placed on 'truth' and consistency. Interviewers intervene and interrupt in order to control both the content of the interaction and the organizational flow of the discourse. In response, politicians may evade questions or attempt to turn them to their own advantage. Such political discourse, however, is mainly carried out in a civil and respectful tone, and at times a politician may be more concerned to present a popular public image or 'personality' than to engage in debate on an issue of political substance.

In this chapter we have examined political discourse largely from the point of view of its rhetoric, recognizing that much of political language is highly stage-managed for and by the media. We have seen that this rhetoric leans heavily on devices frequently used in advertising discourse, both at the level of sound and at the level of words. Meaning, in particular, can be a highly political issue, and we have noted that politicians are frequently concerned to manipulate meaning – reinventing and reinterpreting it in order to colour our perception of political trends, policies, actions or events, and exploiting an expertise in semantic engineering in order to persuade us of, and indeed to construct, political realities. Responsibility and accountability are key issues in politics, and we have seen that responsibility, in particular, is frequently backgrounded and obfuscated by linguistic means. Finally, we have paid some attention to the discourse of debate and interviewing, and this has raised linguistic issues such as questioning and topic management, which we shall need to examine further in subsequent chapters.

We now move on to look at the discourse of law, where we will pay particular attention to the language of courtroom contexts, as well as the language of legal writing. This will allow us to revisit and consider in more detail the language that is characteristic of contest, confrontation and cross-examination.

Further exercises

1   Look back at all the extracts and examples of political discourse in this chapter. As in the chapter on advertising discourse, you will note that we have analysed certain items for their use of one particular discourse device rather than another. It is clear, however, that political discourse functions at many levels simultaneously. Consider how many of the examples could easily have been selected as evidence of the use of several other linguistic devices. Look particularly at your answers to Exercise 2a: having worked your way through the chapter, would you answer any of the questions differently now?

2   Consider the following (edited) excerpt from a speech made by Margaret Thatcher to the Conservative Party conference on 9 October 1980, when she was prime minister.

> As you said, Mr Chairman, our debates have been stimulating and our debates have been constructive. This week has demonstrated that we are a party united in purpose, strategy and resolve. And we actually like one another.

There are many things to be done to set this nation on the road to recovery, and I do not mean economic recovery alone, but a new independence of spirit and zest for achievement. Our great enterprises are now free to seek opportunities overseas. We have made the first crucial changes in trade union law to remove the worst abuses of the closed shop, to restrict picketing to the place of work of the parties in dispute, and to encourage secret ballots...

Decent people do want to do a proper job at work, not to be restrained or intimidated from giving value for money. They believe that honesty should be respected, not derided. They see crime and violence as a threat not just to society but to their own orderly way of life. They want to be allowed to bring up their children in these beliefs, without the fear that their efforts will be daily frustrated in the name of progress or free expression.

Indeed, that is what family life is all about. There is not a generation gap in a happy and united family. People yearn to be able to rely on some generally accepted standards. Without them you have not got a society at all, you have purposeless anarchy.

Consider to what extent Thatcher uses sound play, word choice, structural organization and semantic manipulation to reinforce the messages implicit in this speech.

3   If you have access to the necessary resources, consider building a 'mini-corpus' of political speeches or written communications that you can analyse in detail: most political parties now make texts available in electronic form on their websites, for example. Try to analyse them in terms of some of the discourse devices we have looked at in this chapter. You might prefer to concentrate on one particular party, or to compare language use across two conflicting political viewpoints. What precautions should you take to ensure that you are comparing like with like? In the case of spoken data, can you be sure that you are analysing what was actually said on these occasions?

You do not have to say anything

The discourse of law

All are equal before the law
Declaration of Human Rights (1948)

Introduction

We live in a highly ordered and regulated society. Simply by virtue of being human, we have rights, and the fact that all of us share these rights equally means that each of us has a corresponding responsibility to respect the rights of our fellow humans. These human rights and responsibilities are enshrined in laws.

The language we use to talk about the law betrays a general sense that our laws are handed down to us from a higher power. We are *under* the law; no one is *above* the law. Our laws are, in a sense, sacred and holy. In some cultures this is taken more or less literally. We speak of *obeying* or *respecting* the law: terms that we would normally reserve only for people. Indeed, the law is widely personified: we also speak of an action being judged *in the eyes of the law*, and we commonly refer to the *word of the law*. We say that the law *knows* of no such defence or that it *recognizes* no exceptions; it *forbids, insists on, demands* and *allows* certain behaviours. More artistically, the law is commonly characterized as a goddess, as shown in Figure 3.01 overleaf: we speak of *violating* the law, and we can be brought *before* the law, to face her harsh scrutiny. There is much here that associates the law with religious ritual: there is ceremony, solemnity and mystery.

At the same time, our laws are intricately entwined with our concept of truth, and there is a strong scientific flavour to many of our legal dealings. Laws typically proceed from self-evident truths or principles, and it is no accident that we talk of the *laws* of physics. Legal procedure is seen as being logical and rational: terms are defined and redefined, and exceptions are noted, debated and accounted for. Neither is it an accident that scientists speak of *trial* and error.

The laws of rights and responsibilities govern every aspect of our lives. We have the right to life, and therefore are constrained from taking another's life; we have the right to live free from violence, and so cannot be violent to others. And yet, for the most part, our lives, which are governed by these 'eternal' laws, are largely mundane and secular, and have little to do with the ethereal concerns of science or religion. But similar rights and responsibilities apply to the ownership of property, the running of a business or company, our commercial transactions of buying and selling goods or services, our financial dealings and our use of credit. We have important

Fig. 3.01   Justice

legal obligations with respect to taxes, insurances, the schooling of our children and the registration of births and deaths. Marriage places us under obligations too; indeed, the business of dissolving a marriage is an intricate and expensive legal process. In our daily lives there are innumerable legal issues to consider, whether we are driving or parking a car, using computer software, owning a pet, advertising an item for sale, buying alcohol or tobacco, gambling, watching TV, having sex or erecting a fence. There is almost no earthly human activity that is not subject to some legal restriction or provision.

Even our speaking and writing is bound by law. There are strict laws governing slander and libel, and in many societies it is illegal to speak or write in certain ways – to incite violence or hatred, for example, or to deny the Holocaust. There are laws forbidding the production, dissemination or ownership of certain writings, and in many contexts it is even illegal to tell lies. Contravening these laws leaves us open to punishment, which can, in some societies, mean death; alternatively, there is imprisonment, which can range from months to a lifetime. Fines and awards of damages can similarly vary from the trivial to the astronomical, and there are several other forms of penalty available to the courts that can significantly restrict our personal freedom.

Legal considerations consequently seep into areas of our lives that we might not regard normally as being related directly to the legal domain. Look at the leaflet enclosed in a simple packet of painkillers, for example. The text is of a medical nature, of course; but in the final paragraphs the manufacturers often have to cover themselves against any legal comeback, and you may be surprised at the list of possible side effects that you are advised can ensue from taking a single analgesic pill: the literature for Anadin Original, for instance, warns of the possibility of swollen facial features, bleeding in the stomach, peptic ulcer, gout, wheezing and difficulty in breathing. The ostensibly medical discourse of such disclaimers actually serves to fulfil legal requirements, and the warnings that come with pharmaceutical products are just one example of the multifunctional and multifaceted nature of legal discourse.

Curiously, we have quite an appetite for the law – particularly at the moment in claims for compensation. The twenty-first century seems set to be the age of litigation, with lawsuits increasingly coming before the courts on grounds that frequently look absurd. Recent cases in the USA include an action against an airline brought by passengers who had been troubled by turbulence on a flight; a prosecution against a sporting venue after a spectator was hit by a ball; and a copyright suit against a music company for unlawfully 'bootlegging' silence. Fear of legal liability can lead to equally absurd legal discourse infiltrating our daily lives again. It is one thing to be warned of a medicine's side effects, but on a recent flight I received a complimentary packet of peanuts, whose packaging bore the odd warning: 'Caution, may contain nuts'.

I say it is curious that we have such an appetite for the law because getting involved in a legal dispute can be an exhausting, traumatic and expensive business. It may be that we are all equal before the law, but we do not all have equal access to the finance it demands; indeed some may be more equal than others in this respect. The apparatus of the law is complex and involves the employment and payment of highly skilled professionals. And, on the other side of the fence, facing police interrogation or being subjected to intensive cross-examination in court can be an extremely distressing experience: police and barristers can simply run rings round you if you are inexperienced in these domains, and they are more than capable of putting words in your mouth that you had no intention of saying, if it suits their needs. The language of police questioning and courtroom pleading are, as we will see, widely characterized as both coercive and intimidating.

It is at least partly to avoid being involved in this arena that we feel obliged to ensure the validity of our legal position by employing lawyers to give advice and to draw up legal documents that will protect us against the rigours of the law. In this domain of legal discourse, the language used tends to be characterized very differently. Written legal language, particularly as it appears in legal documentation, is well known to be complex, cryptic and confusing. Indeed, of all the forms of discourse that we examine in this volume, this area of legal discourse is perhaps the most impenetrable (although some areas of medical language can often give it a good run for its money, as we will see in the next chapter). Anyone who has ever been asked to 'read the small print' before signing a legally binding contract will have experienced the obscure and bewildering nature of its language. Characterized by arcane vocabulary, complex and convoluted syntax and endless, apparently redundant, repetitions, written legal discourse – or 'legalese' as it is sometimes disparagingly called – can be hopelessly alien to anyone outside the legal profession.

Exercise 3a

Examine the following example of discourse data (a licence agreement for software) and consider the characteristics that reveal its distinctively legal flavour.

> Adobe and its suppliers do not and cannot warrant the performance or results you may obtain by using the software. Except for any warranty, condition, representation or term to the extent to which the same cannot or may not be excluded or limited by law applicable to you in your jurisdiction, Adobe and its suppliers make no warranties conditions, representations, or terms (express or implied whether by statute, common law, custom, usage or otherwise) as to any matter including without limitation noninfringement of third party rights, merchantability, integration, satisfactory quality, or fitness for any particular purpose. The provisions of Section 6 and Section 7 shall survive the termination of this Agreement, howsoever caused, but this shall not imply or create any continued right to Use the Software after termination of this Agreement.

- What do you notice about the vocabulary used?
- How are sentences structured?
- Can you explain the odd use of capital letters?
- How does the use of punctuation deviate from the prescribed norms applied to other forms of writing – academic essays, for example?
- Why are there so many apparently redundant repetitions?

These are among the questions that we will address when we proceed to examine the discourse of legal writing. Bear in mind your answers to the above questions as the chapter develops.

The law vies with prostitution for the honour of being the oldest profession, and this long history is certainly a factor in conditioning the features of its discourse, including its notorious incomprehensibility. Legal writing, in particular, goes back a very long way: the cuneiform script, created by the Sumerians more than 5000 years ago, appears to have been used predominantly for legal purposes: the majority of the inscriptions that have been excavated have been found to record legal or law-related information (Coulmas 1989).

In England a distinctive legal language has been apparent at least since the eleventh-century Norman Conquest. Early legal writings were constructed primarily in Latin, using a variety of Law Latin that included many Latinized English and Old French words: 'murder' comes from Law Latin *murdrum*, itself a Latinization of Old English *morðer*, meaning a secret killing (Kiralfy 1958). Under Plantagenet rule, French began to take over from Latin in the legal domain, but most English people did not understand French either, as the 1362 Statute of Pleading made plain: 'people have no knowledge or understanding of that which is said for them or against them by their serjeants and other pleaders'. The use of French and Latin tended to serve a secretive function in the law, just as the use of technical, specialist and esoteric language serves to protect professional monopolies in a variety of fields to this day. Indeed, it was 1650 before an Act proposed 'turning the Books of the Law, and all Processes and Proceedings in Courts of Justice into English', and it was some considerable time again before English was finally employed for all forms of legal discourse. This is not to say that the Latin and French terms simply disappeared; many still persist in English legal discourse today and are one of several features, as we will see, that help to keep modern-day legal discourse at some distance removed from ordinary linguistic experience.

In fact, many commentators argue that since it is the language of the law that actually *defines* the profession, by keeping that language inaccessible to ordinary people, legal professionals contrive to protect their own position (see, for example, Goodrich 1987). After all, if we were all able to write our own wills, draw up our own contracts and represent ourselves in courts of law, there would be no place left for notaries, solicitors and barristers. In this respect, then, the language of the law operates as a professional **argot** – a term for the specialist or technical language used by a particular group or profession, which serves to distinguish 'insiders' from 'outsiders' and maintain a social distance between the two.

A further characteristic of legal discourse can be seen as reflecting the requirement for fairness and justice in the law. In order to be seen to be equitable, legal language has to be unambiguous, specific and stable: there must be no room for doubt or indecision in the application of the law, and it must be practised in the same way in different situations at different times. This results in a level of **explicitness** in legal language that is unmatched in almost any other form of discourse. Indeed, while we have seen in previous chapters that language is generally highly dependent on the context in which it is produced, much of legal discourse, by contrast, is relatively inward-looking: the language that is used tends to be highly codified and seldom requires recourse to factors in the outside world for its interpretation. We will look shortly at how this explicitness is particularly discernible in written legal language.

However, as well as being specific and stable, legal discourse must also be able to account for all eventualities: laws ideally need to be expressed in a form that can cover all possible related circumstances and events. This is a difficult demand to fulfil and frequently creates areas of uncertainty in law. In the British legal system, for example, the distinction between *manslaughter* (which is generally defined as causing death by recklessness or negligence) and *murder* (which involves an intention to kill or cause severe injury) is widely seen – wrongly, in fact – to rest on the question of whether there has been 'malice aforethought'. This criterion would tend to lead us to categorize the (relatively novel) crimes of assisting in someone's suicide or hastening a patient's death for essentially benevolent reasons, as falling under the less serious heading of manslaughter: there is, after all, no malice involved here. But in fact the distinction in law is actually based solely on *intention*, and such crimes, no matter how kindly motivated, are clearly intentional and must fall within the scope of the murder charge. Nevertheless, the uncertainty has been sufficient for British juries in recent years to tend to sympathize with defendants in these cases; and it cannot be long before the laws here are altered to make more explicit reference to such circumstances.

There is, then, a tension between two key demands that the law has to meet: first, it must be able to regulate specific aspects of human behaviour with consistency; and second, it has to be adaptable to new cases and flexible enough to account for changed circumstances or novel crimes. This tension, as we shall see, is a central feature of its discourse; it is one that we will examine in some detail.[1]

The linguistic oddity of the tension manifests itself most noticeably in written legal discourse, and consequently we will turn our attention to this area first. Clearly, the spoken discourse of police interviews and courtroom testimony is likely to be very different from the language of the written legal document. But when we move on later to examine the arena of legal speaking, we will find that its discourse is, in its own way, equally remote from the language of our everyday lives; and that this distance is also at least partly a function of the competing demands that the law seeks to fulfil.

Legalese

Written legal language is characterized by the use of a wide array of lexico-grammatical features. While it is difficult to distinguish consistently the lexical from the grammatical, it is practical first to consider aspects of wording and then to examine the syntactic structuring of legal writing.

The word of the law: the vocabulary of written legal discourse

If the language of the law is intended to function as a secretive and exclusive device, as many commentators contend, then the use of a mysterious and esoteric vocabulary is an obvious means by which to achieve this aim. In previous chapters we have had occasion to point out how rare it is for a single word to make a really important difference to the character of discourse (although we have seen several cases in which one does); by and large, we have wanted to say that the meaning of words is constructed in the larger linguistic context and the social situation in which the discourse is produced. Nevertheless, the domain of the law is widely known, and widely castigated, for its use of an abstruse vocabulary. The words *legal* and *jargon* collocate very strongly in English.

Mind you, *jargon* collocates pretty strongly with *medical* and *technical* too; and, incidentally, with *academic*. The truth is that jargon is a feature of many professional fields, and it is worth pointing out that discourse analysis itself is by no means immune from it. Indeed, even the word *discourse* is jargon: when it exists at all in everyday language, it is more or less confined to archaic or literary usage. Equally, the discourse analyst's use of the word *text* does not accord in any convincing way with the word as others generally use it, and a distinction is drawn between *cohesion* and *coherence* that is beyond the scope of the average dictionary definitions of the words (we examine these terms more closely when we consider the discourse of medicine in the next chapter).

Strictly speaking, *discourse* and *text* here are both examples of **terms of art**, as they are words which do have a meaning in everyday life, but which also have a specific and very different meaning inside a particular professional register ('art' in this context refers to a professional trade). Terms of art are fairly frequent in the law: *party*, for example, refers to a participant in a court case; *execution* to the carrying out of a court judgment; and *infant* to someone under 18 years of age.

In part, the prevalence of jargon in legal discourse stems from the long history of legal practice. As we have mentioned, the use of Latin and Latin-based vocabulary is widespread, dating back to a time when Latin (or more strictly, Law Latin) was the language of the law. Many legal rights and principles which are fundamental pillars of modern law were originally formulated in Latin and their names have simply remained that way. *Habeas corpus*, for example, underpins our basic right not to be held indefinitely without trial, and echoes two of the key words contained in the writs once issued by courts to demand that a prisoner be brought before them for examination of the case.[2] The phrase is particularly in evidence in Britain at the time of writing, with the government trying to extend the period for which suspected terrorists can be held without charge, and in the USA and elsewhere while debate rages over the detention of prisoners at Guantanamo Bay. To a lesser extent, the concept of *mens rea*, or guilty mind, features in the debate over the criminal categorization of so-called mercy killings; and the principle of *caveat emptor* (let the buyer beware) still dominates certain types of property transactions. Other Latin words have simply passed into English without translation: 'subpoena' and 'affidavit', for example.

Most of Latin legalese, however, is simply obscure and arcane to the majority of non-professionals: *doli incapax* (incapable of crime) and *duces tecum* (an order to produce a document in court), for example, are beyond the comprehension of the majority of people outside the profession. Much the same is true of many French words that have persisted in legal language: *escrow*, *estoppel*, *demurrer* and *ouster* are utterly alien items to the ordinary citizen. (It should be pointed out, though, that this may be to do with the arcane nature of the concepts they name – we have little trouble with other words derived from Old French, such as *disclaimer*, *assurance*, *verdict*, *evidence* and *merger*.)

Written legalese has also contrived to hang on to several archaic forms of English, and even of Old English: *deem*, *bequeath* and *aforesaid* are all Old English forms, as is the old verb ending '-eth', which is still occasionally presented today in ultra-ceremonial contexts such as national proclamations ('witnesseth' and 'proclaimeth' are two frequently employed examples). Other typically legal archaic forms include verbs such as *devise* and *bestow*, quaint phrases such as *set their hand to* (rather than sign) or curiously old-fashioned wordings in dating a document. Such archaisms undoubtedly lend an air of solemnity, ceremony and perhaps even ritual to written legalese.

We can see evidence of all this in the following example of a will. I reproduce it here in full (including the use of capital letters, and such punctuation as there is), with only the personal details removed. A few words are handwritten; these are shown in italic. I have selected the will partly because it is a perfectly modern example (it was drafted in 1994), but also because it is so very ordinary in its nature: it expresses a wish, after all, for one of the simplest and most common arrangements for distributing one's property after death.

Exercise 3b

Examine the will in detail and try to identify the features of wording that you feel contribute to it being so characteristically a legal document.

THIS IS THE LAST WILL of me (NAME) of (ADDRESS) which I make this *first* day of *June* One Thousand Nine Hundred and Ninety Four

1. I HEREBY REVOKE all former Wills and testamentary dispositions made by me

2. AS Executors of this Will I appoint my Son (NAME) of (ADDRESS) and the partners at the date of my death in the firm (SOLICITORS' NAME) of (SOLICITORS' ADDRESS) or the firm which at that date has succeeded to and carries on its practice and I express the wish that no more than two of them shall prove the Will (hereinafter called "the Trustees")

3. I GIVE the residue of my property to my Trustees UPON TRUST to sell it (with power to postpone sale without being liable for loss) and after payment out of it of all my debts tax and testamentary expenses to hold any of the investments from time to time representing the same (hereinafter called "my Residuary Estate") UPON TRUST to divide the whole of my residuary estate amongst my said Son (NAME) and my Daughter (NAME) as shall survive me and if more than one in equal shares PROVIDED THAT if any child of mine has died before that date (whether before or after the date of this my Will) leaving a child or children living at my death who attain the age of twenty one years then such a child or children shall take by substitution and if more than one in equal shares per stirpes the share of my Residuary Estate which such deceased child of mine would have taken if he or she had survived me and attained a vested interest

4. MY Trustees shall have the following additional powers:-

(a) My Trustees may retain any investments in which my Estate is invested at my death and may invest monies requiring investment in or upon the acquisition or security of any property of whatsoever nature as they think

---

88

fit whether or not providing income (including in particular but without prejudice to the generality of the foregoing insurance policies on the life of any beneficiary or other person and any house or flat and the furnishings thereof as a residence for any beneficiary) and may vary or transpose any such investments in all cases without being liable for loss and in all respects as if they were entitled thereto beneficially and subject to no restriction with regard to advice or otherwise in relation to investment

(b) In addition to all other powers conferred by law my Trustees may at any time and from time to time raise the whole or any part of the vested contingent expectant or presumptive share or shares of any beneficiary hereunder and pay the same to or use the same for the advancement maintenance education or otherwise howsoever for the benefit of such beneficiary

(c) My Trustees may insure against loss or damage by fire and any other risk any property for the time being comprised in my Estate or any trust fund created by this Will or any Codicil hereto for any amount notwithstanding that any person is absolutely entitled to such property and may pay the premiums for such insurance out of the income or capital of my Residuary Estate or out of the income or capital of such property or any trust fund comprising such property and **I DECLARE** that any money received by my Trustees under any such policy shall be treated as though it were the proceeds of the sale of the property insured

IN WITNESS of which I the said (NAME) have signed my name the day and year first above written

(*signature*)

SIGNED by the above named (NAME) in our presence and attested by us in the presence of her and of each other

(*signatures and addresses of two witnesses*)

- What type of vocabulary is employed in the will? Look out for archaisms and technical words.
- How are words formed into compounds in the document? What functions do these compound word formations serve in the discourse?
- How is capitalization used in this legal document and what purposes does it fulfil?
- Which aspects of wording are particularly explicit and how are they used to cover all eventualities?

The will is a large document and needs to be discussed in detail. Consider your answers to the above questions in the light of the analysis that follows.

This document is, as I say, relatively modern and free of legal complication; nevertheless, it makes far from straightforward reading. Undoubtedly this is largely a function of the way it is organized: its lack of punctuation and its use of long sentences and complex grammar. We will refer to these aspects of the document in detail when we come to look at sentence structure in the next section.

But the vocabulary used here is out of the ordinary, too. This is not so much because of the terminology used: there is no bequeathing or devising or setting one's hand – instead we see *appoint, give, sell, divide, retain, invest, raise, pay, use* and *sign*. There is a certain amount of formality, of course – but this is a formal document. Still, the use of such words and phrases as *testamentary dispositions, attain the age, take by substitution, monies, the generality of the foregoing, transpose, contingent expectant or presumptive* and *advancement* are all rather more old-fashioned and formal than perhaps they need to be. There is a certain amount of technical terminology, it is true, but *prove the Will, without prejudice, Residuary Estate, Codicil* and the Latinism *per stirpes* are not exactly excessive; in the overall context it is hard to see that we would gain much by avoiding them.

We do see an odd, unconventional use of capital letters. Certain words are, unexpectedly, always written with an initial capital. We do not write like this ordinarily; initial capitalization is largely reserved for proper names. Why do these words appear in this form? Examine the text again and try to find a reasonable answer. The words that are initially capitalized are: *Will, Codicil, Executor, Trustee, Residuary Estate, Son* and *Daughter*. These are all terms that have been explicitly defined in the document itself (or, in the case of 'any Codicil', will be defined if and when one is added). The will is defined by the use of *this* at the very outset: this document we have in our hands. The executors are named, explicitly, early on, and are then referred to as the trustees by means of an explicit definition: *hereinafter called the Trustees*. The estate is also defined by a similar device: *hereinafter called my Residuary Estate*. Both the son and the daughter are explicitly named too.

What function does this device serve? For the person whose will is being drafted, probably none. It may be noted at the time, but almost certainly as no more than a quaint oddity. For the lawyer, however, it is an important convention. Any reference to the world outside of the document is risky: things may change in the outside world, circumstances may alter. A legal document of this importance needs to ensure that all references to the world of ordinary mortals are nailed down, watertight. The use of capitals in the document is a conventional assurance that these references have been checked, confirmed and defined: there is no doubting who or what they refer to.

This is a convention of significance to the lawyer drawing up the will, and to any other lawyers who may need to see it in the future. But it is not designed to be of value to the non-lawyer. The will is, in a sense, a coded document, and therefore curiously remote from our usual experience. A small point, perhaps, but nevertheless the device of capitalization signals that this document is unlike ordinary documents – it is the product of a craft beyond the range of the ordinary person.

Capitals are used unusually elsewhere in the will. There appears to be a convention that capitalizes the first word or two of each section in the document. This seems rather archaic: you may have seen the device in other contexts, perhaps at the beginning of chapters in novels. Nevertheless, it is uncommon, and serves to remind us, perhaps, that legal documents need to be drawn up in a particularly traditional fashion, rather than in the way that a more run-of-the-mill modern-day paper or report might be set out. Again, you may find this a relatively trivial observation; after all, it does not make any difference to the way we read or understand the document – or does it? We will return to this question later.

What indubitably does make the language unusual at word level is the use of the compounds that are so uniquely associated with legalese: *hereby, hereto, thereof, thereto, hereunder* and, most classically, *hereinafter*. This, for many people, is what a genuinely legal document is supposed to sound like. And yet the terms themselves are, as far as sense is concerned, fairly unnecessary. With the exception of *hereby* (which we will also look at later), they all have meanings that we routinely express in far plainer language, using phrases like 'to it', 'of it', 'below' and 'from now on'. It is worth wondering why a document produced in the 1990s should need to make use of such archaic forms.

A similarly old-fashioned compound word, not used here but characteristically associated with written legal discourse, is *whereas*. The word does appear in every-day language, but normally only in the contrastive sense of 'while on the other hand'; an example might be: 'He's from London, whereas I'm from Liverpool.' In legal documents, however, the word retains its older meaning of since or because. Declarations are apt to begin with a series of *whereas* clauses, appealing to the self-evident truth of the principles on which the declaration bases its logic. The UN's Universal Declaration of Human Rights of 1948 begins this way:

> Whereas recognition...of the equal and inalienable rights of all members of the human family is the foundation of freedom, justice and peace...
>
> Whereas disregard and contempt for human rights have resulted in barbarous acts...
>
> Whereas it is essential...that human rights should be protected by the rule of law...
>
> Now, Therefore THE GENERAL ASSEMBLY proclaims...

In the will, we also find instances of the compounds *whatsoever* and *howsoever*. These are not especially unusual in ordinary discourse, even though they are constructed in much the same archaic way as *hereinafter*. They are of interest to us, though, because they betray the legal profession's concern to fashion their written documents so as to cover all eventualities – a feature we mentioned at the beginning of the chapter.

One of the most characteristic ways of covering all possible scenarios in written legalese is the device of multiple listings with 'or'. Indeed, the will takes account of several such eventualities in this way, including the possibility that the solicitors will no longer be practising at the time that the document will be needed again; that the terms of the will may apply to one or more children; that insurances might be required for a house or a flat; that money might be paid to, or used on behalf of, a beneficiary; that fire might destroy an asset completely or partially; and that money may need to be paid from capital or income or a trust fund. Look at the will again and observe how this is achieved.

Listings like this may seem to be redundant or excessive, but covering all angles is one of the things we pay lawyers to do. This is particularly true with respect to commercial contracts. Look at the following example, and try to note all the listings:

> If a person decides not to install, construct, reconstruct, relocate, alter, or modify the process or process equipment as authorized by a permit to install, the

person, or the authorized agent pursuant to R 336.1204, shall notify the department, in writing, and upon receipt of the notification by the department, the permit to install shall become void. If the installation, reconstruction, relocation, or alteration of the equipment, for which a permit has been issued, has not commenced within, or has been interrupted for, 18 months, then the permit to install shall become void unless otherwise authorized by the department as a condition of the permit to install.

(Proposed Administrative Rule R 336.1201
from March 1996, Michigan Register)

The peculiar lexical characteristics of the text above are motivated by the requirement for contracts to be explicit: the vocabulary seeks to leave no room for ambiguity and to forbid any possibility of uncertainty. The contract specifically lists the activities at issue, whether they be to 'install, construct, reconstruct, relocate, alter, or modify'; and two further explicit contingencies are foreseen, namely that the work 'has not commenced within, or has been interrupted for, 18 months'.

Occasionally this explicitness can get out of hand. This was the wording with respect to maintenance on a simple UK leasehold arrangement:

The tenant shall when where and so often as occasion requires well and sufficiently repair renew rebuild uphold support sustain maintain pave purge scour cleanse glaze empty amend and keep the premises and every part thereof and all floors walls columns roofs canopies lifts and escalators shafts stairways fences pavements forecourts drains sewers ducts flues conduits wires cables gutters soil and other pipes tanks cisterns pumps and other water and sanitary apparatus thereon with all needful and necessary amendments whatsoever.

(*Ravenseft Properties Ltd* v. *Davstone (Holdings) Ltd*, A11 ER 929)

No doubt the form of words was aimed at ensuring that the landlord's position was legally watertight, but in any case it failed, as the document was still taken to court in a dispute as to its meaning.

Written legal language, then, characteristically uses vocabulary in a highly explicit way so as to cover unambiguously any eventualities that can be foreseen. It is when this is not practical or possible that lawyers contrive to allow for all reasonable variations of circumstances by the use of phrases such as *howsoever they may choose* or *of whatsoever nature as they think fit*.

At odds with this tendency is the tacit assumption, handed down from on high, that laws are neutral principles transcending human variation. Legislation depends heavily on the interpretation of the meanings of the words it is couched in; in a very real sense, language *is* the law. The process of enacting legislation involves decisions on what counts semantically as what, and most particularly on what counts semantically as belonging to which category.

Linguistically, the key concept here is that of **hyponymy** – the semantic relationship by which one word may invariably be replaced by another, but not vice versa. *Murder* and *manslaughter* can always be replaced by *homicide*: the crimes are subcategories of the crime of homicide, and semantically the words *murder* and *manslaughter* are hyponyms of the word *homicide*. (In the terminology of semantics, *homicide* is thus a **hypernym** of *murder* and *manslaughter* – it is the **superordinate** term.)

Consequently, much of the discourse of legislation and pleading is character-ized by appeals to the meaning of legal terms and concepts, and specifically (in linguistic terms) to whether or not one term is a hyponym of another. The debate as to whether complicity in suicide is to be treated as murder or manslaughter will depend on precisely such an appeal. The fact that such appeals rely on a sig-nificant degree of interpretation, often highly subjective, means that agreement is often hard to reach. Clearly, different cultures and different legal systems make such decisions in different ways: just as one person's notion of what is *beyond rea-sonable doubt* is not necessarily another's; so one culture's view of what amounts to *justifiable homicide* may not be shared by another. (In France, for example, *crime passionnel* is a legal defence that can be made in murder cases where the crime has been carried out immediately, and without premeditation, on the rise of jealous anger or heartbreak.)

One strategy to achieve harmonization in such semantic appeals involves what can be seen as 'legal fictions', in which novel circumstances are *taken* to be the same as, or similar to, those covered by existing legal rules and regulations (Maley 1994). In law, the discourse strategy of 'deeming' is a typical method by which this process is accomplished: one object, event or activity not covered by existing laws is *deemed* to be the same as another for which legal regulations are already in force. The drunk on a bicycle can be tried under motoring laws if the bicycle is deemed to be a car; the aggressive youth who happens to be carrying a metal comb in his pocket can be brought to trial if the comb is deemed to be a weapon. Similar processes may well be involved in deeming who counts as a terrorist.

The terms of reference of an old law can be 'eased' to allow for the inclusion of a new set of circumstances. In the same way, existing words can have their definitions expanded. Consequently, deeming is common practice in contracts. In writing a contract (or at least having one drawn up for us) we can simply deem that one situ-ation counts as another. The Michigan regulation that we saw earlier, relating to an installer's contract becoming void if installation has not commenced within 18 months, actually goes on to deem what counts as 'commencing'.

> "Commenced", for purposes of this subrule, means undertaking a continuous program of on-site fabrication, installation, erection, or modification, or having entered into binding agreements or contractual obligations, which cannot be cancelled or modified without substantial loss to the owner or operator, to undertake a program of construction of the facility to be completed within a reasonable time.

This is more than just a clarification of 'commencing'. The contract overturns the accepted usage and replaces it with a meaning that would not normally be under-stood from it: it deems that installation has commenced once binding agreements have been made.

A more extreme instance of deeming is seen in the following enigmatic tax accounting regulation. Look at the text and try to work out what it means, if you like; but note specifically that the regulation explicitly engages in the process of deeming a time warp into existence.

The provisions of the preceding sentence shall not be applicable with respect to the taxable year beginning January 1, 1975, or any succeeding taxable year which begins before January 1, 1980; and, for purposes of such sentence, January 1, 1980, *shall be deemed* to be the first January 1 occurring after January 1, 1974, and consecutive taxable years in the period commencing January 1, 1980, shall be determined as if the taxable year which begins on January 1, 1980, were the taxable year immediately succeeding the taxable year which began on January 1, 1974.

(Internal Revenue Code 3302I(2)I)

We might note, finally, the use in this example (and indeed throughout our examples) of the modal verb, 'shall'. This could be seen as a grammatical feature, and therefore better examined in the section on syntax, but the selection of *shall* is genuinely of lexical interest: in every case, it could be replaced by 'must' or 'will', for instance, without changing in any way the grammatical structure of the sentence or utterance in which it appears. The third-person construction with *shall*, constantly used in written legalese, is so atypical in everyday written language as to be virtually non-existent. While characteristic of some dialects, we rarely find 'he shall', 'she shall', 'it shall' or 'they shall' in written form outside the legal sphere. On the odd (quasi-literary) occasion that it is used (Cinderella *shall* go to the ball, for example), it has the flavour of a determined promise – which was indeed its original function, and certainly the one suggested in a legal document. Its usage is archaic and quaint, just like the *devise, bequeath, per stirpes* and *hereinafter* examples that we have seen already. There is almost a flavour of the Authorized Version about the use of *shall*: it somehow 'sounds right' for the ceremony and ritual that accompanies the performance of a legal document.[3]

In summary, then, we see that the written language of the law is characterized by an archaic and arcane vocabulary, and that it also makes use of a technical lexicon that has a specialized semantics. The conflicting functions of legalese (of achieving certainty while allowing flexibility) frequently result in forms of language which are unusually and even outlandishly explicit, but which can also be remarkably vague and open to subjective interpretation or semantic debate. In consequence, the vocabulary of written legalese contributes to the production of a form of language that is very far removed from everyday linguistic experience.

As we turn now to examine the grammatical organization of written legal language, we shall see a similar tendency to produce language that is forbiddingly unfamiliar in terms of its syntactic structure.

The rule of law: the syntax of written legal discourse

When you examined the example of a will in the last section, what struck you most about it? Look at it again. Now that we have taken account of its highly technical vocabulary, its odd use of capitals, its explicit listings of certain key words and the frequency of certain archaic forms, such as *hereinafter* and *shall*, what else strikes you about it?

There is, of course, the question of its overall length. It uses over 600 words, basically to say not much more than that a woman wants to leave all her worldly goods to her children, and that, if those children should die before her, then their own children should benefit accordingly. There is little doubt that, in the world of written legal discourse, size does matter. This is nothing new: throughout history it has been common practice for scribes to charge by the word, and those laws and practices that were created when literary taste favoured the verbose are characterized by even greater length and linguistic redundancy (Mellinkoff 1963). Some of this has undoubtedly survived to the modern day.

Increased sentence length is apparent in almost all written legal discourse. Documents such as wills, deeds and contracts can contain astonishingly lengthy sentences, many of them very sparsely punctuated, making them difficult for the layman to read and understand. The will used here was fairly modest in this respect (although the third sentence does contain no fewer than 174 words): a recent analysis of written legalese found sentences containing more than 270 words, compared with an average of about 28 in written scientific English, itself not a genre noted for its brevity of expression.[4] (The record, as far as I can ascertain, seems to be held by a New Zealand bank whose standard guarantee form contained a single, punctuation-free sentence of 1300 words.)

It certainly does not help matters when a long sentence is left largely unpunctuated. In fact, in an address to the Canadian Bar Association (20 February 1991), Cheryl Stephens from the Canadian Center for Legal Information points out that:

> Research has discovered that the public has more problems with the unfamiliar *organization* of the text in legal documents, the difficult sentence structure and the lack of shared context than they do with the *vocabulary* of the law. Unfamiliar patterns of capitalization, punctuation, paragraph structure and indentation combine to create barriers to understanding the legal document.

In our everyday writing we generally use quite a lot of punctuation to clarify the meaning or reading of longer sentences. However, punctuation is always open to interpretation and the 'rules' of punctuation are by no means universally agreed: a recent British best-seller on the subject of punctuation ran into its own little storm of criticism when it crossed the Atlantic to the USA, where punctuation conventions differ from those of the UK.

A complete lack of punctuation can certainly cause significant confusion. Consider this (fictional) example: 'I bequeath to my granddaughter my diamond necklace emerald ring and pearl brooch'. How many items are being bequeathed here? It could be five, four or three, depending how you read 'diamond necklace' and 'emerald ring'. The 'natural' reading would typically be punctuated in UK English as 'my diamond necklace, emerald ring and pearl brooch'. However, the US convention would normally insist on an extra comma, thus: 'my diamond necklace, emerald ring, and pearl brooch'. This extra comma is sometimes used in UK English, but it is regarded as optional and perhaps even a little pedantic (it is often called the Oxford comma); it is generally added only when absolutely necessary to guarantee the avoidance of a semantically important misreading.

Concern about punctuation in legal documents is not just a question of style and convention, however. Occasionally a case can hang on it. A recent liability suit in Wisconsin turned on whether or not there ought to have been a comma after 'property' in the following regulation, which defined property as: 'real property and buildings, structures and improvements thereon, and the waters of the state'. The defendant (who had a structure on the land but did not own the real estate) contended that since there was no comma, the regulation was ambiguous. He lost his action, on a split verdict, but the case became important in its own small way because it explicitly confirmed the legal principle that:

> rules of grammar and punctuation should not be applied at the expense of a natural, reasonable reading of statutory language, taking into account the context in which it appears and the purpose of the statute, especially when the result would be an expansion or contraction of the statute contrary to its term.
>
> (*Peterson vs. Midwest Sec. Ins. Co.*, 2001 WI 131)

There may be historical reasons why legal documents tend to avoid punctuation as much as possible: in the days of pen and ink the fraudulent addition of a comma could substantially change the meaning of a statement. Punctuation confusions are not confined to lists. Marking off a *which* clause in commas, for example, can change its force from restrictive to purely descriptive. Consider the difference between these two forms:

> The music which I chose got everyone up and dancing

> The music, which I chose, got everyone up and dancing

The first form, without the commas, restricts the subject to only the music chosen by me; it is more or less implicit here that there was some other music too, not chosen by me, which perhaps did not prove so enlivening. The second form, inside the commas, suggests, by contrast, that the music generally was a great success, and, as it happens, was (all) chosen by me – though the fact that I chose it is added almost as an incidental observation.

Believe it or not, such commas have also been at the heart of a US legal dispute. Try to work out whether *fraternal organizations* are excluded or included by the following proviso in a US public accommodation regulation:

> PROVIDED, That nothing contained in this definition shall be construed to include or apply to any institute, bona fide club, or place of accommodation, which is by its nature distinctly private, including fraternal organizations, though where public use is permitted that use shall be covered by this chapter.

Nice legalese, but does the law apply only to the organizations mentioned before 'distinctly private', or does it also apply to 'fraternal organizations', which come after? Does it refer only to fraternal organizations that are distinctly private? Or does the *which*, with its commas, introduce a non-restrictive clause, providing only supplementary description? (Personally, I think it is perfectly clear that they are meant to be included, but this time the Ohio court ruled that the proviso was ambiguous.[5])

The first example given above of the restrictive clause, 'the music which I chose got everyone up and dancing', was a bit misleading, at least when masquerading as a piece of everyday spoken language. You are far more likely to say, 'the music I chose'. By and large, we tend not to break up our utterances with too many intervening clauses, and, when we have to, we normally find the shortest or simplest way of doing it. In the second example, by the same token, you would not say, 'the music, which I chose'; you would probably make two separate utterances, along the lines of, 'the music really got them up and dancing – I chose it, by the way'.

In the same way, the presence of embedded clauses in a written sentence makes for difficult reading. It is a general feature of written language, as opposed to spoken language, that sentences tend to be syntactically more complex. However, professional writing elevates the tendency to a new plane altogether, and this is not just confined to legal discourse: much scientific and academic writing borders on the impenetrable. All the same, in the hands of lawyers, the impenetrable does acquire a flavour all of its own.

Exercise 3c

Examine the following data, a US purchase agreement for a home workshop. Pay particular attention to the syntax employed.

> This Agreement shall be binding upon and enure for the benefit of the successors of the parties but shall not be assignable, save that the Purchaser may at any time assign all or any part of its rights and benefits under this Agreement, including the Warranties and any cause or action arising under or in respect of any of them, to any transferee of all or any part of the Business Assets or to any Affiliate of the Purchaser who may enforce them as if he had also been named in this Agreement as the Purchaser.

- How is the text structured at clause level?
- How are the clauses linked, and which words are used to signal the relationship between clauses?
- Identify the noun phrases in the agreement and examine how they are structured.
- Reflect on your answers to these questions in the light of the following analysis.

Apart from the curious capital letters again, and the strangely archaic vocabulary for an agreement concerning a piece of modern technology (*shall, enure, successors, parties, assign, save, cause, transferee*), you will have noted that this is a single sentence, and 96 words long at that; yet it contains only three commas. You may also have noted the constant listing with *or*, as in 'all or any part of its rights, any cause or action arising under or in respect of any of them, to any transferee of all or any part of the Business Assets or to any Affiliate'.

But perhaps the most obstructive (and most legalistic) aspect of this example is its overall syntactic structure. The sentence starts simply enough, although it is unusual in ordinary writing to combine 'be binding upon' and 'enure for the benefit of' in quite this way, particularly without any punctuation. The syntax then joins this statement to another, using 'but', to point out that the agreement cannot be handed over to anyone else. Immediately, however, there is an exception to be stated – *save that the Purchaser may at any time…* This turns out to be an exception that must itself be qualified with a longish list of possibilities introduced by *including*, before we are told who the rights can be transferred to. This again needs to be expanded with a relative *who*, and this in turn has to be further clarified by an *as if* clause. It depends how deeply you want to analyse the sentence, but there are certainly two clauses very seriously embedded within it, at points where the sense is confusingly fractured and obstructed; and the sentence itself is constructed around some 11 separate clauses. (Embedded clauses notoriously make sentences more difficult to understand: analysis of US Immigration documents reveals that they contain a significantly above-average proportion, raising the suspicion that they are there to construct 'textual barriers' to migrants seeking legal status and residency (Stygall 2002).)

We might also point out that the qualifications and provisos in our example above are lumped together to produce heavy noun phrases, which are unappetizingly hard to digest. What can the purchaser assign? The answer is a noun phrase, 29 words long: 'all or any part of its rights and benefits under this Agreement, including the Warranties and any cause or action arising under or in respect of any of them'. Who can he or she assign them to? Answer, another noun phrase, this time 11 words long: 'any transferee of all or any part of the Business Assets'.

This prevalence of noun phrases in written legal language is also apparent in other written forms of professional discourse. In fact, the device of **nominalization** (expressing processes in noun form) is fairly widespread throughout all written language, and we noted when looking at the discourse of politics that it frequently functions as an obfuscatory mechanism. What makes it so unusual here, in this legal document, is that the language is ostensibly drafted for the layman to read and *understand*. After all, it is up to the layman to say, 'yes, that's clear – I'm happy to sign my name to that, and to agree to be legally bound by it'.

Nominalization is favoured by legal writers not so much for its ability to confuse, but more because it allows them to avoid reference to people, especially ones who have not already been explicitly defined in the document itself. Recall how the Michigan regulation was worded: 'upon *receipt* of the *notification* by the department, the permit to install shall become void. If the *installation*, *reconstruction*, *relocation*, or *alteration* of the equipment, for which a permit has been issued, has not commenced...'

Not a person in sight. But if the wording of this regulation were to be reworked into a more everyday form, a legal writer would be extremely disconcerted. Consider this possible rewording, for example:

> If for any reason you decide not to install this equipment, you must tell us so in writing. Also, if you do not start installing it within 18 months of agreeing to, then you will have to reapply for permission. The same applies if you start installing it, and then have to stop, and do not start again within 18 months. What we mean by 'starting' is this: if you...

What is going to worry the lawyer here is the use of **anaphor** (anaphor, generally, refers to a word or phrase that relies on another word or phrase for its meaning). What, for example, does *it* refer to, in the second sentence? What about *the same* in the next sentence? The same as what? Equally, what does *so* refer to in the first sentence? And look at the second again: *agreeing to* what? No, this just will not do: from a legal point of view there is too much scope for misinterpretation here.

An even louder objection will be made to the *this* of *this equipment*. What equipment? Where? The problem for the legal writer is that words like 'this' depend for their meaning on the context in which they are uttered. (Linguists refer to such terms as **deictic** – the word 'here' is another example, as is 'now'.) From a legal perspective they are problematic as they point to things and places in the outside world that may (and probably will) change, move or be replaced. Deictic terms, like anaphoric terms, are assiduously avoided by the legal writer.

We might recall at this point that politicians also employ nominalization when they want to suggest (for example) that a process or activity of human agency, on which they might be expected to have some controlling function, is actually a fact or a finished product – or sometimes even a natural force, not of human agency, in which it is impossible to intervene. 'Globalization' is an example we have mentioned already in this context. Hand in hand with this use of nominalization, we found, went a tendency to cast sentences and utterances into a passive voice construction – a device that can also serve to obfuscate human agency.

It is noticeable that legal writing also makes frequent use of this device. 'Deeming' is almost always accomplished in the passive voice, for instance, thus avoiding the necessity of having to define who is doing the deeming – as in the Internal Revenue Code example given above: 'January 1, 1980, shall *be deemed* to be the first January 1 occurring after January 1, 1974, and consecutive taxable years in the period commencing January 1, 1980, shall *be determined* as if...'

We suggested, at the end of the section on the vocabulary of written legalese, that there was a tendency towards the ceremonial in the creation of legal documents. In looking at the syntax of written legalese, this suggestion is surely reinforced. The complexity of its structure entails that only 'initiates' are qualified, not just to write the documents in question, but also to read them. The documents are, in fact, really designed for lawyers to read, not laymen. The specialized vocabulary, along with the density of the text, the clustering and nesting of clauses, and the impersonal grammatical formulations, all make the legal document a forbidding and mysterious experience for the outsider.

The legal writer typically exploits conventions familiar only to those inside the profession, and in so doing leaves traces that will guide another practised eye to a quick evaluation of the form and meaning of the document. The use of capital letters is a peculiar instance of this, and especially a device of capitalization that we have not commented on so far, where key structural words (capitalized throughout) mark out the basic logical method of construction of the document. A quick glance in the right places will lead the interested professional to an immediate sense of what is likely to be contained in the document – much as an artisan builder or craftsman is able to 'see' the structure of a building or a piece of furniture without having to dismantle the fixtures or fittings of it. Look back at some of the earlier examples and exercises and note how the essential structure of documents can be made visible through this use of capitalization.

It is no accident that legal documents are often referred to as 'deeds'; nor that a piece of legislation becomes an 'act'. The transformation of an ordinary person's day-to-day requirements or wishes, or of society's mundane public order concerns, into a document or piece of legislation that is fit to withstand the fierce gaze of the law, amounts to a mystery that is almost equal to that of the Communion. The document 'enshrines', with all proper ritual, the ceremonial deed of declaring or deeming or covenanting, or the grave act of passing a piece of legislation or proclaiming a decision of national or international importance.

In the introduction to this book we introduced speech act theory, a pragmatic approach to discourse which rests on the premise that when we speak (or write), not only do we *say* something, but we also *do* something, and not just in the sense that speaking and writing involve physical actions. In using language we intend to convey particular meanings, and our utterances have a certain force that affects the person we are speaking or writing to. In his classic text on this subject, J. L. Austin (1962) explains how language is a form of action that has three distinct aspects. In simple terms, these are as follows:

- *Locutionary act*: the act *of* saying something; refers to the meaningful production of sounds, words and utterances.

- *Illocutionary act*: the act achieved *in* saying something; refers to the *force* of the utterance in a given context.

- *Perlocutionary act*: the act achieved *by* saying something; refers, for example, to the consequential *effects* on the feelings, thoughts or actions of the addressee(s).

In order to interpret and understand speech acts, we need to look beyond the linguistic form in which they are phrased and make reference to the situated discourse in which they are produced. For example, a teacher in a rowdy classroom may use a direct speech act: *Be quiet!*; or, alternatively, employ more indirect phrasing: *Who's talking?* The illocutionary force of her indirect utterance is not so much to question as to command: *Stop talking*. Knowing the norms of the classroom context and sharing in the assumptions of classroom culture, students will not answer, but will react with the perlocutionary act of becoming silent.

As we have seen, language is a social practice, and in making an utterance we also make a statement about our position in relation to society – we 'make a move' in that context, whether by expressing an opinion, adding some factual information into a discussion, promising to meet someone at a particular time, explaining why we have or have not done something, persuading someone to buy a product or vote for a political party, making a friendly greeting or a grumpy dismissal, warning someone of a danger or apologizing for being late.

As mentioned in the introduction to the book, there is a class of utterances where the act of uttering them is genuinely the act of performing the process in question – where the process cannot in fact be achieved unless the utterance is made. These are known as **performative** utterances: 'I apologize' is an archetypal example. The exact form of words is not the issue here; it is simply that the process of *apologizing* is performed verbally, and it is the uttering of the words that constitutes performing the action. The words, in a sense, are the deed – much as the words of a legal document encapsulate the deed of bequeathing or contracting or deeming. If you go back to Exercise 3b you will find several performative utterances used in the will; look out for performative verbs, such as *appoint, give, declare, express,* and consider the purpose served by the use of *hereby.*

It is no accident that the class of performative utterances includes many members that are legal in force or tenor, often involving the conferring of rights or the making of commitments:

> I swear that the evidence I shall give shall be the truth, the whole truth, and nothing but the truth
>
> I sentence you to three years in prison
>
> I hereby revoke all former Wills
>
> I promise to pay the bearer on demand the sum of twenty pounds
>
> I hereby give permission for my son to join this field trip

And many that are religious:

> I now pronounce you man and wife
>
> I christen you Anthony Charles Lynton

We might also note that, while performatives are usually in the first person, this is not exclusively so:

> You are charged that on Sunday last you did steal a bicycle
>
> This court is now in session
>
> This church is hereby de-sanctified

And, indeed, that performatives can nowadays be 'uttered' electronically, as shown in Figure 3.02 overleaf.

You may have noticed that the compound *hereby*, which we have seen and mentioned earlier, often accompanies performatives, carrying the sense of 'by making this utterance' or 'by signing this document'. This assumes that the utterance is made at the right time and place, of course, for context is important here. In order for each of these speech acts to work – that is, to carry out the deeds stated – they have to be articulated by particular persons in particular settings at particular times: certain 'felicity conditions' have to be in place. 'I pronounce you man and wife' simply does not work if uttered to you by a drunk in a park. Look back at the examples above and identify the felicity conditions that need to be in place for the performatives to be successful, or, to use Austin's term, 'happy'.

The allocation of rights to perform speech acts gives us our first insight into the hierarchical power structures that are represented in the spoken language of legal interaction. While it would be wrong to assume that power is wholly predefined or static in social relationships, the differential access to legal knowledge and the imbalance of authority between participants in courtrooms leads to an asymmetry and imbalance in the discourse constructed. In the following section, we will be particularly concerned to examine the relationship between participant roles and the realization and negotiation of power in legal interviews and courtroom testimony.

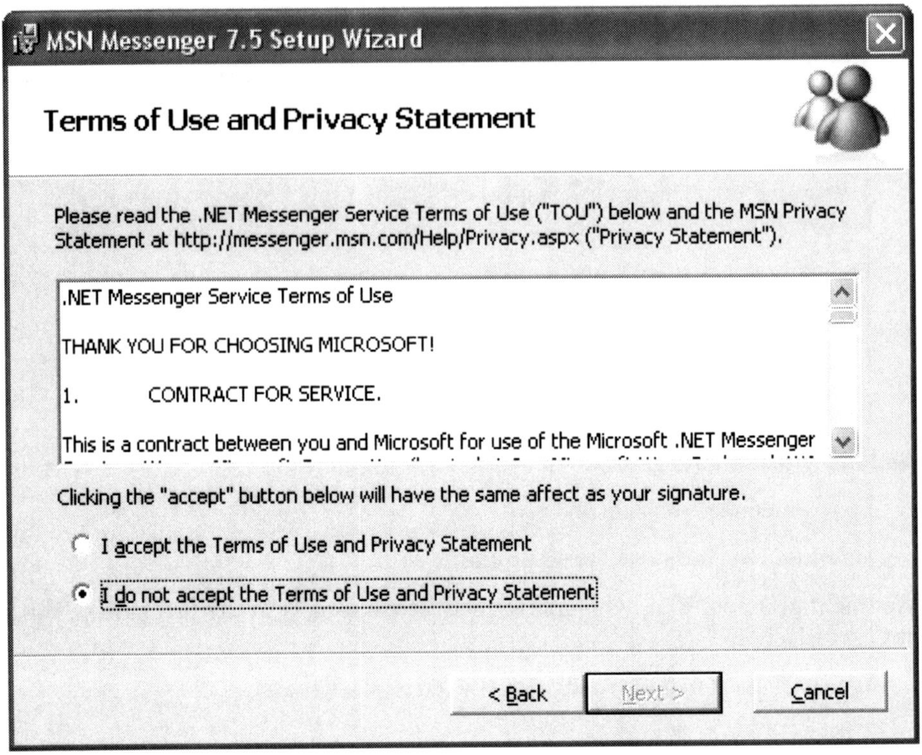

Fig. 3.02   MSN Messenger terms

What you're saying is...: spoken legal discourse

> Anything you say can and will be used against you in a court of law
>
> (US Miranda warning)

If it is true that, as Conley and O'Barr put it, 'most of the time, law is talk' (2005: 129), then it is rather curious to note that one of our society's most sacred legal rights is the right to silence: you really do not have to say anything. In view of this right, it is unsurprising that much of our legal system is devoted to the business of getting you to say something. Once you do, after all, you are fair game.

There are two important aspects to consider in the right of silence. First, you are presumed innocent until proved guilty, and the burden of proof falls on your prosecutors; you are not obliged to help them. The principle of *nemo tenetur se ipsum prodere* (no one can be obliged to speak against himself) still holds, although it is a principle that has to a certain extent been watered down over the years. Second, you are entitled to have someone speak on your behalf – indeed, it is expected that you will appoint a lawyer to do so.

In the USA both these principles are made clear to you when you are arrested, in the Miranda warning, which takes the following form:

> You have the right to remain silent. Anything you say can and will be used against you in a court of law. You have the right to speak to an attorney, and to have an attorney present during any questioning. If you cannot afford a lawyer, one will be provided for you at government expense.

In the UK, since the Criminal Justice and Public Order Act 1994, the caution takes this form:

> You do not have to say anything, but it may harm your defence if you fail to mention when questioned something which you later rely on in court. Anything you do say will be given in evidence.

Compare the two warnings, and consider the differences between them, not only in their content, but also in their syntactic form.

The wording of the UK caution was debated in the House of Lords at the time of its introduction, and Lord McIntosh of Haringey made the following point about its comprehensibility:

> I have only one particular point to make … it concerns the caution. I listened carefully to the Minister as she read it – not only to the words … but also to her tone of voice and the way in which she read it. None of that can appear in Hansard, but I ask the House to consider very carefully whether this is a comprehensible series of words: *If you do not mention when questioned something which you later rely on in court...* In normal speech we do not include a phrase such as "when questioned" in the middle of a sentence without any punctuation and when it is out of the normal order of everyday speech. I suggest that that sentence is not in demotic English and will not be readily understood by a very large number of people who will hear it read to them... I beg the Government to look again at the wording of the caution and to undertake serious research. It is possible to undertake research into how people – not necessarily those with university degrees or PhDs – actually understand the wording.
>
> (*Hansard*, 23 February 1995, Column 1280)

You may like to try rewording the caution for yourself, to see if you can solve the problem outlined above. (It is amusing to note that the Home Secretary of the time apparently struggled to get below an 80-word formulation for his preliminary proposal to parliament.)

The UK warning was changed from its original – *you do not have to say anything, but anything you say may be taken down and given in evidence* – precisely because it was felt to be too easy for criminals to remain silent until they had 'worked out' a defence. The modified caution reflected the right of the court to infer an 'absence of innocence' in a suspect who withheld information that it might seem reasonable for an innocent party to offer. There has long been a feeling, in Britain at least, that the law favours the criminal – experienced and well-financed – over the unfortunate and legally inexperienced victim. This feeling lies behind Tony Blair's pledge, which we examined in the last chapter, to 'create a criminal justice system which puts the victim first, punishes properly the criminal'.[6]

Nevertheless, there is also genuine concern about the possible manipulation or even falsification of spoken evidence that has been taken in the process of police questioning. It is worth reminding ourselves at this point that, in the context of the law, evidence is largely linguistic: crucial decisions regarding guilt or innocence rely on linguistic negotiation. Indeed, speech exchanges in police interview rooms and in courtrooms almost wholly define the events that take place within them, and interviews between police officers and suspects, as well as courtroom examinations, all represent processes of linguistic arbitration.

The police have a vested interest in initiating and controlling any exchanges in which they get the opportunity to get a witness or suspect to talk, and cross-examining barristers have a range of weapons at their disposal to lead the examinee into saying things perhaps better left unsaid. We will look first at the language that characterizes the way police conduct their interviews.

In other words: the discourse of police interviews

In the chronology of crime, the first interactions to take place are between police officers and relevant others: victims are expected to give explicit accounts of the crimes committed against them; those suspected of perpetrating offences will, under caution, undergo interviews and interrogations; witnesses will be interviewed in order for details of unlawful events to be recorded as fully as possible, and they may be asked to give and sign a formal statement. These initial speech encounters are crucial for establishing the course of any later legal processes and procedures. The police interview has been well characterized as the 'upstream' event that sets in motion the course of action that can lead eventually to a trial, often occurring many months and miles 'downstream' (Russell 2002).

Norman Fairclough presents the following data taken from an interview between a police officer (P) and a witness (W). Consider it carefully, and examine how the power relationship is established linguistically.

(1) P: Did you get a look at the one in the car?

(2) W: I saw his face, yeah.

(3) P: What sort of age was he?

(4) W: About 45. He was wearing a…

(5) P: And how tall?

(6) W: Six foot one.

(7) P: Six foot one. Hair?

(8) W: Dark and curly, Is this going to take long? I've got to collect the kids from school.

(9) P: Not much longer, no. What about his clothes?

(10) W: He was a bit scruffy-looking, blue trousers, black…

(11) P: Jeans?

(12) W: Yeah.

(Fairclough 2001: 15)

Much can be learned about the nature of spoken legal interviews from this short extract. Examine, for example, how the police officer uses multiple questions to exert control over the interview.[7] Question-answer structures are an example of **adjacency pairs**, a concept that has been particularly productive in the conversation analysis approach towards explaining the sequencing of discourse. Adjacency pairs are probably best understood by an example. When we give a compliment, for instance, we typically expect a reply, and, if we do not receive one, we may feel that the compliment has been 'wasted'. Similarly, when we greet a friend or acquaintance, we expect a greeting in return. We consider ourselves badly or rudely treated if our compliments or greetings (first pair parts of adjacency pairs) are not 'balanced' with appropriate expressions of thanks or returned greetings (second pair parts). Questions typically function as the first pair parts of adjacency pairs, and they demand responses (second pair parts) that are relevant to the questions asked. Beyond the sequential pairing, questions may also secure the return of the third turn to the questioner.[8] By presenting the witness with a checklist of questions, the police officer therefore exerts considerable control over what follows: control not only of the organization and the ordering of speaking turns in the interview, but also of the topic to be spoken about in each turn.

The power and authority of the police officer is also revealed in the use of interruptions: at lines 5 and 11 the officer interrupts the witness's account of what the suspect was wearing.[9] Furthermore, a little later in the interview, note how the police officer leads the witness into a certain response regarding the suspect's clothes: at line 11, the officer prompts 'jeans' in response to the reference to 'blue trousers', and the witness agrees.

A central goal of the police interview can be seen as the eliciting of a confession from a suspect (Heydon 2005). The interview techniques used by police officers, often with this central goal underpinning them, may place witnesses and (especially innocent) suspects at a significant disadvantage: strict control of structure and content may prevent witnesses and suspects from telling their own story.

Exercise 3d

Examine the following data elicited from an interview between a police officer (P) and a member of the public (S) who has been arrested on suspicion of assault.

(1) P: Do you know where this was?

(2) S: Yeah, Atlas Road.

(3) P: Right, at the north end?

(4) S: Err, I was just looking…

(5) P: Where in Atlas Road?

(6) S: Err, the Northshields pub is…

(7) P: Okay, carry on, carry on.

(8) S: They came up behind us and it happened. ➡

---

(9) P: What?

(10) S: Well, he used an elbow and a kick.

(11) P: Where were you standing at this time?

(12) S: About the distance from you to…

(13) P: How far?

(14) S: Three, four, five feet?

(15) P: What you're saying is that he said you go over and teach someone a lesson?

(16) S: Err, yeah.

- What strategies does the police officer use to exert her authority in the interview situation?
- How do the interview strategies employed by the police officer seek to elicit a confession from the suspect?
- How much scope is the suspect given to present his own account of events?

Think about your answers as we move on to examine first this data and then other discourse strategies distinctive of police interviews of suspects.

Note how the police officer conducts the interview by the continual use of questions (lines 1, 3, 5, etc.). Interruptions occur when the suspect fails to give direct answers, or at least when the suspect's answers are not phrased to the police officer's satisfaction (lines 5, 7 and 13). The interruption at line 7, which, somewhat paradoxically, is made to direct the suspect to continue speaking, is phrased in a manner that would rarely, if ever, be employed in everyday discourse. Finally, at line 15, note how the officer puts words into the mouth of the suspect by restating one of his responses: 'What you're saying is…'

Restating a response is a fairly innocuous device, often occurring in everyday discourse. But the tendency of police interviewers to alter and amend the responses provided by interviewees has been well documented (Shuy 1993). Look at the following evidence from interviews conducted in 1978 between American detectives and Jerry Townsend, who was charged with the rape and murder of women working as prostitutes. Note the way Townsend's response is reinterpreted by the detective at line 3, and consider the meaning of Townsend's final answer at line 4. (You should note that Townsend suffered from severe learning disabilities and appeared always to use the expression *commit suicide* as meaning 'kill'.)

(1) Detective: *Jerry, did you kill these girls up there in Fort Lauderdale?*

(2) Townsend: *No, I didn't commit suicide but, you know, I just put them where they can't be of a use no more.*

(3) Detective: *In other words, you just went ahead and choked them around the neck? Now you have to be straight out.*

(4) Townsend: *Yeah. Yeah.*

(Shuy 1993: 182)

At line 3, Townsend's reference to putting the women 'where they can't be of a use no more' is repeated and reinterpreted ('in other words') by the detective as 'choked them around the neck'. And what about Townsend's final response, 'Yeah. Yeah'? Is this a reply to the detective's question about choking the women or Townsend's reaction to the request for him to be 'straight out'? It is impossible to know, of course, but it is clear that utterances such as that in line 3, which consist of multiple questions, can cause confusion and miscommunication in police–suspect interviews.

Tape recordings of spoken interviews are not submitted to courts directly, but are first transcribed into written records, and it is these written transcripts that form the basis of the court prosecution. Recently there has been considerable controversy surrounding this procedure and, in the UK in the 1990s, many successful appeals were made on the grounds that written records of police interviews had been falsified. Similar storms have plagued the Australian law courts, where a new word has been coined: individuals who have been charged and convicted as a consequence of fabricated linguistic evidence (and particularly as a result of bogus confessions) are said to have been *verballed*.[10]

While discourse analysis cannot yet be used to show deliberate fabrication, other processes involved in the written transcription of spoken police interviews have fallen within its remit. Research has suggested that by the time a case reaches court it has been subject to a 'large number of re-tellings' in several different communicative contexts, including police interviews, grand jury and plea-bargaining sessions, pretrial indictment and arraignment hearings (Cotterill 2002). Perhaps most importantly, the retelling of spoken interviews in written reports can often entail the omission of the suspect's account: researchers have looked at several cases in which elderly people had been accused of minor misdemeanours and found that explanations provided by the suspects at interview did not appear in written reports – personal histories and other potentially mitigating factors were omitted, and only the perspective of the police officer was properly presented (Linell and Jonsson 1991).

Considerable work has been done by Malcolm Coulthard (2002) on the case of Derek Bentley, who in 1952 was charged with the murder of a police officer, even though he had not fired the fatal shot. Analysis of Bentley's statement reveals substantial evidence that the interview *dialogue* that took place between Bentley and police officers was misrepresented as a *monologue* in the written record: specifically, the written statement implied that Bentley had provided information spontaneously when, in fact, his remarks had been phrased as responses to police officers' questions. Coulthard argues that this misrepresentation, and particularly the distortion of the timing and sequencing of the dialogue that occurred as a result of the failure to include officers' questions in the written record, led to an unfair summing-up by the judge at Bentley's trial. Bentley received the death sentence and was executed. Forty years later the guilty verdict was overturned.

The Bentley case was heard *before* the introduction of compulsory tape-recording of police–suspect interviews. But audio-recording does not guarantee justice at court, particularly if the written transcriptions are careful to record suspects' 'bad language' in order to cast doubt on their credibility and status, while police officers can equally have their language 'cleaned up' so as to make them sound fair and friendly.

Discourse features, such as *well, look, I think,* and other linguistic markers of hesitancy are often excluded during transcription (as they are in the transcriptions of parliamentary debates, incidentally). This can result in written records sounding more certain and confident than the original spoken statements. Written records also cannot represent some intonational aspects of language that are crucial to the interpretation of meaning. In consequence, transcription does not produce verbatim accounts of spoken interviews, but rather results in 'interpretations' of spoken exchanges – and it is these written interpretations that are taken forward into courtroom hearings.[11]

Just answer the question: the discourse of the courtroom

The differential power relationships characteristic of police interviews are also found in the courtroom. Those in authoritative positions command particular forms of address; in Britain these can be quite ceremonious: *your Lordship, your Ladyship, your Honour, my Learned Friend.* In many courts there are archaic and ritualistic dress requirements, sometimes even involving the wearing of wigs. Also, the sheer physical layout of the court often reflects the asymmetrical power relations which hold between participants: the judge typically sits in a raised position at the front of the court; barristers, supported by their juniors and advising lawyers, sit on opposite benches; and few participants are permitted to move freely around the court. Witnesses appear only in the restricted space of the witness box; defendants, often flanked by court officers, are confined to the dock. It is in this formal, archaic and forbidding context that our legal duels are fought; and the weapons of choice are words.

In our discussion of written legal language, we saw that considerable attention is paid to defining the meanings of words: we saw, primarily, that written legalese uses a technical vocabulary with specialized semantics. In the spoken discourse of the courtroom, the precise meaning of words, phrases and legal terms is often the subject of deliberation and debate too. A great deal of court time is spent on reviewing and ruling on the semantics of particular pieces of legislation.

We have mentioned briefly the case of the carriage and the bicycle – *Corkery* v. *Carpenter* (1951). Corkery was charged under the Licensing Act of 1872 for being drunk and disorderly while in charge of a 'carriage, horse, cattle or steam engine'; there was no question that Corkery was drunk, and no doubt that he was disorderly – the crucial question was whether his bicycle was covered by the Licensing Act (or, in the linguistic terms that we used earlier, whether *bicycle* is a homonym of the superordinate, *carriage*). The bicycle was duly deemed to be a carriage and Corkery was punished (Maley 1994).

We have also made reference to the debate about murder and manslaughter in the context of a so-called mercy killing. One such case occurred in Britain in 1957, when a doctor, who had administered a large dose of painkilling drugs to a terminally ill patient, was charged with murder. Despite the patient's 'helpless misery', the judge concluded that 'the law knows no special defence in this category'. The legal debate, as we have mentioned, rests narrowly only on *intention*, and not on *malice aforethought*, the absence of which should, in many people's opinion, lead to the lesser charge of manslaughter. But we note again that the application of our laws is

Fig. 3.03 *Time* magazine cover 1998

invariably debated and determined in relation to the meanings of the language which gives them their expression.

Meaning, as we have said many times, can be manipulated. And just as politicians, for example, make selective use of linguistic terms to persuade us of particular political realities, so legal professionals lead us to specific perceptions of events and actions by their own careful selection of words and phrases.

Occasionally politics and the law will overlap in the context of just such semantic quibbling.

The trial of President Clinton was brought on a charge of perjury: Clinton was charged with lying about his extramarital affair with internee Monica Lewinsky. Clinton relied on the defence that oral sex does not constitute sexual intercourse (it is an advanced technique of massage, apparently) and therefore does not amount to infidelity; consequently, his denial of adultery was not perjury. The case therefore depended on the semantic interpretation of *oral sex, sexual intercourse, infidelity* and *adultery.* You might like to work out your own particular answer to the question headlined in *Time* magazine (see Figure 3.03) on 24 August 1998: 'When is sex not "sexual relations"?'

Manipulative verbal games are an everyday part of language in the courtroom. Lawyers and barristers carefully select words with the intention of leading jurors towards particular interpretations of circumstances and situations. Consider the following example and try to gauge how the choice of different verb phrases might suggest a different reading of the action that occurred:

The truck…

bumped into

knocked over

collided with

careered into

hit

struck

crashed into

smashed into

…the pedestrian.

(Adapted from Stubbs 1983)

Nouns and noun phrases can be similarly manipulated to represent a particular turn of events. For example, in the infamous, politically driven McCarthy 'witch-hunt' trials in the USA in the 1950s, the terms *informant* and *informer* were carefully and variably used. Consider the denotations and connotations of these terms. While they both denote individuals providing information, they have rather different connotations: *informant* is perhaps a relatively 'neutral' term, but *informer* is a more dysphemistic expression, associated with the provision of information against, and to the possible detriment of, another individual (Navasky 1982).

Similar manipulation of meaning at word level can be seen in the case of a doctor prosecuted for carrying out a late abortion. The prosecution argued that if the termination had not been performed the *infant* may have lived, and made repeated reference to the *killing* of the *baby boy* and to the *ending of the life* of *the child.* The defence, by contrast, continually referred to the *termination* of the *product of conception,* the *abortion* of the *foetus* and the *disposal* of the *embryo.* These choices of different noun phrases were not accidental, and aimed to conceptualize the process of abortion in starkly divergent ways.[12]

Metaphorical language can also function as such a 'conceptualizing device' in court talk. Research analysing the murder trial of O. J. Simpson has focused on the metaphorical representation of Simpson as a volatile *time bomb*. The prosecution had used the metaphor to represent Simpson as an erratic, unpredictable and dangerous individual who was capable of being a wife beater: 'you know there are certain things that can set him off, that can set that fuse to burning, that can make a fuse shorter and shorter'. In response, the defence took up the metaphor, but applied it in a very different way: 'the fuse…kept going out. It never blew up, it never exploded. There was no triggering mechanism' (Cotterill 1998: 147–8). The lawyers' intentions here were to establish a conceptual framework that would capture the imagination of the jury members, and within that framework to weave two different, persuasive threads of narrative.

In our examination of written legal language we saw how vague linguistic expressions can be employed deliberately in an attempt to allow scope for individual applications of legislation. Similar strategies are used in the spoken discourse of the courtroom: terms such as *intentional* and *reckless* allow considerable room for linguistic and legal manoeuvre. Vagueness and ambiguity can also result from the use of grammatical words that have multiple meanings. It is noticeable, for example, that when summing up for the jury judges often rely heavily on the use of the modal *may*. An example might be: 'you *may* think that driving while in this condition was a negligent way to act' (Stubbs 1983).

Think about this use of *may*. Is the judge using it as an expression of possibility, in the sense of *you may be right* (but equally, *you may be wrong*)? Or is the judge implying that he or she is granting permission for the jury to think this way, in the sense of *you may leave the table (but only after you have finished your pudding)*? If jurors are not sure, misunderstanding is almost bound to result. Given the judge's powerful position of authority, it is hard to resist the impression that he or she is using this modal form to steer the jury in a certain direction and towards a certain conclusion. (The charge would never stand up in court though.)

As we have seen in the previous chapters, certain grammatical constructions are often selected purposefully to obscure or hide the agency of actions. Researchers examining the use of passive constructions in Canadian rape trials have found that the passive form in which the agent of the action is missing (the agentless passive) is frequently employed to detract attention away from the accused: for example, *the woman was attacked*, rather than *the accused attacked the woman* (which most people would agree is the clearest grammatical form to describe an action). Indeed, in court talk, actions are often also nominalized (as in written legalese) and we find the human agency lost altogether: *there was an attack on the woman*. Such syntactic constructions serve to obscure the role of any actor or perpetrator of the crime, and even perhaps to conceal the very nature of the crime itself (Coates et al. 1994). Syntax, we can see, is used just as artfully by the courtroom lawyer as by any politician.

However, certainly the most characteristic syntactic device of the courtroom, and perhaps the most important, is the question form. Just as police interviews are structured around question-and-answer pairs, so too the structure of courtroom discourse is typified by similarly organized examination and interrogation. In the courtroom, as in the police station, the right to ask questions is often limited to the powerful participants: in this case, judges and members of counsel. And while there may be areas of legal discourse in which question-and-answer sequences are cooperative (between lawyers and clients, for instance), questions in cross-examination are characteristically confrontational.

Leading questions are generally disallowed in courtroom examination, but this does not deter lawyers from phrasing their enquiries in a way that predisposes certain answers. Research into the use of questions in several high-profile court cases in the USA shows that open-ended questions (e.g. those phrased by *why, where, when*) tend to elicit narrative-style responses from witnesses; by contrast, closed-ended questions (e.g. those that can be answered by *yes* or *no* or some other minimal answer) tend to limit the length and content of responses (Harris 2001).

A well-known book of linguistic advice for lawyers warns against using questions beginning with *why* and *how*, since 'such questions hand over entirely to the witness'. Instead, lawyers are advised to use questions that are more restrictive and so allow the examiner to stay in control of proceedings. The following are typical:

> When you heard the noise you have described, you were at the corner of Shaftesbury Avenue and Cambridge Circus, correct?
>
> After you witnessed the document, you say Mr Downing folded it and put it into a long envelope. That's right, isn't it?
>
> Do you agree that it was raining at the time?

(Cited in Evans 1998: 88–9)

We will return to a consideration of the precise syntactic structure of such questions in a moment. For now, it is important to understand that the way in which a question is asked may influence the answer that is given. Compare the syntactic forms of the following interrogatives:

> Where were you on the night of 14th September?
>
> Were you in the Cambridge Arms on the night of 14th September?
>
> On the night of 14th September you were in the Cambridge Arms, weren't you?

Note how the first example, an open-ended 'wh-' question, allows a free response to be expressed – any place or location can be specified by the respondent. The second rendition is more 'conducive': the alleged place of the crime, the Cambridge Arms, is stated explicitly, and only a minimal *yes* or *no* response is requested. Finally, examine how the third example is actually quite coercive: the question contains the complete proposition, *you were in the Cambridge Arms*, followed by the negative tag form, *weren't you*, which calls only for a confirmation or denial of the proposition. (Recall how, in the last chapter, the political interviewer Jeremy Paxman exploited the power of a question containing a complete proposition when interviewing Tony Blair about the invasion of Iraq.) Interestingly, it has been shown that, particularly in asymmetrical speech exchanges, it takes more linguistic work to deny than to affirm propositions; consequently, questions that contain complete propositions like this strongly predispose affirmative answers (Atkinson and Drew 1979).

Exercise 3e

Examine the following data taken from the Oklahoma bombing trial of Terry Nichols, which took place in December 1997. The extract is part of the defence's cross-examination of the witness Steven Burmeister. Burmeister's evidence was crucial to the trial, since he had worked as part of the chemical evidence recovery team immediately following the bombing.

(1) Q. And you tested glass fragments; is that right?

(2) A. Yes.

(3) Q. Did you pick up any foam?

(4) A. Not off of the surface, but I did remove some foam from the protected areas of vehicles.

(5) Q. And did you test that for high-explosive residue?

(6) A. Yes.

(7) Q. Did you find any?

(8) A. No.

(9) Q. Did you pick up some plastic?

(10) A. I don't recall whether I retrieved any particular plastic pieces, myself.

(11) Q. A number of plastic pieces were retrieved; correct?

(12) A. Yes.

(13) Q. And they were sent to your laboratory; correct?

(14) A. Yes.

(15) Q. How many of them were sent to your laboratory?

(16) A. I have no idea of the number of pieces of plastic.

(17) Q. Hundreds?

(18) A. I really can't come up with a number.

(Criminal Action No. 96-CR-68.
Reporter's Transcript, *Trial to Jury*, volume 22)

- How does the attorney phrase his questions and how do they function in the discourse? What implications does your response to this question reveal about the relationship between linguistic form and function?

- Rank the attorney's questions according to the degree to which they are conducive or leading.

- What is the most noticeable feature of Burmeister's responses to the attorney's questions?

Consider your ideas in the light of the following analysis.

Note the employment of yes/no questions in the above cross-examination (lines 3, 5, 7 and 9) and note that, while they elicit minimal answers at lines 6 and 8, in other instances the questions do not educe answers of *yes* or *no* (lines 4 and 10). Look also at the phrasing of the defence lawyer's questions at lines 1, 11 and 13: the syntactic structures of these interrogatives contain complete propositions (at line 1, 'you tested glass fragments'; at line 11, 'a number of plastic pieces were retrieved'; and at line 13, 'they were sent to your laboratory') and function as questions only because of the final tag forms (*is that right* at line 1, and, at lines 11 and 13, the positive truth tag, *correct?*). Such questions call for a simple affirmation or denial of the presented 'facts' and so serve to further restrict the witness's testimony; note that Burmeister responds with a simple *yes* answer to all these questions (lines 2, 12 and 14). At line 15, the defence counsel asks a question calling for a minimal numerical response and, when no answer is forthcoming, attempts to coerce the witness by the suggestion of a particular figure, 'Hundreds?' (line 17).

Careful phrasing of questions therefore allows lawyers a certain degree of control over both the length of the ensuing response and the content of what is expressed in courtroom testimony. Furthermore, jurors' impressions can be directed in particular ways by presuppositions that are embedded within questions (again, we have come across devices exploiting hidden presuppositions in both our previous chapters). The following extract is from a rape trial heard in the US courts, in which it was alleged that the victim had been attacked while *partying*, and focuses on the ensuing debate about the meaning of the term. Examine it carefully, paying special attention to the phrasing of the questions.

(1) Defence Attorney: Is it not true…partying among people your age does not mean go to a party?

(2) Victim: That's true.

(3) Defence Attorney: It implies…to many people that implies sexual activity, doesn't it?

(4) Prosecuting Attorney: Objection, Your Honour.

(5) Judge: Overruled.

(6) Defence Attorney: To many young people your age that means sexual activity, does it not?

(7) Victim: To some, yes, I guess.

(Adapted from Matoesian 1993: 166)

Notice how the defence attorney coerces the victim into agreeing that the term *partying* involves sexual activity. In the first lines we see a straightforward declarative – 'partying among people your age does not mean go to a party' – with a negative truth clause prefixing the statement – 'Is it not true?' The ensuing interrogation includes questions which contain complete propositions with attached negative tags: 'that implies sexual activity, *doesn't it?*' and 'that means sexual activity, *does it not?*' (lines 3 and 6). It can be argued that the inclusion of statements in tag questions actually makes responses almost irrelevant.[13] Certainly, in the above extract, the way the questions are phrased boxes the victim into a corner and manoeuvres her into a position where she can do little more than agree with the propositions presented (line 7). As a consequence the jury's impressions are directed away from the responsibility of the suspected assailant and towards the liability of the victim – a result that, as Matoesian (1993) argues, leads to the 'revictimization' of women in rape trials.

Finally, consider how at line 4 the adjacency pair, articulated in the defence attorney's question and the victim's response, is breached by an *objection* from the prosecution. This shows that, as noted above, adjacency pairs do not necessarily have to neighbour each other, and, more importantly, that the allocation of **speaking turns** is relatively fixed in courtroom procedures.

In everyday speech encounters we follow a certain etiquette of taking turns at speaking. Patterns of turn-taking, along with many other aspects of the structuring of social interaction, are studied in the approach of **conversation analysis**. This approach, which we reviewed briefly in the introduction to this book, seeks to examine not only how conversational behaviour is (sequentially) organized and structured, but also how it relates to the creation of social roles, social relationships and a sense of social order.

In relation to the taking of turns in conversational exchanges, seminal work by the conversation analysts Harvey Sacks, Emanuel Schegloff and Gail Jefferson reveals that we tend to follow specific routines for taking a turn at speaking. First of all, we recognize that there are only certain places when it is appropriate to take the conversational floor – without, for example, interrupting or intruding on the speaking turn of another. In fact, Sacks, Schegloff and Jefferson find that a conversational participant who is already speaking is allowed a significant degree of control over the ensuing interaction: a current speaker may allocate the next speaker by, for example, addressing a question to a particular conversational participant, or by using non-verbal clues such as gaze. If the current speaker in a conversation does not select a next speaker, then any participant is free to self-select themselves. Largely unconsciously, we use all sorts of signals to show that we wish to take a turn at speaking: finishing a current speaker's sentence for them, uttering 'background' expressions of assent or dissent for the current speaker (for example by the use of *mm, yeah, no, but*) and, non-linguistically, by engaging in rapid nodding or taking a sharp and loud inhalation of breath. Finally, if the current speaker begins to relinquish the turn and no other speaker self-selects themselves to speak, then the current speaker may continue (and indeed may feel obliged to continue).[14]

Consider how spoken exchanges and turns at talk are managed in the institutional context of the courtroom, and how asymmetrical power relations between participants are played out in court talk. Note, for example, how the supreme position of judges allows them both to exercise full rights over the turn-taking rules and also to break the rules if they so desire: judges may, and often do, select the next speaker; they can self-select at any point (even if this means intruding on or interrupting the speaking turn of another participant); and, in principle, they may continue to talk for as long as they wish. Counsels for the defence and prosecution are also allocated a substantial amount of speaking time: they present opening and closing addresses, as well as conducting examination and cross-examination of witnesses and defendants. Like judges, they have the right to determine the next speaker in court proceedings and, as we have seen, often do so through the particular construction of questions. They may also select themselves for speaking turns within certain constraints: as is illustrated in the rape trial extract above, as well as having their own defined time to speak, opposing counsels may interject at other times in order to raise objections and other points of order. By contrast, witnesses and defendants are highly constrained as to when they are entitled to speak: when taking a speaking turn, they do not have the right to select the next speaker; they may not select themselves at any point; and their turns at talk are strictly confined to speaking spaces determined by judges and members of counsel.

One important effect of this constraint is the severe limiting of opportunity for witnesses and defendants to initiate or introduce their own topics, and this in turn allows little room in which to express or explain any background information that might be felt to be relevant or mitigating. Furthermore, the courtroom requirements for brevity and strict control result in regulations that further constrain the construction of testimony: for example, witnesses are prohibited from repeating the words of others (this is 'hearsay', and the rules demand that testimony is based purely on first-hand experience); and evidentiary rules generally bar witnesses from expressing their personal attitudes, beliefs and opinions.

We see, then, that just as the writing of the law is far removed from other forms of written discourse, the spoken interaction that takes place in courtroom contexts is very remote from our experience of other types of speech exchanges. The manner in which we structure our everyday interactions is radically different from the organization of courtroom proceedings, and many of the topics of our common conversations are banned from testimony in courts of law. Questions are framed in forms that coerce restricted answers. As a consequence of all these factors, witnesses have limited opportunities to present an extended or narrative account of events. Indeed, attempts by defendants and witnesses to fully tell their story are characteristically met with warnings from the court to 'just answer the question'.

In this chapter we have examined a variety of forms of legal discourse and we have considered how the language of the law typically fulfils contrastive functions: to be, for example, fully explicit and yet at the same time deliberately vague. We have seen that the forms of language used to serve such apparently contradictory purposes, together with the use of archaic, arcane and ritualistic forms, results in a cryptic code of legal language that is divorced from other, more common, discourse practices. Examination of the specialized semantics of legal language has shown that, just as in the discourse of politics, the meanings of words and expressions may be semantically manipulated or engineered for particular effect. In all the data we have analysed, it has been important to take into account the highly conventional, institutionalized and asymmetrical nature of legal interactions: we have studied authority in legal discourse and have considered how the language used in legal settings can serve to nourish and perpetuate the power differential between those inside and those outside the legal profession. Indeed, we have seen how the language of the law is instrumental in defining and protecting the almost sacred position of legal professionals. Finally, analysis of the language used in the courtroom context has revealed how justice is primarily a process of linguistic negotiation, how guilt and innocence are decided on linguistic evidence, and how the structure of court talk favours those who speak with a voice of authority and how it restricts or 'silences' others.

In the next chapter we turn to a consideration of the language of medicine. We will look at both the spoken and the written discourse of this professional genre and examine further how power is played out in the arena of medical consultation, examination and investigation.

Further exercises

1   Look back at all the examples of legal interviews and interactions included in this chapter. Examine the speech exchanges from the point of view of the interviewer (police officer, barrister or attorney) and consider how they perform 'speech acts' – that is, when they say something, they also do something. Carefully examine the relationship between the forms of language used and the ways in which these forms function in the situated discourses. Where possible, think particularly about the (potential) *illocutionary force* of the utterances used in police interviews and courtroom examinations.

2   Examine the following reader-unfriendly excerpt from the legal conditions of a loan made by an Australian bank. Feel free to subject it to ruthless analysis.

> In the event of default in the payment of this or any other Obligation or the performance or observance of any term or covenant contained herein or in any note or other contract or agreement evidencing or relating to any Obligation or any Collateral on the Borrower's part to be performed or observed; or the undersigned Borrower shall die; or any of the undersigned become insolvent or make an assignment for the benefit of creditors; or a petition shall be filed by or against any of the undersigned under any provision of the Bankruptcy Act; or any money, securities or property of the undersigned now or hereafter on deposit with or in the possession or under the control of the Bank shall be attached or become subject to distraint proceedings or any order of process of any court; or the Bank shall deem itself to be insecure, then and in any such event, the Bank shall have the right (at its option), without demand or notice of any kind, to declare all or any part of the Obligations to be immediately due and payable.

3   Depending on where you are, it is normally possible to visit courtrooms when the court is in session. Arrange to attend a trial for a day and see the legal and linguistic processes at work in real life. There is no substitute for this. Be aware, however, that there are generally strict regulations about the taking of notes. In some cases it may be possible to obtain transcripts (but note that even these may not transcribe the speech exchanges verbatim). Try to identify the discourse strategies that reflect the asymmetry of power in the courtroom. Are there any points at which unexpected shifts in power are represented in the discourse?

Doctor knows best

The discourse of medicine

The life of a sick person can be shortened not only by the acts, but also by the words and the manner, of a physician
AMA Code of Medical Ethics (1847)

Introduction

We accord more status, power and authority to the medical profession than perhaps to any other field. Doctors are widely seen as being able to tell 'what the future holds' for us, and we respect them accordingly. Consulting a doctor about a health issue is characteristically a fraught experience, as the working of our bodies are a mystery for most of us: we cannot help fearing that any problem, no matter how trivial it might appear initially, could turn out to be life-threatening or symptomatic of some deeper and potentially devastating disorder. Doctors, in a real sense, hold our lives (and deaths) in their hands.

The authority we grant to medical professionals is in many ways on a par with the revered status that society has traditionally given to ministers of the church, and indeed the notion of *ministering* is deeply entwined with health care generally. Healers are held in religious awe in many societies, and even in a Western democracy where medicine is viewed more mundanely as a branch of biological science we nonetheless hesitate before questioning a doctor's diagnosis or decision: seeking a second opinion is not a course of action that patients embark on lightly.

The authority of Western physicians can trace its roots back to Hippocrates, and even to Aesculapius, the half-god in whose name the Hippocratic oath was partially sworn:

> I swear by Apollo the physician, by Aesculapius, Hygeia, and Panacea, and I take to witness all the gods, all the goddesses, to keep according to my ability and my judgement, the following Oath…

The concept of Aesculapian authority, in fact, is often invoked to account for the high regard in which doctors are held.[1] Under this schema, the physician's right to respect is viewed as tripartite: the doctor is invested with *sapiential* authority, the right to be heard based on wisdom (or knowledge and expertise); with *moral* authority, which derives from the principle that physicians act not on their own interests, but rather on the basis of the needs and interests of their patients; and with *charismatic* authority, a term widely used in other disciplines and one which stems originally from the unity between medicine and religion, but which nowadays rests on a recognition of the sheer magnitude of the issues (not least, death) with which the doctor has to deal on a daily basis.

This mysterious and arcane aspect of the medical profession, however, must seem somewhat at odds with our modern understanding of health care as a public service, funded largely from taxpayers' money and available to citizens as a basic right. There has been, over the last few decades in particular, a marked shift towards the involvement, empowerment and autonomy of patients in all areas of their medical treatment. Communication and information are now key issues in public health. The 2006 conference of the Royal Society of Medicine (RSM) in London (see Figure 4.01) is to address 'Patient Involvement, Empowerment and Information', and this choice of topic is a direct response to the UK government's White Paper of January 2006 entitled 'Our Health, Our Care, Our Say'. (Given what we have noted in previous chapters, it should be no surprise to find this particular choice of wording.)

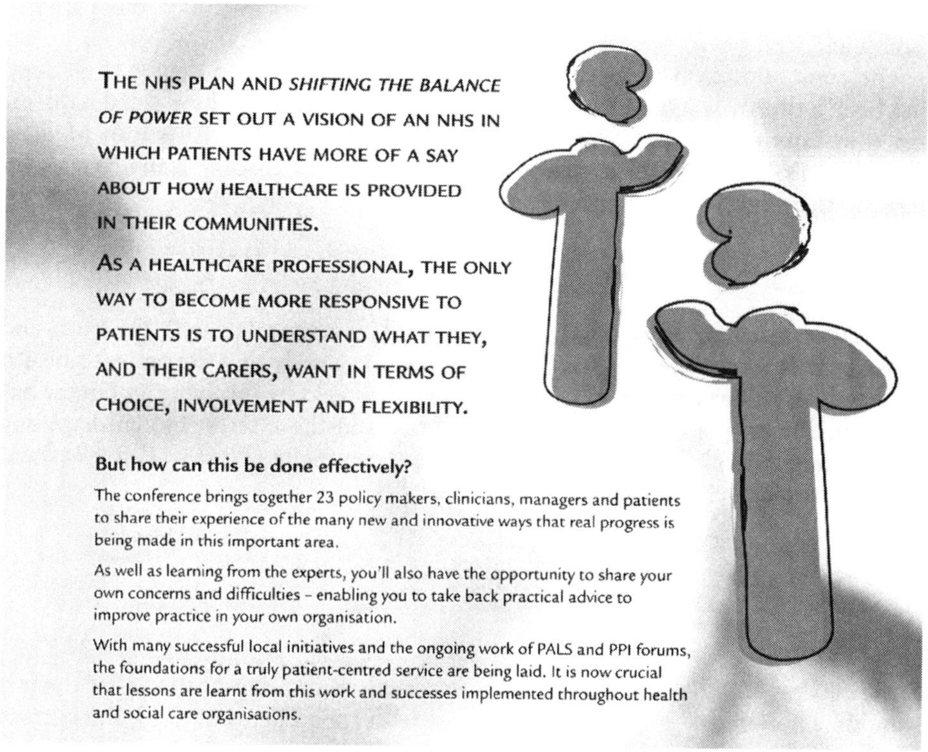

THE NHS PLAN AND *SHIFTING THE BALANCE OF POWER* SET OUT A VISION OF AN NHS IN WHICH PATIENTS HAVE MORE OF A SAY ABOUT HOW HEALTHCARE IS PROVIDED IN THEIR COMMUNITIES.

AS A HEALTHCARE PROFESSIONAL, THE ONLY WAY TO BECOME MORE RESPONSIVE TO PATIENTS IS TO UNDERSTAND WHAT THEY, AND THEIR CARERS, WANT IN TERMS OF CHOICE, INVOLVEMENT AND FLEXIBILITY.

But how can this be done effectively?

The conference brings together 23 policy makers, clinicians, managers and patients to share their experience of the many new and innovative ways that real progress is being made in this important area.

As well as learning from the experts, you'll also have the opportunity to share your own concerns and difficulties – enabling you to take back practical advice to improve practice in your own organisation.

With many successful local initiatives and the ongoing work of PALS and PPI forums, the foundations for a truly patient-centred service are being laid. It is now crucial that lessons are learnt from this work and successes implemented throughout health and social care organisations.

Fig. 4.01   RSM conference leaflet 2006

Medicine is widely understood to be a complex and specialized branch of science, and its discourse inevitably features a reliance on equally specialized and complex language. Indeed, in many respects, an analysis of medical discourse will lead us along some of the avenues we followed in studying legal language. Like the language of the law, medical discourse is a professional register that is characterized by archaisms (including many Latin terms), a technical and formal vocabulary, and specialized semantic sets. The spoken exchanges of medical consultations also share similarities with their legal counterparts: talk between doctors and patients is constructed according to particular communicative routines, often realized in ritualized language, and demonstrably reflects an asymmetrical distribution of power.

There has been considerable interest and debate in the last decades of the twentieth century and the early years of the twenty-first as to how much patients actually need, or want, to know about their medical conditions. The deeply scientific nature of medical thinking makes it difficult for the doctor to be able to communicate medical concepts and frameworks to the unscientific patient, just as it can make it bewilderingly forbidding for a patient to enquire meaningfully into a doctor's diagnosis. Recent interest in the medical potency of a 'positive attitude' on the patient's part has encouraged many practitioners to try to impart to patients some comprehensible medical background within which their illness can be contextualized. However, much of medical language tends to occupy a blurred area between the technical and the everyday; in consequence, misunderstandings and miscommunications inevitably abound, often to the detriment of the patient's health and well-being.

The communication of medical information, especially from doctor to patient, has been a thorny subject for millennia; the medical world has long faced a dilemma over how much detail should be given to a patient. The American Medical Association's code of ethics quoted at the top of this chapter actually goes on directly to prescribe that the physician has:

> a sacred duty to guard himself carefully in this respect, and to avoid all things
> which have a tendency to discourage the patient and to depress his spirits.

This is tantamount to saying that a doctor should be economical with the truth, and in the patient's best interests too. The implication is clearly that the patient's health – indeed, his or her chances of living – may be damaged by receiving an honest but unfavourable prognosis. Economy with the truth in the interest of civil harmony underpinned much of ancient philosophy, especially Plato's *Republic*, and Hippocrates himself is reputed to have advised:

> concealing most things from the patient while you are attending to him [and]
> revealing nothing of the patient's future or present condition. For many
> patients...have taken a turn for the worse...by forecast of what is to come.
>
> (*Decorum*, XVI)

Such maxims stand in stark contrast to our modern-day expectation that doctors should be honest and open in their dealings with their clients. Indeed, the current version of the AMA code no longer invokes the older, rather Platonic viewpoint, declaring instead that:

a physician shall deal honestly with patients and colleagues…patients have a
right to know their past and present medical status and to be free of any mistak-
en beliefs concerning their conditions…

(Code of Ethics 2000: xiv, 174–5)

We see a tension here – one that we can perhaps characterize as a tension between
care and *cure*. On the one hand, patients naturally want (and feel entitled, as part of
their care) to understand the nature of their illness and the rationale behind their
proposed treatment, and doctors will be keen to communicate information that is
likely to help patients deal with illness in a positive and productive way. On the
other hand, it can be extremely difficult for doctors to put such information across
in a comprehensible, useful and timely form, and they may feel that receiving
unwelcome or traumatic news is not actually in the patient's best interests. This tension is likely to be even more evident when set against the hectic pace of modern
clinical practice, where settings and timings can be less than conducive to communicative care. Added to which, not all doctors have communication skills to match
their surgical or diagnostic expertise.

We will look at medical discourse with this tension in mind, and our analysis
will fall broadly into the two areas mentioned in the code of ethics: words and
manner. More precisely, we focus first on the language choices used by the medical profession in their dealings with patients, and examine, for example, how the
language that doctors choose to employ, and the voices that they choose to adopt,
impact on the patient's experience of (and perceived benefit from) the medical
encounter.

After pausing briefly to consider a case study demonstrating the difficulties
faced by the medical profession in communicating with the public in the face of
a general health scare, we then go on to look at the discourse of medical consultations and examine how doctors and patients typically sequence and organize their
language in the context of medical interviews. Here we will try to gauge how this
reflects (and possibly helps to create and sustain) the asymmetrical distribution of
power in the doctor–patient relationship, and to judge how the fundamental tension between the discourses of *care* and *cure* can result in medically detrimental
miscommunication.

Linguistic schizophrenia: the language choices of the medical profession

The secrets of medicine…are bound up in its language; decoding the elements
of medicine's language may, *pari passu*, decode the fundamental nature of
medicine.

(Rita Charon 1992: 115)

As we begin our analysis of medical discourse, we should recall that discourse does
not naturally lend itself to being 'analysed' in separate linguistic categories. The
following exercise will exemplify this issue clearly.

Exercise 4a

Examine the following data carefully and try to locate why, according to Peter Tate's widely acclaimed *The Doctor's Handbook*, it represents 'dysfunctional' medical discourse.

(1) Doctor: Well, Mrs Arthur, there is nothing to worry about. You have multinodular goitre, but this is a benign condition. There are a couple more tests we need to do just to be on the safe side. I will arrange for a special scan and a biopsy of that biggish lump. Is that OK?

(2) Patient: So are you sure it's not serious, doctor?

(3) Doctor: Oh yes, speak to the nurse about the arrangements for the tests and I will see you in a month. Goodbye.

(4) Patient: Well, goodbye doctor, er thank you.

(Adapted from Tate 2003: 13)

- Examine the doctor's choice of words. What influence are they likely to have on the patient?
- What concerns does the patient have and how does she address these to the doctor?
- What is the overall tone created by the language used by the doctor?

In the light of our analysis of written legalese, you will probably have noted how, at the level of vocabulary, the doctor presents his diagnosis in language that is in many respects alien to the patient: technical terms such as 'multinodular', 'goitre', 'benign' and 'biopsy' are particularly obscure, and even 'special scan' may cause confusion if spoken with no accompanying explanation.

You may also feel that there is a paternalistic tone to the doctor's treatment of the patient. It is hard to be sure, just reading it on the page, but from the breezy opening, 'there is nothing to worry about', through the 'couple more tests we need to do' and 'I will arrange for a special scan' (both of which serve to exclude any participation from the patient in the process), to the dismissive 'speak to the nurse' and 'I will see you in a month', there seems to me to be a strong flavour of 'doctor knows best' – a feeling reinforced by the brisk goodbye, which clearly startles the patient, as evidenced by her 'goodbye doctor, er thank you'.

There is also the problem of what is not said. In concentrating solely on the medical 'facts' of the patient's condition, the doctor fails to address the patient's personal concerns, or to provide the reassurance she seeks about the seriousness of her illness and about her future well-being. Noticeably, the doctor does not explain why she needs to have further tests, other than 'just to be on the safe side' – from which a patient is surely entitled to infer that there is still some uncertainty. And yet, when she checks if he is 'sure it's not serious', he immediately answers 'yes'.

Interestingly, Tate comments that although the patient will probably attend the examination (out of fear), she is quite likely to default on treatment over the longer term.

Finally, did you consider the way the doctor chooses to present his diagnosis: 'you have multinodular goitre, but this is a benign condition'? Even allowing for the technical vocabulary, might the patient have understood the situation differently if he had said: 'you have a benign condition, which we call multinodular goitre'? This is an issue that we will return to towards the end of the chapter, but it is worth mentioning at this point since it shows how the various features and levels of language that are of interest to the discourse analyst are all inevitably and inextricably intertwined. Of course, it may also suggest that the doctor is concerned first with the technical diagnosis and naming of the disease, and only second with the impact of that diagnosis on the patient.

Why is the doctor choosing to speak in this obscure, paternalistic and dismissive way? It may be that, as Peter Tate explains, for 3000 years the authority attributed to physicians has been reflected and replicated in the dominance of paternalistic styles in which doctors take a didactic 'parental' role with patients. Indeed, some commentators argue that the unequal distribution of knowledge, power and influence in the practice of medicine is so acute that doctors and patients actually inhabit different 'worlds': they operate within entirely separate realms of experience, function within divergent frames of reference and, crucially, speak with different voices – doctors converse in a professional voice of 'medicine', while patients articulate the personal voice of 'lifeworld' (Mishler 1984). These linguistic voices are so distinct and disparate that doctors have to become 'bilingual', to be fluent in both registers. Some doctors may be so immersed in their medical world that they struggle (or fail to see the need) to switch codes effectively; if so, their patients are left at a severe disadvantage, in only having recourse to the language of everyday experience and not being conversant in the register of medical discourse.

This is not to say that 'medical language' is homogeneous or that the professional voice of doctors is uniform or unvarying. Recent research in Chile has shown that, in any single medical consultation, doctors may represent themselves in a variety of voices: the *doctor* voice – used, for example, to seek information, to review or to assess; the *educator* voice – used to communicate medical facts and information about treatment; and the *fellow human* voice – used to show understanding and to provide reassurance (Cordella 2004). This last point shows that professional and personal voices may overlap and intersect in interesting ways: doctors who are aware of the inaccessibility of their professional language will often use technical terms and translate them into lay terms within single utterances:

Have you noticed any changes in your vision?... In your eyesight?

Symptoms might suggest episodic, eh, partial small bowel obstruction

(Henzl 1990: 86)

Nevertheless, as numerous commentators have reported, the professional medical voice remains the norm. William Donnelly's observation on the medical language used in American teaching hospitals is particularly telling in this respect:

> Words that pathologize human situations seem much more popular than plain
> language for the human experience of illness. Words like apathy, anxiety,
> denial, depression…come easily to the physician's tongue. We seldom hear
> determined, discouraged, hopeful, optimistic, pessimistic, courageous, brave,
> valiant, sad, happy, and the like…

(Donnelly 1986: 86)

We see, then, that doctors' professional voices tend to articulate a somewhat narrow biomedical view of the world, in which the expression of human interest, values or concerns assumes a lower priority than the reporting or diagnosing of medical 'facts' – much as we saw in our earlier 'dysfunctional' example. The importance of this point cannot be overstated, since the fact-based impersonality of the world that lies behind this discourse can cause doctors to miss opportunities to display the personal, compassionate and empathetic understanding that has been shown to be crucial in medical care (Frankel 2002).

With that in mind, examine the following doctor–patient interaction and consider what remains unsaid, as well as what is said explicitly:

(1) Doctor: Has anyone in your family ever suffered from heart disease?

(2) Patient: Yes, my dad and my brother both died from heart attacks.

(3) Doctor: Your brother? How old was he when he died?

(4) Patient: Only, only forty-eight, it was awful he was so young. And that's why, that's why I'm so scared about this sort of throbbing sensation.

(5) Doctor: When did you first notice the palpitations?

Notice how, at line 4, the patient expresses his feelings and emotions about his illness, talking, for example, of his fears related to the symptoms he is suffering. This presents the doctor with an ideal opportunity to communicate empathic understanding: for example, to express support, comfort or possibly reassurance about the patient's fears. However, at line 5, the doctor does not take up the feelings raised by the patient, but prefers to concentrate only on the medical facts of his condition: there is a yawning gap between the doctor's medical voice, used to construct specific diagnostic discourse, and the patient's personal voice, which seeks to express relevant lifeworld experience.

Already we see, then, in the 'voice' of the medical profession, language choices that construct a discourse which is unfamiliar and remote from that of everyday life, and which appears to be separated from lifeworld by an abyss that only the most articulate can cross. The remoteness of this language is evidenced not only at the level of what is said – including the choice of words and phrases, which we will address shortly – but also, as we have just noted, at the level of what is not said, or, more importantly, what is 'left out'. Before we look at the vocabulary, phrasing and labels that do reach us from across the gap, we will turn our attention briefly to some of what can get lost en route.

The construction of medical narrative

Storytelling lies at the foundation of the expression of personal experience and is integral to how patients describe and explain their medical conditions in consultations. However, *anecdotal* is treated as a pejorative word in medicine since, by definition, individual narratives refer to single instances of experience that do not contribute to the 'science' of medicine (Hunter 1991). Doctors tend to prefer 'hard data', and consequently their written records and case histories are designed to condense patients' personal narratives into medical facts.

To fully appreciate the difference between the two worlds – of medical fact and personal narrative – read the following extract a couple of times and try to get a feeling for the anguish of the elderly woman who told this story to her doctor.

> Patient: I had – you know what – one day I was in the subway and I had such terrible pain in the heart, just like – it was at night and I stood there and I didn't say nothing. Here I – oh my God – but the pain, the pain was terrible, I never had such a pain. So the girls must have noticed – they get up, the train stopped, and they said, 'Is anybody on this train not feeling well' – like that – and I didn't open my mouth, I kept quiet the pain was terrible. So, I went down, I had a little business to do on Wall Street, so I made it. I went to Wall Street but I sat down. But the man in the cashier he says, 'Miss, you all right?' I says, 'Yes, I'm all right', and I still wasn't, I said I didn't want to go no ambulance and doctors I mean hospitals...'

This is an extract from the doctor's written version of the encounter:

> Doctor: HPI: 87 yo W w/hx/o A fib x yrs, ?CAD, for routine f/u. Rare CP not assoc w/exertion relieved By NTG...
>
> A+P: 1. AF: check echo, Rate OK on dig
>
> 2. CP: Very atypical. Continue NTG prn

(Adapted from Charon 1992: 122–4)

Comparison of these two pieces of data shows how the patient's lifeworld stories and anecdotes are translated into the professional language of medicine. The doctor's version focuses on the patient in relation to 'healthy' humans: the patient's chest pain is described as 'very atypical'. The focus of attention is shifted away from the patient herself and towards the condition that makes the patient 'abnormal'. This, as we will see shortly, is only a step away from a diagnostic discourse strategy that presents the patient *as* the disease. In her authoritative review of medical discourse, Suzanne Fleischmann (2001) observes that of the many different forms of medical writing (from prescriptions to encyclopaedias), it is medical case histories that have demanded most attention, and it is in this area where, because of the prevalence of a discourse of 'doctor knows best', there has been the loudest call for reform in medical writing practices. It is well beyond the scope of this book, however, to do more than note the existence of the problem and reflect that it is perhaps symptomatic of the difficulties presented when two worlds collide.

By their nature, case histories are condensed documents that summarize large amounts of information. It is interesting again to see what is included in the doctor's synopsis and what is left out, since much can be lost in translation, and indeed doctors have frequently been found to suppress elements of a patient's case that challenge their theories (Donnelly 1997). Case histories also tend to present the patient's voice as subjective and the doctor's voice as objective: research has shown that while doctors tend to *note, find* and *observe*, patients tend to *complain, claim* and *deny*. Case writing also contrives to depersonalize patients, either by categorizing them simply as instances of disease, or by submerging their identities as people by the use of agentless passive grammatical constructions (a device we have met several times already) or by making technology the grammatical agent, as in 'the CT scan revealed an abnormality' (Anspach 1988).

Interestingly, it is not just patients whose narrative expression of experience may be restricted by a narrow biomedical view of the world. Doctors practising in new sub-disciplines of medicine can be constrained by the biomedical model and the restricted vocabulary that it offers. Reporting on his own work in family medicine, Dixon points out that there are plentiful means of referring to medical pathology, but only limited terms for describing social and psychological problems. His conclusions are important:

> What I recorded, but did not 'see', were upper respiratory infections, hypertension, anxiety states, general malaise; what I saw, but could not record, were people, their friends and families, with problems...
>
> (Dixon 1983: 363)

Wording and phrasing in medical discourse

The vocabulary of medical discourse, like that of the law, is characterized by a reliance on specialist terminology; and, again like written legalese, medical discourse is well known for its conservation of archaic and arcane terms. Many observers have commented on the preservation of Latin terms in medicine, and examples range from anatomical and physiological terms, such as *vertebra, cranium, humerus* and *dorsum*, to the prolific use of Latin-derived abbreviations in written prescriptions: 'tid' (*ter in die* – three times a day); 'ac' (*ante cubum* – before meals); and 'po' (*per os* – by mouth). Words derived from ancient Greek are also common: *oestrogen, odontology, pancreas* and *pandemic* are just a few examples. The preservation of some of this archaic language borders on the inexplicable: what can possibly be gained by referring to the *dorsum* of the hand rather than the *back* of the hand? Other forms – particularly the Latin abbreviations noted above – could arguably save precious time, but many would counter that their inherent ambiguity presents a hazard to patient safety, and insist that plain English is the least ambiguous form of communication in these areas (Dunn and Wolfe 2001): in fact, the use of esoteric and arcane vocabulary may lead not only to mystification, but even to miscommunication in the discourse of medical care.

The use of technical vocabulary, and, as we have suggested, especially those technical words and phrases that fall within the scope of everyday discourse, can also lead to ambiguity in speech exchanges between doctors and patients. Try, for example, to define the following terms: *eating disorder; stroke; palpitation; schizophrenia; hysteria; depression; epilepsy*.

Research aimed specifically at assessing the potential of medical jargon to cause misunderstanding in medical consultations has found significant differences between professional and lay interpretations of common medical terms such as these (Hadlow and Pitts 1991). For example, the term *eating disorder*, which among medics is understood as a set of complaints represented by physiological and psychological factors regarding instability in appetite, was widely understood by patients as relating to *indigestion* or even *stomach ache*. Medical and folk interpretations of the term *schizophrenia* are equally divergent: while the condition has proved difficult to define, medical interpretations primarily revolve around issues relating to disturbances in form and content of thought, turbulence in mood and mental disposition, and difficulties in establishing a sense of self and a relationship to the external world. In contrast to this complex medical interpretation, more than half the patients sampled in the research were happy to describe the condition as *where a person has two personalities*. Overall, patients only revealed 'correct' medical understanding of medical terms in about a third of cases, and the widest gap between the interpretations of physicians and patients occurred with commonest psychological terms: *depression, migraine, hysteria, eating disorder*. Such terms clearly have different meanings for medical and lay users, and consequently their use in doctor–patient speech exchanges is likely to give rise to considerable ambiguity and misinterpretation.

While patients may be mystified by medical jargon, they can be equally bemused by language that is informal or ambiguous.[2] Research has suggested that parents of sick children feel particularly disempowered by medical information that is presented in vague terms. Parents who were informed that their children had a *virus* suffered anxiety rather than reassurance: labelling an illness in such a general and ambiguous manner seems not to be helpful unless appropriate explanation is also offered (Kai 1996).

We have observed before that complex, technical or 'difficult' subjects frequently lend themselves to figurative expression. Indeed, we have noted figurative language being used to deal with death, sex and bodily functions in previous chapters, and since these topics are regularly raised and rehearsed in speech exchanges between doctors and patients, it is not surprising that the use of symbolic language in medicine is generally frequent. Metaphors are especially common, and body parts are particularly likely to be represented metaphorically: the human heart, for example, can be represented as a *pump*, the digestive system as *plumbing*, and the urinary tract as *waterworks*. This type of metaphorization, even if rendering the medical concepts more 'concrete', can nevertheless contribute to a feeling that the doctor's treatment of the patient is similar to that of a mechanic working on an inanimate object, leading to a sense of dehumanization in patients.

One metaphorical framework that is particularly prevalent in the discourse of medicine likens medical practice to a *war* in which doctors do *battle* with diseases and in which patients follow doctors' *orders* to *fight* the enemy within. Patients are cast into the role of 'occupied territories' in which the disease is operating, and, as a result, patients and their personal concerns are pushed into the background while space is cleared for the foregrounding of the struggle between doctors and diseases. As Suzanne Fleischmann observes, 'in the highly competitive "scientific" world of medical research, illness-sufferers risk being eclipsed in biomedicine's crusade against disease – a state of affairs that is both reflected in and furthered by its language' (2001: 476). All the same, while it is doctors who battle diseases, blame for defeat tends to be placed (linguistically) at the feet of patients: 'he raised his enzymes, he dropped his pressure, he failed chemotherapy' (Donnelly 1986).

We have commented too on the sensitive nature of topics raised in doctor–patient interaction, and doctors display an understandable concern about discussing bad news in medical consultations. As a result, discourse devices which seek to soften the impact of diagnoses are common. Abbreviations can be used to avoid saying unwelcome words explicitly: *STDs* are treated in *GUM* clinics. Euphemism is common too: bereavement counsellors may well refer to the *loss* or *passing away* of a *loved one*. Some doctors even choose to avoid the word *cancer* when possible, substituting terms such as *growth, tumour* or *condition*. While such language may be designed to protect patients from harsh realities, its non-literal nature can also lead to misinterpretation or misunderstanding; we will see evidence for this towards the end of the chapter when we come to look at the discourse of diagnosis.

Of course, it is not only doctors who engage in symbolic linguistic representation of disease and death. By and large, people in everyday life are reluctant to mention cancer, for example, and it is not uncommon in the USA to hear the disease still referred to as *the big* C (though for many doctors the big C now also refers to communication). Similarly, we ourselves are generally keen to find ways around referring to sexual diseases: research undertaken in the late 1990s with a group of patients suffering from herpes found that half the group had never raised the issue of sexual disease with their sexual partners, and that the discourse of those who had mentioned it tended to involve metaphor, jokes or indirect language:

> You don't have any social diseases, do you, ha, ha, ha?
>
> You don't have anything like that, do you?
>
> Is there anything that's going to affect me if we're going to have sex that I should know about?
>
> (Cited in Pliskin 1997: 97–100)

Sometimes the language used in these contexts can be so indirect that the maxims of conversation appear to be broken. As we said when we mentioned these maxims in the introduction to the book, the essentially cooperative nature of conversation means that in such cases the conversational participants will endeavour to interpret meaning by trying to infer the *conversational implicature* of the utterance. If, for example, just prior to hopping into bed, one partner asks the other, 'Is there anything about you that I should know?', then the maxim of relevance would (normally) rule out this question being a request for information on tastes in food or foreign holidays; consequently another implied meaning is sought that would seem to be more relevant – namely, 'Is there a possibility that you have any sexually transmissible diseases?' By the same token, if the reply is equally indirect, such as, 'I haven't been a hermit', conversational relevance will be sought in a similar way.

Reluctance to speak about sexually transmitted diseases is a serious matter and is widely recognized as a key factor in their continued spread and proliferation. Indeed, the cultural taboo on discussing such diseases means that it is actually more likely that two people will engage in sexual intercourse than that they will enter into discourse about STDs. Since herpes and other STDs are highly socially stigmatized, sufferers are extremely reluctant to disclose their condition, fearing social exclusion if labelled with the name of the disease.

Naming and labelling in medical discourse

The naming and labelling of objects, events or people, as we have seen in previous chapters, frequently leads to the establishment of assumptions and expectations about the character and nature of what has been named. This is evidenced in medical discourse: a patient who has been labelled as *schizophrenic* is expected to display certain behaviours, and similarly, once a patient's illness is named as, for instance, *angina*, then particular medical processes and treatments almost inevitably result. Choice of names and labels can be subtly devastating. The doctor who refers to 'this unfortunate 72-year-old woman' may well thereby be sentencing her to 'a slow but certain death' (Charon 1992). Equally subtle can be the process whereby patients are (perhaps unconsciously) labelled by, or reduced to the status of, their illness: *the peptic ulcer in room four needs his IV changed.*[3]

There may, of course, be an element of grim humour in this practice. Certainly, medical training hospitals are notorious for their black humour, and grisly pejorative terms are in widespread use within their walls: *brainstem preparations*, a description of terminally ill patients, and *CTD*, an initialism for 'circling the drain', are two particularly gruesome examples (Anspach 1988). Such labellings, whatever other functions they serve, clearly contribute to the dehumanization of patients and their personal concerns and circumstances, and can further reinforce the direction of the doctor's focus towards the specific medical condition, while the patient is rendered almost invisible.

Indeed, the naming of diseases as distinct entities (*infections, ulcers, cancers*) may itself also contribute to the abstraction of personhood from patients: such linguistic representations imply that diseases exist separately from the patients who are 'carrying' them. Furthermore, the representation of illness as a *thing* rather than as diagnostic *construct* may also lead doctors to particular perceptions. A friend informs me that his doctor recently told him, 'together we can beat this thing', when the *thing* in question was not an infection (which might perhaps be more understandable), but a genetic condition. Similarly, some diseases are regularly presented as discrete entities *because of* the different names given to them, even though (as in the case of certain blood disorders, for example) they are more properly understood as conditions that evolve one from the other. By the same token, a single name may be given to a condition consisting of a number of diverse disorders (such as schizophrenia, which we have already noted as a term widely misunderstood by the layman). Suzanne Fleischmann observes that 'such situations can have significant repercussions for recipients of these diagnoses, in that potentially important differences regarding treatment and prognosis may be obscured by the common signifier' (2001: 490).

The language of medical discourse, then, betrays a gulf between the medical world and the world of everyday life. Doctors talk to us across this gap, and much can be lost in transmission. The language that characterizes the medical world relies on a vocabulary that is forbiddingly technical, obscure, restricted and occasionally archaic. The immense difficulties of communicating issues that are bound up in this biomedical model result in discourse that is plagued by ambiguity and indirectness, and the fact that these issues are of literally vital importance to the patient means that any miscommunications that ensue can be devastating. Medical discourse is largely constructed within a scientific framework that subtly dehumanizes the patient, with its concern for the labelling and naming of objective 'facts', and strains under the tension of the conflicting aspects of *cure* and *care*.

The tension between these twin features of medicine will, of course, be most particularly evident in the context of a health issue that causes major public concern, when the medical profession finds itself in the position of having to reassure a worried public that everything is being done to provide them with the best possible medical treatment. In looking briefly at such a case, we will not only see further evidence of the tension mentioned above, but also receive a reminder – if we needed one – that health care is a major political issue, and one that in times of difficulty, especially in the face of threatened lawsuits, will need to exploit the power of advertising, with the ostensible purpose of 'educating' rather than per-suading the public. Given that all five of our areas of study are involved here, it makes sense to look at such a case now, and to afford it a little more time and space than an ordinary exercise.

Everything you need to know: a short case study in persuasive medical discourse

In 1998 a group of researchers headed by Dr Andrew Wakefield at the Royal Free Hospital in London published a paper suggesting that parents perceived a link between MMR immunization and autism.[4] The three-in-one MMR (measles, mumps, rubella) immunization has been (and still is) standard medical practice in Britain since 1988, and in the USA since the mid-1970s; it is widely supported by the medical profession in many countries, not least because it tends to ensure high take-up rates throughout populations that might otherwise default on one or other of the three inoculations it contains. The Wakefield paper attracted considerable criticism at the time of its publication, but also engendered significant media inter-est.

Research into the issue was undertaken on several fronts, most of it questioning the validity of the paper's claims. Nevertheless, as often happens in such cases, the story refused to go away: Dr Wakefield published further claims and the issue became a political and medical hot potato. Importantly, take-up of the combined MMR vaccine in Britain fell. What is more, in 2001 Dr Wakefield was allegedly forced to resign his post at Royal Free, after being told that his work was 'not in line with the hospital's policy'.[5]

By this time, it is fair to say, the waters had become muddied, with public hostility and suspicion aroused towards the MMR vaccine for a wide range of not altogether coherent reasons: there were suggestions, for example, not only that the vaccine 'caused' autism (and other conditions such as Crohn's disease), but also that it had not been tested properly in its initial stages; that the main motive behind its adoption was that it was cheaper than giving single doses; that it contained

Fig. 4.02   Gillray cartoon 1802

dangerous levels of mercury; and that other countries had discontinued or decided against its use.

The medical profession faced a severe challenge here, and it will be instructive to examine briefly some of the language they used in addressing it. The difficulties were formidable, not least because the profession needed to tailor their message to a mass audience that had several different lines of resistance (a problem we have already noted as being a central challenge for the advertiser). It is interesting to note, too, that the government's initial response was to throw money at an advertising campaign, and to announce a bigger and better multi-media campaign when this initial effort proved unsuccessful. The second campaign, however, was hastily scrapped (and indeed denied) in the face of severe public criticism of the government's continuous and record-breaking use of the media. Instead, a campaign of 'education and information by front-line medical staff' was deemed to be the most effective way of promoting the MMR message; a judgement based at least partly on clear evidence that people trusted their doctors more than they trusted politicians.[6]

While few would dare to dispute the macro-scale value of mass vaccination, the decision for individual parents over whether or not to vaccinate their child is a highly personal and emotional one. Inoculation has always been a practice tinged with some horror. The great nineteenth-century smallpox inoculator Edward Jenner was widely and wildly lampooned in the early stages of his work (as illustrated in Figure 4.02), and when in 1853 the Vaccination Act made it compulsory for all children to have the vaccine, there were riots. A programme of 'education and information' about inoculation is by no means guaranteed to be successful.

With the context now established – admittedly only in a sketchy fashion, as is necessary in a book of this limited scope – we can begin to look at the (written) language and discourse that the medical profession used to achieve their aim. The main line of attack took the form of an information pack, given to front-line health professionals for distribution and dissemination to the public. The pack opened impressively with a 'statement of support'.

Exercise 4b

Examine the *Statement of Support for MMR*. Consider the techniques that are being used to persuade readers of the benefits of the vaccine.

Statement of support for MMR

MMR – Getting to grips with the facts

This statement supporting the use of the MMR vaccine has been endorsed by the following organisations.

Royal College of Paediatrics and Child Health

Royal College of General Practitioners

Royal College of Nursing

CPHVA Community Practitioners and Health Visitors Association

Faculty of Public Health Medicine

BMA British Medical Association

Department of Health

All of us who work in the NHS and the independent professional bodies concerned with children's health have a duty to minimise risk when advising on tests or treatments. We minimise risk by ensuring that recommended medicinal products and vaccines have undergone careful tests and trials. This allows doctors, nurses and health visitors to be confident that they are recommending and using the safest and most effective vaccines to protect our children from disease.

If you are the parent or grandparent of a young child, you may be concerned about the recent stories casting doubt on the safety of MMR immunisation, and the suggestion that having the measles, mumps and rubella vaccines separately would be safer.

Doubts about the safety of MMR vaccine have centred on two questions. Is there a link between MMR and autism? And would separate vaccines be safer than MMR?

Does MMR cause autism?
Autism was well known long before MMR was used in this country. More cases of autism are being reported now, but the increase started before MMR was introduced and there was no step change in autism rates when MMR immunisation started.

Professor David Hall
President
Royal College of
Paediatrics and Child Health

Professor David Haslam
Chairman
Royal College of
General Practitioners

Beverley Malone
General Secretary
Royal College of Nursing

Jackie Carnell
Director
Community Practitioners and
Health Visitors Association

Professor Sian Griffiths OBE
President
Faculty of Public
Health Medicine

Ian Bogle
Chairman of Council
British Medical Association

Professor Sir Liam Donaldson
Chief Medical Officer
Department of Health

Sarah Mullally
Chief Nursing Officer
Department of Health

Dr Jim Smith
Chief Pharmaceutical Officer
Department of Health

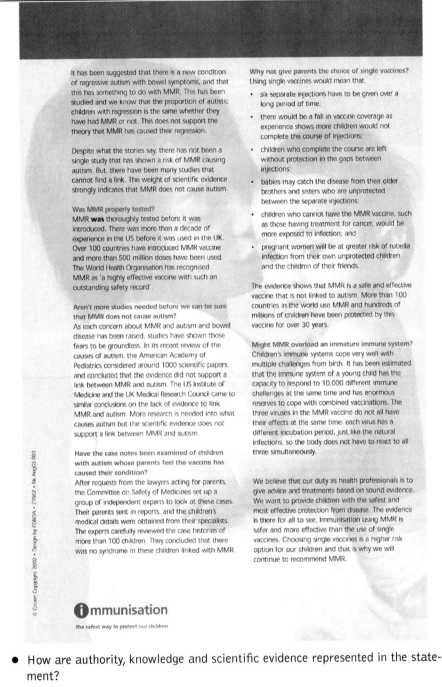

It has been suggested that there is a new condition of regressive autism with bowel symptoms, and that this has something to do with MMR. This has been studied and we know that the proportion of autistic children with regression is the same whether they have had MMR or not. This does not support the theory that MMR has caused their regression.

Despite what the stories say, there has not been a single study that has shown a risk of MMR causing autism. But, there have been many studies that cannot find a link. The weight of scientific evidence strongly indicates that MMR does not cause autism.

Was MMR properly tested?
MMR **was** thoroughly tested before it was introduced. There was more than a decade of experience in the US before it was used in the UK. Over 100 countries have introduced MMR vaccine and more than 500 million doses have been used. The World Health Organisation has recognised MMR as 'a highly effective vaccine with such an outstanding safety record'.

Aren't more studies needed before we can be sure that MMR does not cause autism?
As each concern about MMR and autism and bowel disease has been raised, studies have shown those fears to be groundless. In its recent review of the causes of autism, the American Academy of Pediatrics considered around 1000 scientific papers, and concluded that the evidence did not support a link between MMR and autism. The US Institute of Medicine and the UK Medical Research Council came to similar conclusions on the lack of evidence to link MMR and autism. More research is needed into what causes autism but the scientific evidence does not support a link between MMR and autism.

Have the case notes been examined of children with autism whose parents feel the vaccine has caused their condition?
After requests from the lawyers acting for parents, the Committee on Safety of Medicines set up a group of independent experts to look at these cases. Their parents sent in reports, and the children's medical details were obtained from their specialists. The experts carefully reviewed the case histories of more than 100 children. They concluded that there was no syndrome in these children linked with MMR.

Why not give parents the choice of single vaccines? Using single vaccines would mean that:

- six separate injections have to be given over a long period of time;
- there would be a fall in vaccine coverage as experience shows more children would not complete the course of injections;
- children who complete the course are left without protection in the gaps between injections;
- babies may catch the disease from their older brothers and sisters who are unprotected between the separate injections;
- children who cannot have the MMR vaccine, such as those having treatment for cancer, would be more exposed to infection; and
- pregnant women will be at greater risk of rubella infection from their own unprotected children and the children of their friends.

The evidence shows that MMR is a safe and effective vaccine that is not linked to autism. More than 100 countries in the world use MMR and hundreds of millions of children have been protected by this vaccine for over 30 years.

Might MMR overload an immature immune system?
Children's immune systems cope very well with multiple challenges from birth. It has been estimated that the immune system of a young child has the capacity to respond to 10,000 different immune challenges at the same time and has enormous reserves to cope with combined vaccinations. The three viruses in the MMR vaccine do not all have their effects at the same time: each virus has a different incubation period, just like the natural infections, so the body does not have to react to all three simultaneously.

We believe that our duty as health professionals is to give advice and treatments based on sound evidence. We want to provide children with the safest and most effective protection from disease. The evidence is there for all to see. Immunisation using MMR is safer and more effective than the use of single vaccines. Choosing single vaccines is a higher risk option for our children and that is why we will continue to recommend MMR.

ⓘmmunisation
the safest way to protect our children

- How are authority, knowledge and scientific evidence represented in the statement?
- How is the target audience addressed?
- How are questions employed, and for what reason?

The health information provided by the medical authorities on MMR can be seen in much the same light as a piece of social advertising. Its primary function is to target a specific audience (in this case, parents and grandparents of infants) and make them think and, crucially, behave in certain ways. To fulfil this function successfully, the medical profession has to represent itself as both knowledgeable and authoritative. Note how the *Statement of Support* chooses to represent the authority of the bodies who are endorsing the vaccine: not only are the logos of the professional organizations given, but so too are the signatures of professors, doctors and other accredited individuals.

The certainty of their knowledge is also implicitly represented in the title of the statement: they are providing parents with the *facts*, which may be contrasted with the *stories* that have given cause for concern about MMR. These stories are held responsible for raising fears of a link between MMR and autism, and they are firmly rejected: they are 'groundless' and 'lack evidence'. By contrast, the facts endorsed by the supporting agencies have been ascertained by 'careful tests and trials' and are backed up by 'the weight of scientific evidence'. Notably, while the stories merely *suggest* links to autism, the facts *show* and *conclude* that there is no such link.

Observe how numbers are used, too. '100 countries' use the vaccine, '500 million doses' have been given, '1000 scientific papers' have been consulted, cases of 'more than 100 children' have been reviewed (by experts) and 'hundreds of millions of children' have been protected by the MMR vaccine for 'over 30 years': this is truly the weight of the scientific evidence, which is 'there for all to see'. By contrast, the flimsiness of the opposing view is implicit in the statement that 'there has not been a single study that has shown a risk of MMR causing autism'.

Unsurprisingly, the discourse is structured in a question-and-answer format. This is a tried and tested device; it features strongly in promotional brochures, for example. Indeed, the fact that it does so ought to give us a clue as to the nature of what sort of discourse we are looking at: it is a sales pitch. Our ability to see this connection is underpinned by a concept known as **intertextuality**. Discourse analysts, as we have mentioned many times now, tend to be interested not only in how language is used within texts, but also between texts. We touched on the concept obliquely when looking at political discourse: we noted, for example, that what a politician says in one speech will often be judged by reference to what was said in another speech.

However, the point can be taken further. For any particular discourse there is a set of other texts which are potentially relevant and so may be integrated into the dis- course (Fairclough 2003). Ways of speaking and writing, when repeated frequently enough, tend to become relatively fixed, or as Barbara Johnstone calls it, 'routinized' (2002: 101); the familiarity of these discourse routines within one genre (e.g. pro- motional discourse) leads us to interpret a similar instance of the routine in an apparently different setting (e.g. medical discourse) as being part of, or strongly associated with, the first genre.

As well as being promotional, the question-and-answer device clearly depends on a presupposition. *We know*, it suggests, *the questions that you want to ask* (very often, though, the questions are not put precisely in the way that you might have chosen to put them). The strategy allows the seller to tailor a carefully chosen form of words by way of reply to 'your' question, while simultaneously appearing to under-

Top 10 myths about MMR | Top 10 truths about MMR

'I am unsure about having my child immunised with MMR because ...

	Top 10 myths about MMR		Top 10 truths about MMR
1	...getting protection by catching the diseases is better than having the vaccine.'	1	MMR immunisation is the safest way that parents can protect their children against these serious diseases, as infants, young children and their families are particularly vulnerable.
2	...the vaccine contains three viruses; given at the same time this is too much for young children.'	2	Over 500 million doses of MMR have been used in over 100 countries around the world since the early 1970s. The World Health Organisation recognises MMR as a highly effective vaccine with an outstanding safety record (*WHO, 2001*).
3	...other countries around the world recommend that MMR be given as three separate vaccines.'	3	No country in the world recommends MMR vaccine to be given as three separate injections.
4	...measles, mumps and rubella are rare in the UK so there is no need to immunise.'	4	Children who are not immunised with MMR increase the chance that others will get the diseases, for example, before MMR, pregnant women would catch rubella from their own children.
5	...MMR causes autism and bowel disease.'	5	The evidence is that MMR vaccine does not cause autism or inflammatory bowel disease (IBD). There are now numerous studies that do not support a link between autism and IBD and the MMR vaccine (*CSM, 1999; Gillberg and Heijbel, 1998; Taylor et al., 1999; Davis et al., 2001; DeWilde et al., 2001*).
6	...there was a scientific paper that showed a real link between MMR and these diseases.'	6	The Wakefield *et al.* Lancet 1998 study actually said 'We did not prove an association between MMR vaccine and the syndrome described' and none of the studies undertaken since has found a link. Berelowitz, one of the contributors to the Wakefield study has subsequently said 'I am certainly not aware of any convincing evidence for the hypothesis of a link between MMR and autism...' (*Berelowitz, 2001*).
7	...giving the MMR vaccines separately reduces the risk of side effects.'	7	Single vaccines in place of MMR put children and their families at increased and unnecessary risk. The combined vaccine is safer as it reduces the risk of the children being infected with the diseases whilst waiting for full immunisation cover.
8	...the vaccine was not properly tested before it was licensed.'	8	The normal procedure for licensing was used for MMR and the vaccine was thoroughly tested before being introduced into the UK routine immunisation programme in 1988.
9	...my child has already received one dose so there is no need for a second one.'	9	Two doses of MMR vaccine are needed to give children the best protection before they go to school. Ninety per cent of those who did not respond to the first dose are protected by the second. Those with low antibodies after the first dose will be boosted.
10	...my son doesn't need protecting against rubella; my daughter doesn't need protecting against mumps.'	10	There are very few children who have a true contraindication to receiving the MMR vaccine (see UK Health Department's *Immunisation against infectious diseases* 1996 for definitive list).
	All of the above are wrong.		**All of the above are correct.**

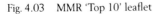

ⓘ mmunisation

the safest way to protect our children

www.immunisation.nhs.uk
www.mmrthefacts.nhs.uk

Fig. 4.03   MMR 'Top 10' leaflet

stand and empathize with your concerns – we might recall at this point our comments about synthetic personalization from the chapter on the discourse of advertising.

In the *Statement of Support for MMR* some of the questions do seem to be fairly unexceptionable: 'Does MMR cause autism?' 'Was MMR properly tested?' The answers seem pretty straightforward, too: 'MMR does not cause autism'; 'MMR was thoroughly tested'. (It is worth noting, if only briefly, that the certainty of the last answer would not be shared by all medical professionals: in 2000, Peter Fletcher, a former principal medical officer at the Department of Health, reported that 'being extremely generous, evidence on safety was thin', and that 'the granting of a product licence [for MMR] was premature'.[7]

Other questions in the text, however, can hardly be described as the ones that most parents were bursting to ask: 'Have the case notes been examined of children with autism whose parents feel the vaccine has caused their condition?' seems to me to be a tangled and rather legalistic construction, and looks suspiciously as if it might have been included largely because the answer is so unequivocally and impressively 'yes'. I leave you to examine the other questions for yourself in a similarly critical light.

The information pack also features an eye-catching *Top 10* chart (see Figure 4.03). Note that the *stories* of the previous document have now developed into full-blown *myths*; and that the *facts* have hardened into *truths*.

You will have noticed the classic contrastive juxtaposition of 'true' and 'not true' in the structure of this text. We have seen this structuring device several times already in our analysis of other genres of discourse, and I hope you will not be too surprised to be reminded that it was particularly prevalent in the discourses of politics and advertising. In discourse analysis terms, the device is operating to create **cohesion**.

Cohesion typically depends on the provision of explicit linguistic linking devices that serve to show how different parts of a text relate to each other and give the text its structure and 'texture' (Halliday and Hasan 1976). These links can be as unremarkable as a pronoun (linking one noun phrase to another) or a conjunctive link such as 'and' or 'but'. At a slightly more sophisticated level, links can be created by the use of substitution:

> Doctor: Do you expect to maintain this diet over the longer term?
>
> Patient: I hope *so*.

In this example, 'so' is substituted for the clause, 'to maintain this diet over the longer term'.

In a similar way, textual ties may be created through ellipsis, where the omission of 'relevant' text means that interpreters have to look to the larger discourse or the wider context to 'fill the gap' and so understand the meaning of the text:

> Doctor: Are you willing to undergo further therapy?
>
> Patient: I *am*.

Clearly, in this case, 'I am' is understood to mean 'I am willing to undergo further therapy'.

We noted in our discussion of written legalese that devices such as anaphoric reference, substitution and deletion tend to be avoided by lawyers, who prefer to use frequent repetitions of words and phrases to signal cohesion, thus creating a highly explicit and context-free text that is very far from our everyday experience.

Cohesion can also be achieved by linking devices used across a whole text: the 'true versus not true' strategy used in the *Top 10* chart makes the 'texture' of the text very clear. Not that anything is left to chance: just to ram the point home, we are reminded at the bottom of each list that 'all of the above are wrong', and 'all of the above are correct': this, we might note, is the language of absolute certainty.

On closer inspection, though, some of the 'truths' do look a little slippery: the juxtaposition at item 7 in the *Top 10* is rather crooked, for example. The question we are (supposedly) asking is about the risk of side effects of MMR; the answer actually concerns the reduced risk of catching one of the diseases while waiting for a separate jab. It may be a *truth*, but it does seem to be masquerading as a slightly different truth to the one we were expecting to hear. Of course, using a clear and repetitive structure to disguise a shift away from an accepted line of reasoning is a device we have met before, particularly in political speech-writing. You might like to examine item 4 too, and ask yourself if the myth and the truth here are entirely contradictory.

Incidentally, the widely held suspicion that MMR is essentially a cost-saving form of vaccination is dealt with in a separate *Frequently Asked Questions* section. Look at the way the topic is treated:

> Isn't MMR used just because it's cheaper than single vaccines?
> MMR is recommended because it is the safest and most effective way to protect children against these three diseases. It has nothing to do with cost. If cost was a factor in the vaccine programme, then the Meningitis C vaccine – which is far more expensive than MMR – would never have been introduced.

Again we find the question-and-answer device at work. But would you have put the question quite like that? The addition of the word *just* makes the question much easier to answer, does it not? And anyhow, the answer provided in the text is still rather unsatisfactory. Why do the medical authorities not simply say: 'No, MMR is recommended because it's the safest and most effective way to protect children against these three diseases. It has nothing to do with cost'? Evidently they fear that we might not be prepared to just 'take their word for it' – some further justification seems to be called for. But why do they feel the need to invoke the particular example of the meningitis vaccine? What has it got to do with the MMR jab? And how much scientific detail does the average parent know about this meningitis vaccine anyway?

Some insights into these questions are provided by a consideration of **coherence**. Apart from its most usual meaning – the degree to which a text *makes sense* to you – discourse analysts use the term coherence to refer to how the text connects with the world, and this includes connections which are not necessarily made by the text itself, but which we ourselves provide by interpreting the text against the background of our own knowledge, assumptions and expectations. Consider a simple example:

A: That's the telephone.

B: I'm in the bath.

A: Okay.

(Widdowson 1978: 29)

In this example, there are no explicit linguistic links. However, despite the absence of cohesive ties, we have little trouble in recognizing the text as a meaningful dialogue. For example, we understand that A's first utterance is a request for B to answer the phone, and we interpret B's response as an excuse not to do so. In this way, we make assumptions based on our expectation that discourse is coherent.

In the same way, the justification contained in the answer about meningitis is only coherent to the average person if they *assume* that this vaccine has several features in common with MMR – perhaps, for example, that there was similarly a cheaper but less safe alternative that was rejected. As we mentioned in the introduction to this book, our cooperative tendencies lead us to seek meaning when it is not given explicitly: are we perhaps being invited here to *assume* that the rationale behind the adoption of the expensive meningitis vaccine is in all important respects the same as the rationale behind the adoption of the MMR jab? For unless we do make this assumption, the point about the meningitis vaccine is, arguably, incoherent.

I do not mean to suggest for a moment that MMR is in any respect an improper drug, or a less safe or effective method of inoculation than any other, and I have no idea what the alternatives to the meningitis vaccine might have been. I am as much in the dark about it as anyone else. My concern is that in presenting the argument for MMR in a facts-versus-myths structure, and a question-and-answer format, the medical profession is inevitably tempted (perhaps unwittingly and probably with the very best intentions) to cherry-pick the 'facts' and to indulge in the occasional sleight of hand in answering the 'questions'. The structure and style is so redolent of advertising and political discourse (and I suspect it was created at least partly by PR wizards), that it actually falls foul of the very traps it was trying to avoid in the first place. After all, the 'informing and educating' initiative was adopted in preference to a slick advertising campaign precisely because it was felt that the public would be suspicious of government-backed hard sell. As a spokesman for the Public Relations Standards Council said when the advertising plans were shelved:

> The public are very canny, and they know that anyone who is advertising on an issue as significant as this is really admitting that we cannot convince the journalists, so we are going over their heads to reach you directly.

(BBC Radio 4, 22 December 2001)

There is much more that could be said about the language of items elsewhere in the information pack (you will see in the Further exercises at the end of the chapter that I suggest you look into this in more detail). The deeper you go into it, the more vague the language gets, especially in terms of risks, and expressions such as *rarely* and *very little* crop up more often, in contrast to the rather absolute language of the more eye-catching documents; also, some questions are answered in fairly technical terms, beyond the grasp of the average, non-scientific, worried parent.

All the same, as well as representing themselves as knowledgeable and their facts as authoritative, the writers of the document are at pains to point out that they do understand the position of parents. As we have seen elsewhere, in order to establish a relationship with readers, organizations tend to represent themselves with the pronoun 'we' and their target audience with the personalized 'you'. In the *Statement of Support*, for example, the relationship is established as '*we* must do *our duty* for *you*' (or, perhaps more accurately, for *your children*). It is interesting, though, that reference to those who are to have the vaccination are not *yours*, but *our* children; and many of the documents in the pack carry the strapline, *the safest way to protect our children*.

It is by no means clear, in fact, that the information pack is really in the business of giving information or indeed aiming to educate: certainly the style and structure of many of the documents owe much to the persuasive devices of advertising and politics, and they go well beyond simply providing parents with information to enable them to make their own decisions about the vaccine. As Fairclough (2003) comments, in contemporary culture many texts that have one primary purpose (e.g. informing) simultaneously fulfil the function of promoting. Most tellingly, the pack includes an article written for professionals by the principal medical officer at the Department of Health urging them to 'actively recommend the vaccine' and warning that allowing parents to make their own choice is 'really dangerous'; 'how do they choose?' is his rhetorical question.[8] Rightly or wrongly, the 'information' pack ends up being deceptive, in claiming to be *providing information* when its real aim is more accurately to *convince* parents that MMR vaccination is 'the right thing to do'.[9]

It may be the right thing to do, of course. But I think the discourse here reflects much of the context in which it was constructed – a context in which the authorities' instinct was to advertise and persuade, but also a context in which the medium of advertising itself has become so associated with seduction and spin that it risks being a counterproductive channel for the communication. It also betrays strong signs of the conflict that we have noted throughout the chapter so far: the conflict between the urge to *cure* the patient, based on a scientific and fact-based biomedical model, and the need to involve patients in the construction of their *care*. We will see further signs of this tension as we now turn our attention to the way the profession typically structures and sequences the doctor–patient interaction of the medical consultation.

What can we do for you? The structure and sequencing of doctor–patient interactions

In the context of the medical consultation, doctor and patient both contribute to communicative routines that are designed to seek and give information. The classical model of such speech exchanges suggests that patients are typically expected to provide information about their symptoms, and doctors are required to be proactive in seeking out pertinent information from their patients. Once a diagnosis and plan of treatment has been made, doctors will then impart this to their patients. Finally, patients may request further information about the doctor's decisions and diagnosis (Ong et al. 1995: 904).

It is possible to identify different stages or phases of communication in the course of medical interviews, with each phase being characterized by different discourse structures. An 'ideal sequence' of medical interviews, for example, might consist of *opening, complaint, examination* or *test; diagnosis, treatment* or *advice*; and *closing*. Naturally, deviations from such an ideal structure will be frequent: both patients and doctors are likely to change the planned schedule of the consultation by local, moment-by-moment negotiation of discourse organization (ten Have 1989).

In an effort to assess and improve interactions between doctors and patients, several *interaction analysis systems* have been designed and used to investigate the dynamics and salient characteristics of speech exchanges. Recognizing a distinction between task-oriented actions and social, interpersonal and emotional behaviours, interaction analysis systems tend to fall into two types: *cure* systems, which aim to assess doctors' instrumental, goal-oriented activities, including, for example, asking questions, giving directions and providing assessments; and *care* systems, which seek to measure social and emotional behaviour and concentrate on the analysis of language used, for example, to express sympathy, encouragement and reassurance.

It is important to say at once that this distinction between 'cure' and 'care' does not precisely reflect the two aspects that we have characterized as producing a tension in medical discourse. Our analysis treats 'cure' as representing the tendency of medical professionals to be primarily concerned with the 'world' (and language) of the science-based biomedical model of medicine, perhaps to the detriment of clear or empathetic communication with the patients they are trying to cure. Equally, we would characterize 'care' as the concern to beneficially involve, inform and empower, in the process of their health care, the patients who constitute the 'market' for the health services provided, and who ultimately fund its activities.

It may also be that distinguishing between analysis systems along the lines of 'cure' and 'care' is rather simplistic, since any aspect of a doctor's behaviour, linguistic or otherwise, is always likely to draw on both goal-oriented and social or emotional elements. Certainly it can be argued that interaction analysis systems tend to concentrate rather too narrowly on the forms, or limited functions, of specific aspects of talk, as opposed to the purposes of discourse structures and strategies within the larger construction of communication in the medical consultation.

Nevertheless, in our analysis of doctor–patient interaction, it makes sense to begin by looking at the structure and content of those instrumental behaviours which seek a 'cure', and to concentrate especially on the way in which, prior to diagnosis, *information is exchanged* between doctors and patients. We will then move on to examine those discourse strategies which are characteristically employed to construct *interpersonal relationships* (i.e. to provide 'care' for the patient), particularly in the context of addressing patients' lifeworld concerns about their medical problems. We will conclude, finally, with an analysis of the discourse structures characteristic of medical *decisions and diagnoses*, which typically need to accommodate elements from both aspects.

Enquiring and informing about illness

Elliot Mishler has examined a range of consultations between doctors and patients, and identifies the prolific use of exchanges that have the following structure:

1 doctor question

2 patient response

3 doctor assessment and/or next question.

The example that follows shows a typical speech exchange in which information is elicited and provided within this structure. Consider how the pattern is realized in the language used, and recall that in our chapter on legal discourse we considered the notion of **adjacency pairs**:

(1) Doctor: What can we do for you today?

(2) Patient: Um, well, since last week, I've had this dreadful backache and it's not, it's not getting better.

(3) Doctor: So, that's quite a few days. Is the pain sharp or is it more of a dull ache?

Note that at line 1 the doctor asks the patient a **question** to which, at line 2, the patient provides a **response**; following this question-answer adjacency pair, at line 3 the doctor gives a brief **assessment** followed by a **further question**.

This basic structure may be realized differently in other situations and settings. The communicative routine may be **reduced**, for example, if doctors do not express assessments explicitly but convey their evaluations implicitly by proceeding immediately to their next question. Alternatively, the structure may be **expanded**, for example, by a request from the doctor for clarification or elaboration of the patient's response. Examine the next extract, and try to identify how the doctor–patient consultation follows the pattern we have outlined.

(1) Doctor: And where do you get that?

(2) Patient: Well, when I eat something wrong.

(3) Doctor: How, how soon after you eat it?

(4) Patient: Well…probably an hour…maybe less.

(5) Doctor: About an hour?

(6) Patient: Maybe less… I've cheated and I've been drinking which I shouldn't have done.

(7) Doctor: Does drinking make it worse?

(Adapted from Mishler 1984: 84)

Note how, at lines 3 and 7, the doctor communicates her acceptance and assessment of the patient's responses implicitly, by posing further questions, and how, at line 5, she seeks clarification of the patient's response by asking him to be more precise about the timing of his bouts of illness.

Mishler argues that the three-part interactional routine of 'doctor question, followed by patient response, followed by doctor assessment' is 'the basic structural unit of discourse in medical interviews' (1984: 68), and adds that it is an organizational structure by which physicians impose their authority and control in speech exchanges with patients. Certainly the three-part discourse arrangement secures doctors more talking time than their patients: in every two turns taken by the doctor, the patient is given only a single space for speaking, and statistical evidence shows accordingly that a large percentage of consultation time is taken up with doctor talk (Ong et al. 1995).

Within this talking time doctors ask many questions. Indeed, research shows that on average doctors pose up to 91 per cent of all enquiries in medical consultations (West 1984). As we have seen in our examinations of political and legal discourse, questions frequently function as powerful discourse devices, controlling the sequencing of speaker turns as well as restricting the topic of responses and the ensuing interaction; questions allow the questioner to control the organization of *who* speaks and *when* they talk, and also to manage the content or topic of *what* is spoken about.

Typically, doctors' use of successive questions serves to specify the nature of a patient's medical condition, concentrating, for example, on the location, timing and frequency of the patient's pain. By contrast, patients tend to use language in a more narrative form to express their emotions and anxieties; when they do ask questions it is frequently to seek reassurance.

Exercise 4c

Consider how the doctor manages the organization of interaction in the following example of a medical interview.

(1) Doctor: What can I do for you?

(2) Patient: Well I come for my stomach because it's getting worse and worse.

(3) Doctor: Yes, and how's that?

(4) Patient: When I get up in the morning then I feel so sick that I just have to sit down for half an hour, uh, to get better and I just don't know anymore where it is. Whether it's my stomach or my belly.

(5) Doctor: What do you mean by 'feeling sick'? Of course that sounds a bit vague, doesn't it? Feeling squeamish?

(6) Patient: Yes, not really squeamish, that I would have to vomit. It's just cramps.

(7) Doctor: Cramps. In the belly, right?

(8) Patient: Stomach, belly. It's everywhere. Sometimes in my back.

(9) Doctor: Yes?

(10) Patient: And, uh, if I press my stomach then it really hurts.

(11) Doctor: Yeah, well then, shall I have a look?

(Adapted from Bax 1986: 102–3)

- How does the doctor structure the medical interview?
- What position is the patient placed in as a result of this structure?
- What difficulty does the patient face in seeking to tell his own 'story'?

Notice first how the doctor directs the structure of the discourse by asking questions which demand a reply from the patient: the doctor's questions put the patient in a 'responding' position and the replies provided are restricted to the topic initiated by the doctor. Notice also that the definition of what is, and what is not, regarded as a semantically relevant topic is increasingly tapered to the doctor's agenda: at line 5, the doctor asks the patient to be more specific about the sickness he is suffering and, in trying to pinpoint the nature of the illness, suggests to the patient that he may be 'feeling squeamish'. Similarly, at line 7, the doctor's question aims to identify the location of the discomfort suffered by the patient and makes a specific proposal as to the place of the pain: 'In the belly, right?'

We have already discussed how, in asymmetrical speech exchanges, it is more difficult for 'non-powerful' participants to deny, rather than to affirm, a suggestion or proposition made by a more 'powerful' person. Here we see evidence of how difficult the patient finds it to deny the doctor's suggestions: at line 6, the patient initially affirms the doctor's proposition of 'feeling squeamish', before managing, perhaps through fear of misdiagnosis, to politely disagree with the phrasing, 'not really squeamish'. Similarly, at line 8, the patient does not appear to be able to deny straightforwardly the doctor's proposal regarding the location of the pain, 'In the belly, right?', but instead rephrases the doctor's proposition into a more general form: 'Stomach, belly. It's everywhere'. We see, then, that by means of particular questions, selective sampling from the patient's responses, and the proposal of specific suggestions, the doctor contrives to guide the discourse along a route towards a swift diagnosis. This raises the question whether, particularly in the light of the difficulty that patients have in denying doctors' propositions, this discourse structure directs the doctor to the right decisions or whether it may lead to misdiagnosis.

The discourse in exercise 4c is somewhat reminiscent of the interviews between police officers and witnesses. Police officers typically present witnesses with a checklist of questions, allowing little room for manoeuvre or departure from the officer's pre-defined routine of interrogation. Interviews between physicians and patients can look rather similar, particularly as the questions posed by doctors do not always seem to follow on from each other (or indeed from the responses provided by patients); this can create a 'disconnected' discourse, sometimes leaving patients bemused and bewildered.

Such disjointed discourse can also result from sharp topic transitions in medical interviews. Doctors may realize greater power in speech exchanges with patients by frequently making *unilateral* topic transitions – one-sided switches that are not negotiated with patients. Such topic changes allow doctors to control the semantic subject matter of the discourse (Ainsworth-Vaughn 1998). Examine the next extract and see how this is achieved, and at what cost.

(1) Doctor: If we're going to really...chip away at your cholesterol, if you decide you want to do that, uh together with me, then...I say there's not a whole lot of other options in terms of medications for your cholesterol.

(2) Patient: Yeah so you prolong your life for what, you know?

(3) Doctor: Do you have, do you have an appointment to see a therapist soon?

(Adapted from Ainsworth-Vaughn 1998: 70)

At line 2, the patient raises the question of whether a life in pain is a life worth prolonging. However, the doctor does not answer the patient's question but rather poses his own question in return. In making this unilateral topic change the doctor is implying that the patient's lifeworld enquiry regarding the quality of her existence has no relevance to the medical context of the consultation. This typical discourse structure results in patients' narratives of illness being absorbed into doctors' medical frames of reference and so leads to the 'evaporation' of the lifeworld and the personal experience it expresses (Davis 1988).

What of the forms and phrasing of questions used by doctors? We have already mentioned that the way in which a question is put into words may predispose a particular response: in the last chapter we discussed in some detail how lawyers aim to phrase their questions so as to restrict the responses that witnesses and defendants are able to provide. Numerous studies of the discourse of medical consultations suggest that doctors use similar strategies. There is a strong tendency to ask closed-ended questions: for example, those that merely require confirmations, perhaps with 'yes' or 'no', or those that have a simple either/or structure. Look back at the extracts we have examined thus far and try to find examples of questions phrased in these ways.[10]

In the context of the medical consultation, even apparently open-ended 'wh-' questions are frequently realized in a way that restricts the response that can follow. In one of the extracts above, we find, 'how soon after you eat it?', which calls for a simple numerical figure; and 'where do you get that?', which requests the straightforward naming of an area of the body. These contrast with other, less constraining, open-ended 'wh-' questions that encourage more narrative-style responses, particularly those calling for reasons or explanations, such as, 'why do you think you are getting these headaches?' or 'what do you think brought it on?'[11]

As we have said, patients ask considerably fewer questions than doctors.[12] Indeed, even parents of sick children are cautious of questioning the authority of health professionals and 'taking up the doctor's time' (Kai 1996). Rather than asking questions, patients tend to use their speaking spaces primarily to provide replies and responses – if they can manage to use their speaking time, that is. Research shows that patient contributions are frequently interrupted by doctors, with one analysis showing almost 70 per cent of patients' initial statements of concerns being interrupted, usually by narrowly focused, closed-ended questions (Frankel 2002). Just like witnesses in the courtroom, patients in medical consultations are rarely given the opportunity to tell their own story or, more precisely in the medical case, to raise and rehearse their lifeworld concerns and fears and to have these addressed. Such silencing of the lifeworld can lead, as we have seen, to the objectification of patients, their dehumanization and disempowerment.

There has been some recent medical recognition that the social and linguistic divide between doctors and patients may hinder patient care and even obstruct progress towards a cure. The USA has seen a particular backlash against the traditional authoritarian role assumed by doctors and, in consequence, there has been a shift away from paternalistic doctor-centred approaches, towards more patient-centred principles and practices. In these practices, the formation of 'healthy' doctor–patient interpersonal relationships is considered crucial and, since successful communication is widely seen as holding the key to creating and sustaining constructive and 'caring' reciprocal relationships, the social 'etiquette' of medical communication has been put under the microscope. We will turn our own attention to it now.

Constructing interpersonal relationships

What types of communication strategies build successful doctor–patient social relationships? Studies looking into this question point to the importance of discourse strategies such as careful listening, humour, expression of empathy and an engagement with the lifeworld experience expressed by patients (see, for example, Barry et al. 2001). Other endeavours on the part of medical professionals to reduce the social distance between themselves and patients have taken the form of engaging in social talk and using conversational styles of language: patients are addressed by their first names, doctors make enquiries about the health and well-being of patients' families and, as against the technical-medical language reported above, doctors favour the use of informal and idiomatic vocabulary, including the use of figurative language to discuss awkward topics or to soften the blow of harsh news. More generally, doctors endeavour to create rapport by being 'polite' with patients (Mitchum 1990).

As we mentioned in the introduction to this book, **politeness theory**, as developed by Brown and Levinson (1987), examines how people manage interaction in a way that engages with what Goffman (1967) refers to as **face-work**. If, in our everyday speech encounters, we need to ask a favour, issue an instruction or make a promise, for example, these activities may well involve making 'face-threatening acts'. Similar pressures are posed in medical consultations and particular strategies are used to mitigate the impact of face-threatening acts. For example, attention may be paid to the positive face of patients by expressions of shared sentiment: 'I fully understand why you are worried about taking this medication, I'm sure I'd feel the same way myself'. Alternatively, we might choose to employ a negative politeness strategy, perhaps using a deferential form that seeks to mitigate any threat that our request entails: 'I know it's a nuisance, but could I possibly ask you to wait outside for a moment?'

An analysis in terms of politeness strategies can be revealing in looking at examples of indirect speech in the discourse of medical consultations. Consider carefully the following extract from the point of view of face-work. The extract is of a speech exchange between a counsellor and a pregnant client who is considering whether to have an amniocentesis test. The patient has just informed her counsellor that she would not terminate her pregnancy should the test prove positive.

> Counsellor: Okay, all right. So you would continue the pregnancy, you would not terminate the pregnancy at that point. Okay, in the event that you would be someone who wanted to terminate the pregnancy...um, for people who don't want to terminate the pregnancy, you know, obviously if the test gives you normal results then you're 'whew', reassured, and it's a lot less stressful to be pregnant for most people after they get good news.

(Adapted from Benkendorf et al. 2001: 205)

146

Notice how the counsellor hesitates and uses face-saving forms of 'hedging' – 'okay', 'um', 'all right', 'you know' – to soften the direct imposition of her own view of the value of the amniocentesis test. Note also how the counsellor uses indirect and impersonal reference to 'someone', 'people' and 'most people' so as to mitigate the potentially face-threatening act of persuading the patient to take the test. However, while the use of indirect language may be used to maintain 'value neutrality' in the consultation, it may also lead to confusion on the part of the patient, who is left to infer which of the factors that apply to *most people* are actually relevant to *her*. As Benkendorf et al. conclude, 'what the counsellor does not do, by choosing more impersonal and indirect language, is explore what having a child with chromosome abnormality would mean to this client' (2001: 205).

We have noted before that tag questions can be used as controlling devices. (You may recall that tag questions typically present a proposition in declarative, non-interrogative form, with a yes/no question tagged on to the end: 'You're American, are you?' is an example, as is, 'in the belly, right?'). However, in her aptly named article, 'But basically you're feeling well, are you?', Susan Harres (1998) discusses the use of tag questions in medical interviews and finds that, while they may be used by doctors to control speech exchanges with patients, they can also sometimes function as expressions of empathy – as in, 'that must be very painful for you, is it?' The same seems to be true of rhetorical questions: we have seen many instances in which rhetorical questions perform powerful discourse functions, but (again, in the right setting) they can function to mitigate doctors' commands: 'why don't we arrange some tests', or 'why don't we arrange for you to visit a specialist therapist?' (Notice also the use of the pronoun 'we' in these examples.)

It is worth pausing here to consider how this point shows the complexity of relating forms of language to linguistic functions and discourse purposes. In the previous chapter we saw that tag questions in the courtroom can function as powerful discourse devices: we looked at examples such as, 'you were in the Cambridge Arms, weren't you?' and considered how such questions place the respondent in the position of simply agreeing with or denying the proposition included in the question. At the time, we remarked that tag questions have also been associated with powerless speech; particularly as used by women, tag questions have been viewed as an expression of tentativeness or diffidence and as a reflection of women's hesitancy to state anything in a conclusive way. Here, in our examination of medical discourse, we can see tags being used in ways that are both controlling and supportive. In this respect it is important to distinguish between different types of tag questions: consider the difference between tagging a statement with a positive question, 'is it?' and a negative question, 'isn't it?' Equally, we might distinguish between tag questions that can be characterized as speaker-oriented and seeking information (*modal tags*) and those that are listener-oriented and used for social purposes (*affective tags*). Most crucially, though, we should bear in mind that tag questions (and indeed all linguistic forms) fulfil different functions depending on the context in which they are uttered, and can serve many different purposes in the construction of social roles and relationships in situated discourse (Holmes 1984).

Context is clearly of paramount importance here: much of the 'caring' quality of 'that must be painful for you, is it?' simply derives from the content and context (consider the difference if the question were 'that is manageable, though, isn't it?'). Equally, 'why don't we arrange some tests' may be softer than, 'I am going to arrange some tests', but neither phrasing genuinely offers much opportunity for the patient to disagree with the doctor. It is also worth considering that rhetorical questions used in this way may well represent (and be perceived as) no more than a superficial gesture. Indeed, a more productive communicative strategy in this area might simply be the avoidance of some of the negative aspects we have considered so far (such as authoritarian interrupting and topic-shifting) rather than the deliberate introduction of synthetic features of personalization.

Anyway, many medical professionals working in the field of communication studies are at pains to point out that the construction of good interpersonal relationships entails far more than the doctor's adoption of a pleasant bedside manner. Specifically, the shift from paternalistic (doctor-centred) medical practices towards more patient-centred approaches has been associated with a move towards the construction of interpersonal relationships that are more evenly balanced.

Exercise 4d

Compare the following two extracts, which exemplify the two different styles. Try to isolate the key elements that characterize the two approaches.

Doctor-directed approach:

(1) Doctor: Well you seem to have shaken off another of these infections, but that's the third year. It can't go on like this. You really have to stop smoking.

(2) Patient: It's not easy, doctor.

(3) Doctor: I know it's difficult, all my smoking patients tell me this, but if you keep trying you will be successful.

Shared approach:

(1) Doctor: Are you still smoking?

(2) Patient: I'm afraid so, doctor.

(3) Doctor: This last infection didn't put you off then. Do you think the smoking is connected to these chest infections you've had?

(4) Patient: I dare say. I wouldn't mind stopping, but it's not easy to give up.

(5) Doctor: I know it's very difficult. Quite a lot of my patients say that. Have you ever tried to give up?

(Adapted from McKinstry 2000: 867–71)

- What are the main differences between the two consultations?
- How is the relationship between doctor and patient managed in the two speech exchanges?
- How important do you think it is for patients to be given the opportunity to contribute to the assessment of their medical condition?

Notice how in the directed approach the doctor takes control over the interview by declaring that the patient's illness is a result of her own behaviour, and telling the patient that she *has to* give up smoking. Expressions such as, 'It can't go on like this', reflect the doctor's powerful position over the patient, and his declaration that 'if you keep trying, you will be successful' implies that the doctor has more knowledge about the patient than she has herself. By contrast, in the shared approach, the doctor invites the patient to consider the relationship between her smoking habit and her illness. He enquires whether the patient has ever attempted to give up smoking, and tries to show some understanding by acknowledging the difficulty of the process, in a subtler, less absolute manner than the doctor in the directed approach.

There is a growing body of evidence to suggest that patients who are encouraged to voice their own ideas and concerns in consultations are more likely to be satisfied with their medical care than patients who are treated by more traditional doctor-directed methods. More importantly, it also appears that the active participation of patients may actually increase the effectiveness of their treatment: patients (or *clients*, as they are increasingly referred to in patient-centred approaches) attain better medical outcomes if they are offered the opportunity to collaborate with their doctors in constructing a dialogue. This appears to be particularly true of the way in which diagnoses are reached in the discourse of medical consultations, and we turn our attention to this phase of the consultation now.

Decisions and diagnoses

The role of language and communication in medical diagnosis is of immense importance: not only is it a crucial component in the understanding of illness, but many would argue further that it plays a vital part in its construction. As Elliot Mishler (1984) points out, the illness that is 'discovered' in the medical interview is constructed, not found. When doctors reach a diagnosis, this represents their interpretation, organization and prioritization of observations made. Doctors' diagnoses are dependent on what they ask and what they hear (as well as on what patients report and do not report) and these factors may be as important as the results of physical examinations and tests.

We have seen that doctor questions and patient answers are prototypical of the information-gathering stage of the medical interview. By contrast, once the doctor has reached a decision on the patient's medical condition, declarative statements are the most common communicative means of articulating diagnoses. The structure of the discourse following diagnosis generally involves the doctor elaborating on the medical judgement, with the patient responding by, for example, seeking further information regarding the decisions reached. It is widely held that communication at this stage is of critical importance, and, especially if it involves bad news, one which many professionals find difficult and challenging.

The potential for miscommunication and misunderstanding is particularly acute at the diagnostic stage. Doctors do not always have a single, definitive answer to the patient's problem and may need to explain several possibilities and circumstances; this may well involve the use of highly technical language (Mitchum 1990). As a result, patients frequently encounter difficulties in comprehending doctors' diagnoses and it is not uncommon for patients to leave a consultation unable to recall or understand what their doctors have said.

The timing and sequencing of the discourse of diagnosis has been found to be vital to a patient's comprehension of, and agreement with, a doctor's decisions or recommendations for treatment. It is especially important at this stage that the diagnosis provided by doctors be contextualized within the rest of the medical interview and, when relevant, within previous consultations: it has been found, for example, that contextualized diagnostic information that emerges from the prior exchange of information and discussion is more likely to be accepted by patients than decisions which are disconnected from the topic and content of the preceding interaction (Frankel 2002).

When the news is bad, the ordering of the information given in diagnosis, together with explanation and prognosis, can be particularly vital. For example, news of serious illness may leave patients too shocked and dismayed to be able to register any information given after the bad news has been received. Evidence of this is presented in an early study by Ley (1979), who observed that sequencing of information in a doctor's discourse has a strong influence on a patient's recall of what has been said. Specifically, patients tend to remember statements given first and to be more likely to forget information presented later. Commenting on this research, Frankel (2002) provides the example of two groups of cancer patients. The first group was informed of their medical condition by the typical structure of diagnosis followed by prognosis: 'You have thyroid cancer and in 85 per cent of cases you can expect to make a full recovery.' The second group received the information in the reverse order, with prognosis provided before diagnosis: 'You have a medical condition from which 85 per cent of people make a full recovery. It's called thyroid cancer.' Variation in the serial position of the presented information was found to have a significant effect: the first group, who had been informed of diagnosis followed by prognosis, generally recalled that they had cancer and that it would be fatal. The second group, who received their prognosis before the diagnosis, generally recalled that they had cancer, but that there was a high chance of a full recovery. The structure, and particularly the sequencing, of information given during diagnosis is therefore crucially important, not only for patients' understanding of their medical condition, but also for their beliefs about and attitudes towards their illness and prognosis.

What about the content of the information given within this organizational structure? Research from many medical fields shows that patients want to know what is wrong with them, what treatment can be provided, and what the future holds. In the case of patients suffering from serious illnesses, the need for such information, be it good or bad, is especially great. However, despite the value that patients place on receiving information, research suggests that many doctors still adopt the Platonic or Hippocratic philosophy we discussed at the beginning of this chapter: physicians may deliberately withhold information from their patients because they fear that total disclosure will cause negative reactions from patients and so may interfere with their recovery. As a result, doctors often concentrate on diagnosing illness as an objective problem and present purely medical information to patients (for example, naming the type of disease, its stage of development and type of treatment). By contrast, patients typically define their illness in terms of its personal relevance (for example, the possibility of recovery, level of pain and side effects of treatment). The tension between the medical (professional) and lifeworld (personal) realms of experience is particularly visible here, and can result in miscommunication between doctors – who believe that they have given precise and relevant information – and patients – who feel that they have not received the type of advice that they need and value. The reaction of this young patient's reaction at having her lifeworld experience ignored is most telling:

> It was like she [the doctor] didn't hear. One time I came out of here and I was crying because I didn't understand what was happening to me and I felt really small, like a worthless sort of human being.
>
> (Cited in Coyle 1999: 117)

The way information is communicated in the discourse of diagnosis can also lead patients into a false sense of optimism about their illness and prognosis. Researchers report on a group of seriously ill patients in North America who had far higher estimates of their survival than did their physicians: three-quarters estimated their likelihood of living six months at 90 per cent, while their physicians' estimate was only 50 per cent (Haidet et al. 1998). Further research, aimed at investigating why patients display such false optimism, particularly examined whether their mistaken confidence was based on miscommunication between doctor and patient. The following extract was found to be typical of discourse discussing treatment after a 'bad news' diagnosis.

> Doctor: You want to undergo therapy?
>
> Patient: Have I a choice, doctor?
>
> Doctor: [shakes his head]
>
> Patient: I've got my back to the wall.
>
> Doctor: I'll try to arrange that you can start tomorrow. With this kind of tumour we cannot afford to lose time.
>
> (Adapted from The et al. 2000: 1377)

In consultations in which doctors have to inform patients of serious illness and poor prognosis, a number of factors combine to give the patient a more optimistic outlook than their medical condition warrants. For example, while doctors often mention that there is no cure for a patient's condition, they nevertheless tend to conceal the prospects of terminally ill patients. Instead, as illustrated in the extract above, patients are informed about the therapy or treatment that is available to them. Unfortunately, patients tend to have a more positive interpretation of the meanings of the terms *therapy* and *treatment* than do their doctors. When doctors state, for example, that 'the cancer can be treated', they may mean there are therapies that can prolong life or, at least, make life more comfortable. By contrast, patients hearing news of relevant therapies and treatments tend to infer that, in undergoing the prescribed course of medical care, their condition can be cured. In this way, false optimism is jointly constructed: by doctors, who do not want to be the bearers of bad news; and by patients, who do not want to hear it (The et al. 2000).

This brings us back to the crucial theme of miscommunication in medical consultations. In this chapter we have identified many aspects of language that have the potential to confuse, depersonalize and even devastate patients: from the use of technical jargon and archaic terms, including obfuscating abbreviations, to the employment of vague and ambiguous linguistic expressions. We have also seen that the manner in which doctors manage medical interviews and consultations can lead to misunderstanding. In traditional 'paternalistic' approaches, the use of disconnected questions, commands, interruptions and unilateral shifts of topic may prohibit patients from engaging in extended and meaningful discussion of their medical conditions and concerns. In particular, the imposition of the biomedical framework and the abstract professional voice of medicine almost inevitably leads to the evaporation of patients' personal lifeworld narratives.

The abstraction of personhood from patients is also a result of medical conceptualization and categorization: from the employment of figures of speech that represent the patient as their disease, to the use of 'war' metaphors which symbolically represent medical care as a battle between doctors and diseases, displacing the patient and the patient's concerns. Furthermore, we have considered how illness may itself be constructed communicatively, and how the representation of diseases as entities, for example, leads doctors towards fixed conceptions and perceptions of illness. We have also noted the concerns of health professionals who find that the biomedical approach, and the narrow vocabulary it offers, is not conducive to or even capable of meaningfully explaining their patients' medical conditions.

Examination of patient-centred medical approaches reveals an array of communicative methods through which doctors may seek to establish more even and equal relationships with their patients. Discourse strategies such as the use of informal or idiomatic language, as well as particular socially oriented and affective communicative routines, can be adopted to facilitate the construction of equally balanced reciprocal relationships. However, perhaps because of societal expectations and presuppositions about doctor–patient relationships, attempts at personalization are often perceived as synthetic or patronizing. Above all, the medical profession still struggles with the conflicting demands of care and cure, and, in spite of a general move towards a market-led model of *health care*, our traditional regard for the physician as *healer* means that changes in language alone are not sufficient to overcome the widely held preconception that 'doctor knows best'.

Further exercises

1 As always, look back through the chapter and examine all the data and examples given. How much linguistic evidence do you find for the tension between *cure* and *care*?

2 Examine the following leaflet (pp. 153–155), published by the Health Promotion Agency of Northern Ireland, and consider it in the light of everything we have looked at in the chapter. Look at it not only as an example of medical discourse; remember also that its functions may well be to advertise, to make a political point, to establish a legal position and indeed to educate.

3 Find a similar information pack on another medical issue (or from another culture) and examine it critically. Do you think it is inevitable that such materials will always go beyond the mere provision of information? If so, why?

"Every parent wants the best for their child. I know that deciding what is best can sometimes be difficult. Some of the worrying things said about MMR vaccine recently may have caused you some doubts about whether giving your child MMR is the right thing to do. Unfortunately newspaper headlines don't always give the full story. In this leaflet we have given you the facts to help you make up your mind.

"I have no doubt that the best thing you can do for your child is to give him or her the MMR vaccine. This is the safest way for you to protect your children against the dangers of measles, mumps and rubella".

Dr Henrietta Campbell CB
Chief Medical Officer - Northern Ireland

Health
Promotion
Agency

Adapted with permission from material published by Health Promotion England. Produced by the Health Promotion Agency for Northern Ireland on behalf of the Department of Health, Social Services and Public Safety.

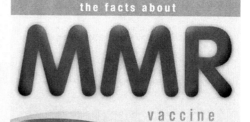

the facts about

MMR
vaccine

protect your child **be wise - immunise**

This leaflet contains the facts about the MMR vaccine. If you want to talk over this information please contact your GP, health visitor or practice nurse. You may also find it helpful to visit the immunisation website at www.immunisation.org.uk

What is MMR?

MMR vaccine protects your child against measles, mumps and rubella (German measles). It is given to children at 15 months and again as a booster before they go to school. Since MMR was introduced here in 1988 the number of children catching these diseases has fallen to an all time low.

Measles, mumps and rubella can all have serious complications.

* Measles can cause ear infections, respiratory problems and meningitis/encephalitis (inflammation of the brain). It has a 1 in 2,500 – 5,000 chance of causing death.

* Mumps can cause deafness usually with partial or complete recovery and swollen, painful testicles in older boys and men. It was the biggest cause of viral meningitis in children.

* Rubella can also cause inflammation of the brain and can affect blood clotting. In pregnant women it can cause miscarriage or major health problems for their babies such as blindness, deafness, heart problems or brain damage.

It is important to remember that without the MMR vaccine nearly every child will get all three diseases.

Does MMR have any side effects?

As with all medicines, there are some side effects associated with vaccinations. Most of these are minor and last for only a short time, for example, redness and swelling at the injection site.

MMR contains three separate vaccines in one injection. The vaccines work at different times. About a week to 10 days after the MMR immunisation some children become feverish, develop a measles-like rash and go off their food – as the measles part of the vaccine starts to work. Your child may, very rarely, get a rash of small bruise-like spots due to the rubella part of the immunisation about two weeks after MMR. This usually gets better on its own but if you see spots like this, show them to your doctor. About three weeks after the injection a child might occasionally get a mild form of mumps as the mumps part of MMR kicks in.

Occasionally, children do have a bad reaction to the MMR vaccine. About 1 in 1,000 will have a fit caused by a high temperature due to the measles part of the vaccine. There is no evidence that this causes long term problems. A child who has measles is 5 times more likely to have a fit as a result of the illness.

Vaccines can also cause allergic reactions. These are very rare, about 1 case in 100,000 immunisations. Although they are worrying when they happen, treatment leads to a rapid and full recovery.

Encephalitis (inflammation of the brain) has been reported in about one case in every million immunisations. This is no higher than the chance of any child developing encephalitis without the vaccine. But measles causes encephalitis in 1 in every 5,000 children who get the disease.

Comparisons of the side effects of MMR with the side effects of having measles, mumps or rubella show that the vaccine is far safer than the diseases.

Complications	Rate after natural disease	Rate after 1st dose of MMR
Fits (due to high temperature)	1 in 200	1 in 1,000
Meningitis/inflammation of the brain (encephalitis)	1 in 200 to 1 in 5,000	1 in 1,000,000
Conditions affecting blood clotting	1 in 3,000	1 in 24,000
Death (depending on age)	1 in 2,500 to 1 in 5,000	None

Facts about the MMR vaccine

- MMR vaccine protects children against measles, mumps and rubella.

- In nearly 30 years, 500 million doses of MMR have been given in over 93 countries. It has an excellent safety record.

- There is no evidence of any link between MMR and autism or bowel disease.

- Giving the vaccines separately may be harmful. It leaves children open to the risk of catching measles, mumps or rubella.

- Where MMR is available, no countries recommend giving all the vaccines separately.

- In 1987, the last year before MMR was introduced in the UK, 97,000 children caught measles and 19 died. A recent outbreak due to low vaccine uptake in Dublin left two children dead.

- Measles is a highly infectious disease and it kills and disables children.

- Mumps was the leading cause of viral meningitis in children under 15 years before the MMR vaccine was introduced. Now it is virtually eliminated.

- Rubella damage to unborn babies is devastating – in many cases pregnant women catch rubella from their own or their friends' children.

- MMR protects your child and your family against measles, mumps and rubella. If children go unprotected, by waiting to have all the injections separately, the diseases will come back.

If your child missed their MMR appointment you can get the immunisation at any time.

What about the reports of links between autism and MMR?

Although autism is increasingly recognised now, the increases were going on long before MMR was introduced. Parents often first notice signs of autism in children after their first birthday. MMR is usually given to children at about this age, but this doesn't mean that MMR causes autism.

A major study of all autistic children born since 1979 in North London was set up to look at the possible link with MMR. There was no sudden increase in rates of autism when the vaccine was introduced in 1988. The study concludes that MMR vaccine did not cause autism.

As a result of this and other studies, doctors here and around the world have agreed that there is no link between MMR and autism.

What about reports of links between bowel disease and MMR?

Careful independent studies in the UK and abroad have led to the conclusion that evidence is firmly against any link between the MMR vaccine and bowel disease.

Have children been followed up long enough after MMR to know it's safe?

In the USA, MMR has been given for nearly 30 years and over 200 million doses have been used. In Finland, where children have been given 2 doses of MMR since 1982, reactions reported after MMR were followed up over 14 years. There were no reports of permanent damage due to the vaccine. In fact, MMR has been shown to be a highly effective vaccine with an outstanding safety record.

Wouldn't it be better for children to have the vaccines separately?

Giving the vaccines separately would mean having six injections instead of two and would leave children exposed to two of the diseases for at least a year. These diseases can be serious and even fatal. It has been said that giving the three vaccines together overloads children's immune systems. This is not the case. Children's immune systems make excellent responses protecting them against these diseases.

No country in the world recommends MMR being given as three separate vaccines. There is no evidence that giving the vaccines separately is any safer, so we could be causing harm without doing any good.

The support of a wide range of medical and nursing professionals for the MMR vaccine is shown by the following statement:

"As professionals intimately involved in the long-term care of children, as well as in the immunisation programme, we wholeheartedly endorse the current policy of using the combined MMR vaccine".

Joint statement issued on behalf of the

Royal College of Paediatrics and Child Health

Royal College of General Practitioners

Royal College of Nursing

Community Practitioners and Health Visitors Association

Faculty of Public Health Medicine

- There is no evidence of any link between MMR and autism or bowel disease.

- MMR protects children from three serious illnesses by two injections. This ensures the children get maximum protection in the most effective way.

- You can get more information from your GP, health visitor or practice nurse. Please do not hesitate to ask.

The discourse of education

We but teach bloody instructions, which, being taught, return to plague the inventor
Shakespeare, *Macbeth* 1, 7

Introduction

In social terms, education has much in common with medicine. Teachers are trained professionals and schooling (like health care) is seen as a crucially important right which should be available to all children and funded by public taxes. Teachers are still held in relatively high regard in most areas of society, though by no means with the reverential awe that is often granted to doctors. Education, like medicine, has long been a political football, and over recent decades has similarly become more 'marketized' and subjected to (often contradictory and incoherent) government targets that largely reflect this ideological shift.

Parents and children themselves have gradually adopted a more consumerist approach to education, and there has been a significant move towards a market-driven curriculum in schools, with employment prospects underpinning much of educational practice and thinking. The traditional 'power' of teachers – in classroom terms, as professionals to be respected for their learning – has been severely eroded in the tidal surge of demands that this knowledge should be economically and commercially beneficial to the consumers and funders of their services.

At the end of the last chapter we saw how both the constraints of discourse and the social constraints that operate in particular institutionalized contexts do not merely derive from a 'powerful' participant's control over communication, but rather are embodied in our own cultural assumptions regarding the communicative customs that are appropriate in the discourses of different organizations. As we now turn our attention to the educational profession we will find that the discourse conventions of learning and teaching are deeply embedded in our cultural consciousness. We have particular expectations of what teachers and students should do (and not do) as well as what they may say (and not say); this places teachers and students in set *subject positions*, in which particular social roles are played out in the practice of education (Fairclough 2001).

In order to succeed in school, students are obliged to conform to rules and regulations that are required, but, in many cases, not made explicit. These conventions, including the regulation of communicative interaction in the classroom, as well as the construction of written work, are culture-specific, of course, but many of you reading this book will be familiar with at least some of the following:

- Written work is subject to particular formal conventions, including the use of Standard English.

- The content of both written work and spoken interaction is pre-defined by the nature of the subject matter being studied, and frequently also by the teacher's control over the semantic substance of discussion. Writing or speaking on 'off-topic' matters is usually discouraged, and often disallowed.

- Turns at talking are conventionalized. For example, in higher education, attendance at traditionally structured lectures involves maintaining silence when the lecturer is speaking, while at the same time showing attentiveness by means of sporadic eye contact, nodding or note-taking, for instance.

- At most levels of compulsory schooling, terms of address between teachers and pupils are non-reciprocal. Teachers are permitted to call students and pupils by their first names, while pupils are normally expected to address their teachers by their title plus surname (e.g. Mr Smith) or by other formal means of address such as 'Sir' or 'Miss'.

- Young children are not permitted to call out an answer to a teacher's question, but rather are required to raise their hands in a bid to offer responses. With hands up, children must then wait to be selected by the teacher before speaking.

This is not to imply, of course, that teachers are free to conduct classroom communication as they wish. Individual teachers are required to fulfil certain roles and engage in particular practices in accordance with the ethos of their school, and, as we have said, to meet ever-changing government guidelines, requirements and targets. In many cases conflicting pressures are placed on teachers by such regulations: a recent study of the National Literacy Strategy in the UK reveals that the inclusion of a recommendation for teachers to meet short-term objectives is at odds with advice to encourage active student participation in classroom discussions (English et al. 2002). Furthermore, as well as satisfying conditions imposed from 'above', successful teachers must also meet the expectations of their students, and these may in turn present contradictory pressures. On the one hand, students expect good teachers to control the class, to be challenging and to ensure that students achieve to the level of their highest ability. On the other hand, and at the same time, students require that teachers be interesting and entertaining (Foster 1995).

In order to meet these diverse expectations, teachers talk. And they talk for a lot of the time (it has been estimated that primary school pupils communicate directly with their teachers for as little as one and a half minutes per hour of classroom time).[1] In fact, teaching *is* talking; in Western societies at least, it is more or less impossible to imagine a silent teacher. Teachers talk to ask questions, to give instructions, to direct responses and to provide evaluations – and these are just a few of the purposes of teacher talk.

157

Exercise 5a

The following extract is taken from a junior school lesson in mathematics. Examine the discourse and consider what makes it such a typical example of classroom interaction.

(1) Teacher: Well, now, what about right angles? Has anybody heard of right angles before? Have you, Amy?

(2) Amy: No, I've seen one, but I think...

(3) Teacher: No, okay, no. Does anyone know what a right angle is? Has anybody heard of it?

(4) Students: [silence]

(5) Teacher: What about you, Tony?

(6) Tony: Err [pause].

(7) Teacher: Come on now.

(8) Tony: Is it like a square corner?

(9) Teacher: A square corner, but some corners don't need to be square, do they? All of you think now and tell me what we've learnt so far about corners.

- How does the teacher control the structure of the lesson?
- Why does the teacher ask questions?
- How would you describe the pupils' responses to the teacher's questions?
- What linguistic strategies are used by the teacher and the pupils to arrive at the 'right' answer?

We will return to a fuller discussion of the particular organization of classroom interaction later. For now, note that speech exchanges between teachers and pupils, such as those shown in the extract above, display many of the features typical of asymmetrical speech encounters: we see, for example, an interrogation-like structure to the discourse; the use of closed-ended questions calling for minimal responses; instances of controlling speech, such as commands; and differentially distributed patterns of intrusion and interruption.

This imbalance between participants is in part a reflection of the differential knowledge of teachers and pupils. Traditionally, teachers have been perceived as the 'holders' of knowledge, and teaching as the *transmission* of this knowledge to students and pupils. The transmission-based model of teaching is based on a particular conception of knowledge as a body of discrete, disconnected and correct 'facts' that can be passed on from teachers to students. Teachers are placed in the position of imparting the knowledge and students are expected to 'accumulate' this knowledge by memorizing the information and engaging in routines of (rote) learning, repetition and reproduction.

> She gives us a new topic and she draws a diagram and she explains what she has done in a pretty complex way and then tells us to open our textbook and try and do it by ourselves, keep on looking at what she had done on the board, and you try and do it in your book the same way.
>
> (Year 10 mathematics student, cited in Campbell et al. 2001: 181)

In contrast to such 'transmissive' (teacher-directed) pedagogical practice, student-centred education involves more active and collaborative learning. Knowledge is not seen as a discrete entity that can be transmitted from one individual to another, but as dynamic and flexible understanding that is constructed within meaningful discussion and debate. Student-centred education relies on more interactive and *discourse-intensive* teaching styles in which teachers and pupils cooperate in composing the dialogue of learning and the construction of meaning.[2] In interactive classrooms, heuristic methods (encouraging students to learn for themselves) are valued, and teachers and pupils work together to form a 'learning community'. Interactive teaching methods therefore seek to establish different social roles for teachers and pupils, to enable more reciprocal social relationships and to provide possibilities for the development of non-conventional subject positions. These methods are typically noted and appreciated by pupils.

> I like to do things that have to me a purpose in life. I want to know why things happen… He [the teacher] makes us do it by working through things and he makes us think how to do it. Other teachers that I have just like to tell us about the things and then say do this, and it doesn't help you to understand it. He makes us understand it more.
>
> (Year 11 mathematics student, cited in Campbell et al. 2001: 178)

Similarly:

> [My teacher] creates a friendly environment. It's fun when you're not afraid of saying something and making a mistake. It doesn't matter because she will say it's okay, just try again. She doesn't make you stress or anything… Her classes are fun. She's my favourite teacher.
>
> (German student, no year given, cited in Campbell et al. 2001: 184)

The opportunity for pupils to engage in such exploratory and collaborative communication is crucial to educational experience: if teaching is talking, then it is equally true that learning is largely linguistic. The opportunity for students to engage actively in the construction of discourse is vital for the shaping of experience into knowledge and understanding. Indeed, according to the influential (social) constructivism theory of education, the most valuable learning takes place when we build new information and skills on to the foundation of our existing knowledge and understanding. The opportunity to use language to make this link is crucial to cognitive development. Furthermore, since learning is not merely a matter of 'adding' information to our existing store, but rather involves reshaping and re-evaluating our own understanding to formulate new interpretations and meanings, then the

opportunity for engaging in exploratory and collaborative talk is particularly important. Referring to work undertaken with primary school children, Barnes and Todd
conclude that 'talk is flexible: in talk [students] can try out new ways of thinking
and reshape an idea in mid-sentence, respond immediately to the hints and doubts
of others, and collaborate in shaping meanings they could not hope to reach alone'
(1995: 15).

The facilitative role of language for learning is by no means restricted to the primary years. As schooling becomes more specialized and subject-specific, the variety
of mediums of expression that are an everyday experience for primary level pupils
– art, drama, music – are restricted to specific lessons and may disappear from the
syllabus of those concentrating on other subject areas. Therefore language becomes
a vital means of rehearsing ideas and advancing understanding: reading, listening,
discussing, note-taking and essay-writing become especially important. What is
more, students' knowledge is primarily assessed by linguistic means: answering
teachers' questions, constructing written coursework, sitting examinations, and so
forth.

At advanced levels of education, the way in which students articulate their
knowledge is seen to hold the key to the development of independent and critical
thinking. In spoken interaction, for example, students are expected to present
papers, engage in debates and form critical questions in discussions. In such contexts, tutors are typically advised to take a back seat in interactions and allow students to initiate and instigate their own dialogues. In this respect, the tutor's role
is often defined as a *coordinator* of the activity inspired by students. However,
even at the most advanced levels of education, teacher coordination of communication may still be a form of teacher control. As a result, as Norman Fairclough
explains, educational practices result in 'the inculcation of particular cultural
meanings and values, social relationships and identities, and pedagogies' (1995:
220).

This inculcation takes place in and through language. But what language is seen
as appropriate by the educational establishment and in the classroom context?

As if it matters: the language of education

In this section we will focus on three key linguistic areas where educational authorities exert significant control over what is deemed to be appropriate in the context
of the classroom. These are language (tongue), dialect and style. We will look at each
issue separately.

Language

**Lunacy of school where pupils speak 59 languages.
Now the new head teacher insists it's...ENGLISH ONLY**

Fig. 5.01   *Daily Express* headline, 22 February 2006

At the time of writing, the *Daily Express*, a British tabloid newspaper, carried a report on one head teacher's stand against providing tuition in ethnic minority children's home languages. Under the headline shown in Figure 5.01, the article explains how the head has abandoned science teaching in 'foreign languages', since such support had not been found to increase students' performance in science exams. Reporting on the 'lunacy' of a school where pupils speak 59 languages, the newspaper praises the head teacher's actions as 'a victory for common sense' (*Daily Express*, 22 February 2006).

What is assumed in this 'common-sense' view? In fact, there appear to be several interrelating threads of reasoning regarding the head teacher's abandonment of minority language tuition. First, and most obvious, it is assumed that the benefits of teaching science in children's home languages can always be measured by pupils' performance in science exams. If no added value can be identified here, then such support is considered to be a failure. Second, and as discussed explicitly in the article, it is supposed that minority language tuition does not prepare pupils for future working life: the head is reported as saying 'when these young people leave school they will be going into a very competitive job market'. This 'common-sense' judgement rests on more deep-rooted cultural presuppositions about the role of education: as mentioned above, and as Fairclough explains, education (like other institutions) is increasingly being market-driven and incorporated into consumer culture. 'Common sense' thus demands that students acquire language skills for their own occupational opportunities and, by implication, for the economic prosperity of society (1995: 23). Finally, the head teacher is praised for her common sense when she insists that linguistic uniformity will lead to the 'integration' of ethnic minority pupils. This in turn entails that supporting cultural difference and diversity leads to segregation and, as the article puts it, to the 'erosion of national cohesion'.

We might pause to note that the selection of particular words in the report contrives to colour our perception of the circumstances described. Why is multilingualism, in a school in a multicultural society such as Britain, described as 'lunacy'? And what is the connotation in describing a migrant language such as Turkish, which has a long history and heritage in the UK, as 'foreign'? (It is worth remarking that for 70 per cent of pupils in this school, English is actually their second language; for them, perhaps, English is the foreign language here.) More importantly, we should observe that the 'common sense' underpinning the arguments for 'English only' is not by any means a self-evident truth: it rests on a number of highly debatable assumptions. For example, we might take issue with the notion that the value of minority language tuition can be assessed and measured adequately by a pupil's performance in science exams. Furthermore, while few would wish to dispute that schooling should prepare students for later life, many would warn of the dangers of looking to achieve this aim in a curriculum aimed narrowly at providing students with skills for the job market. Even those who give priority to vocational education would recognize that languages are an important resource in our increasingly information- and communication-driven society. And not all would agree that diversity is the enemy of consensus, or that variety leads to conflict or a lack of national cohesion: do we all have to be the same, act the same and speak in the same way in order to live together in harmony?

This is not to say that English should not be the medium of instruction in British schools (although we might note that there is already diversity of practice, with some schools in Wales, Scotland and Ireland using Welsh, Scottish and Irish Gaelic, respectively). However, it is important that decisions about such matters, and particularly decisions about the language support that ethnic minority students should receive, are made with proper consideration of the needs of students and of teachers. Such decisions should not be grounded in suspect 'common-sense' assumptions that are proposed as 'natural', but are, in fact, 'naturalized': in other words, where *one* way of seeing the world becomes adopted as the *only* way of doing so (Fairclough 2001).[3]

In fact, we are currently being bombarded with the 'common-sense' view that linguistic diversity leads to disintegration. In 2002 the Home Secretary caused an outcry in Britain by publishing an essay arguing that British Asian parents should speak English to their children at home, so as to prevent 'schizophrenic' rifts between generations of families.[4] It is worth noting that similar advice given to Welsh-speaking parents in the late nineteenth and early twentieth centuries, along with a ban on speaking Welsh in school, were important factors leading to the decline of the language (which is now undergoing a remarkable level of revitalization – not least because of its adoption in schools). Incidentally, the Labour government's response to the *Daily Express*'s story in 2006 was that 'English language fluency is a priority for all pupils'. This seems to be in stark contrast to their attitude when the school launched the mother-tongue tuition initiative, at which time Stephen Twigg (junior minister in the Department for Education and Skills) lauded the idea as 'very much the kind of good practice we want to promote'.[5]

Dialect

It is not just diversity in languages which is perceived to present a challenge to the established sociolinguistic order; so too is dialectal diversity within English. What type of English were you expected to use at school, particularly in constructing written pieces of work? The answer (in Britain) is invariably Standard English: a dialect with its origins in the East Midlands, developed as an embryonic written standard by around the end of the fourteenth century, and later codified through the proliferation of dictionaries and other prescriptive documents during the eighteenth and nineteenth centuries. It is maintained today in a number of institutions, including the media and, of course, education.

Debates surrounding the teaching of Standard English have a long history, as has the related issue of whether (and how) students' home languages and dialects should be supported by schools. Traditionally, views on this matter have been polarized and discussions have revolved around a disjunctive question: should Standard English be taught *or* should pupils be allowed to express themselves in their own regional and social varieties of English? Recent debate has been somewhat more considered, reflecting the requirement that in the interests of life opportunity, for example, students should learn Standard English, and in the interests of self-esteem, for instance, due recognition should also be given to pupils' own dialects. In line with this principle, educational acts, reforms and guidelines prescribe that Standard English should be *added* to the linguistic repertoire of students rather than replacing students' own dialects; and students should learn to recognize when it is appropriate to use the standard as well as, by the same token, when to use their own languages and dialects.

However, as we have already discussed, well-accepted educational theory suggests that students do not learn by simply 'adding' information to an already established store, but rather reinterpret and reshape existing ideas and knowledge in the light of new information. In this respect, it seems unlikely that Standard English can simply be added to students' linguistic repertoire without influencing the way in which students view their own dialects. Furthermore, the fact that Standard English is prescribed as being 'appropriate' for prestigious public discourses, while other languages and dialects are relegated to use in informal and private domains, adds to the potential devaluation of languages other than English and of dialects other than the standard.

Attempts merely to add Standard English to students' linguistic repertoire are therefore likely to lead to a process of replacement, unless taught in a way that engages students in critical analysis and interpretation. For example, pupils could be encouraged to undertake judicious examination of the place of Standard English in today's society and also to examine critically the processes that led to standardization; for example, to explore how, as Dick Leith discusses, the development of Standard English originally involved 'the cultivation, by an elite, of a variety that can be regarded as exclusive' (1983: 33). What is more, the idea that Standard English should be used where 'appropriate' is based on misconceptions about the nature of dialectal variation: for example, the argument rests on the mistaken belief that dialects of English are used in 'clearly distinguished contexts, according to clear-cut conventions, which hold for all members of what is assumed to be a homogeneous speech community' (Fairclough 1995: 243). In reality, there is no such simple fit between dialects and the situations in which they are used. Indeed, dialects themselves are far from homogeneous. All speakers, no matter which dialect they speak, use a range of different styles, depending on a complex matrix of conditions, including: the social context of interaction; the participants involved and the social relations that hold between them; and the activities and purposes carried out within the interaction.

Style

As well as promoting English (rather than other languages) and Standard English (rather than other dialects), particular linguistic *styles* are often required in academic writing. Student writers are expected to follow certain conventions that govern both the type of knowledge represented and the way in which knowledge is expressed. They are often provided with essay-writing guides that provide advice on academic style, but the reasons for the conventions are rarely spelled out in such documents. Consequently, rather than look at essay-writing guides, it will be more useful for us to examine tutors' criticisms of student writing: it is in tutors' evaluative comments, after all, that we can identify the academic conventions that are actually imposed on student writers. We will consider three typical examples.

163

This is an interesting discussion but you fail to fully get to grips with the
question asked or to provide proper evidence and justification for the claims you
make. Your bibliography is incomplete and you will lose marks for this in the
future.

In universities, as in other educational institutions, it is teachers who have control
over the content of what students write – or, at least, who have the authority to
determine the writing that will contribute to awards and qualifications. A teacher
may choose to exert strict control by assigning just a single essay title, or provide
more scope for students by presenting a list of topics for students to choose from, or
even allow students to select their own titles and topics. I consider myself to be a
fairly forward-thinking teacher and always try to give students the freedom to
explore their own areas of interest in their writing. My usual strategy is to present a
list of possible questions, the last one being: *An essay on a relevant topic of your
choice*. However, perhaps because of a lack of trust in students' ability to know what
is or is not *relevant*, I invariably add a proviso: *Please make sure to check your title with
me in advance*. Forward-thinking or not, I clearly contrive to maintain a measure of
control over the content of students' writing.

Furthermore, the level of control does not stop at the prescription of topics. As
the tutor's feedback above reveals, in constructing essays student writers are expected to provide and make reference to *proper evidence* and to *justify* the claims they
construct in their essays. But what counts as proper evidence, and what type of justification is required? Roz Ivanič and John Simpson (1992) observe that only certain
forms of knowledge are seen as acceptable in academic essay-writing and that,
specifically, a student's own opinions and personal experience are often dismissed
unless they are supported by 'objective' evidence – in the form of quotations or
other references to 'legitimate' sources, for example. As in the field of medicine,
anecdote is a dirty word. And, as the feedback above shows, woe betide any student
who fails to list in their bibliography all the sources they have used.

Of course, these customs and conventions may be justified. For example, when I
add my proviso to essay lists I believe that I do so for student-centred reasons. I fear
that my students may waste their time in constructing pieces of writing that will not
be considered relevant or appropriate by the university. However, this does not
detract from the truth that 'legitimate knowledge' is institutionally controlled; and
this is a control which results in limited opportunities for student writers to draw on
their own experience, to present their own lifeworld knowledge and, just as importantly, to write in their own personal voices. Look at the following tutor's comment
and note that it is not just *what* is said that is constrained by academic writing conventions, but also the *way* in which knowledge is expressed.

You raise many interesting points but the essay lacks structure, organization and
coherence; you need to provide more explicit signposting for the reader. Also,
be careful to avoid informal and idiomatic language in writing your essays.

For student writers to be successful, they are expected to follow particular conventions for structuring and organizing the content of their writing: for example, an
essay must include (at a minimum) an introduction, main text and conclusion. Like
many other teachers, I often advise students to 'tell the reader what you are going to

do, do it, then tell the reader that you have done it' – in other words, to provide the type of *explicit signposting* mentioned above. While I might go on to point out that this is just one example of how to structure a piece of writing, I still tend to emphasize that it is nevertheless archetypal and that students will not go far wrong if they choose to adopt it.

What about the 'informal and idiomatic language' mentioned above? I regularly 'correct' the use of informal vocabulary (avoid 'kids' and use 'children'), and I also warn about the use of sexist or ethnocentric language (avoid the use of generic 'he'). But where does informal language overlap with personal expression? And, if the boundary can be identified, should personal expression be corrected too?

Exercise 5b

Look at the following example of writing produced by a British AS-level (16-year-old) student and marked by his history teacher. (Note the underlining added by the teacher to clarify the comment made at the end.)

> I now plan to conclude my essay. <u>As I am sure</u> you can see from the evidence <u>I have</u> portrayed, <u>I do not entirely agree</u> with Thucydides. He thinks that the cause of the Peloponnesian war was the growth of Athenian power. <u>I think it was</u> the so-called 'causes of complaint', namely Epidamnus and Potidaea… <u>But actually this is not my view, I truly believe</u> that the question of whether Sparta was justified or not is the wrong one and cannot be answered, as neither side really wanted to go to war.

> Don't use the word 'I' in an essay, it looks bad and you will lose marks for it

- Do you agree with the history teacher's marking and comment? Why?
- Have you ever used the word 'I' in an essay or similar piece of writing?
- How do you suppose the teacher would have wished the student's opinion to be expressed?

We might note that the student has clearly (some would say, too clearly) followed the advice about signposting, anyway. But his use of the personal pronoun 'I' is considered incorrect, as the teacher's final comment on the essay confirms. Perhaps for similar reasons, the student's use of 'my view' is also underlined as an erroneous or, at least, inappropriate expression in academic writing. But why does the use of 'I' and 'my view' *look bad*, and why should students lose marks for employing such expressions? Ivanič and Simpson (1992) consider this question and argue that academic writing conventions dictate an impersonal and objective style in which the writing is presented as existing independently of the writer. Student writers are expected to adopt a depersonalized voice, thereby creating an image of themselves as having an 'objective' view.

Furthermore, as well as making decisions on whether to use the first-person singular pronoun, students also have to consider how much commitment or responsibility they should display in respect of their statements. For example, strength of commitment can be varied by the selection of *modal* verbs. Compare these:

> This leads to decreased stability...
> This *will* lead to decreased stability...
> This *may* lead to decreased stability...
> This *can* lead to decreased stability...

Similarly, definiteness can be varied by *hedging* devices. Compare these:

> There are *three variables* that we have to consider and they are political stability, size of population and patterns of land ownership.

> In discussing whether aid works we have to consider *a number of variables, such as* political stability.

> (Cited in Clark 1992: 133)

In fact, the traditional requirement for objectivity in academic writing frequently leads student writers to employ language that suggests a *lack* of personal commitment to the ideas expressed: becoming a proficient academic writer entails the acquisition of a detached voice. This is the skill that the young student cited has not yet achieved when he writes: 'I truly believe that the question of whether Sparta was justified or not is the wrong one'. Few undergraduates would express themselves in this way: they have already learnt that, in academic writing, it does not do to care too much or to boldly express *true beliefs*. Indeed, as Ivanič and Simpson conclude, 'academic writing usually discourages people from identifying and exploring personal experiences which they feel strongly about – as if it's better if it doesn't matter' (1992: 166).

Bearing in mind the conventional constraints that prohibit personal representation and voice in academic writing, look at this final example of a tutor's comment on a student's essay.

> Large parts of this essay have been copied from other works. You will shortly hear from the chairperson of the university disciplinary panel who will wish to interview you on account of the plagiarism in this assessed work. You should seek advice from your personal tutor at your earliest convenience.

If anecdote is a dirty word in medicine, then plagiarism is the deadly sin of academic writing. A student who downloads an essay from the internet and presents it as their own may be suspended from an institution or have qualifications and awards withheld. In my experience, wholesale plagiarism is rare. However, students can be disciplined not only for blatant plagiarism, but also for copying even small parts of texts from books or other sources without explicit acknowledgement that the text has been copied (by the use of inverted commas, for example). Many students subject to such penalties claim not to have engaged in deliberate cheating, and in some cases genuinely believe they have done nothing wrong. Perhaps this is not surprising: the prohibition of plagiarism does not sit easily with other conventions for academic writing. As we have seen, student writers are required to employ an impersonal style in which the writer becomes detached from the writing, and also to justify their opinions by reference to 'legitimate' sources of knowledge. Academic writing conventions thus place students in a position in which they have to engage in a fine balancing act: student writers are required to retell the 'legitimate' knowledge of others, but not to do so too closely.

This may appear to paint a rather bleak picture, but if student writers are provided with the opportunity of engaging in critical analysis of traditional academic conventions, they may gain the knowledge and confidence to be able to make an informed choice about whether or not to conform to traditional customs: through critical language awareness, students can come to see that 'ultimately they have a chance, through their essay writing, to explore ideas and make a positive contribution to the thinking in their discipline rather than simply reproducing the orthodoxies' (Clark 1992: 131).[6] Furthermore, in resisting dominant conventions, language use can contribute to changing social orders and practices. In fact, such change may already be in progress: Fairclough observes a shift in academic writing styles in which there is 'pressure for specialized academic identities to give way to private domain or "lifeworld" identities' (Fairclough 1995: 230).

In discussing medical discourse we considered how similar lifeworld experience may either be supported or ignored in spoken exchanges between doctors and patients. As we now turn to a consideration of the spoken interaction of the classroom we will be interested to examine the opportunities that students are given to be active in their own learning and to represent their own lifeworld experience. We will find remarkable similarities between the structure of classroom interaction and that of the medical consultation.

Interrogatives rhetorically formulated: the question-and-answer routines of classroom interaction

According to John Sinclair, whose ground-breaking linguistic research into classroom interaction we will discuss shortly, teachers have more free choice of what they say, and more authority to constrain what others say, than those working in any other profession – with the possible exception of judges. Courtney Cazden agrees and comments that in traditional classroom contexts, 'the most important asymmetry in the rights and obligations of teachers and students is over control of the right to speak' (2001: 82).

Look at the following data elicited from a primary school religious education class and examine how the 'right to speak' is realized in the turn-taking practices of the teacher and his students.

(1) Teacher: Now, who can tell me about Lent, what happens in Lent?

(2) Pupil: When Jesus was…

(3) Teacher: Hands up, hands up and I'll tell you.

(4) Pupils: [raise their hands]

(5) Teacher: Yes, Jenny.

(6) Jenny: Um, I think… [pause]

(7) Teacher: No, Amy?

(8) Amy: Is it when Jesus went in the wilderness?

(9) Teacher: Yes, right, good, when Jesus went into the wilderness for 40 days.

In classrooms, as in courtrooms and medical consultations, speaking turns tend to be distributed unevenly in accordance with the hierarchical power relationships that hold between participants. Teachers, like judges (and doctors, as we have seen), maintain full rights over the routines of turn-taking. As illustrated at lines 1, 3, 5, 7 and 9, teachers may select themselves for a speaking turn at any point. At line 7, the teacher's self-selection interrupts a pupil who is pausing to consider her answer, showing that the speaking turns of pupils are liable to sudden termination. By contrast, pupils have more limited rights to speak. For example, in the above extract, pupils are not permitted to nominate themselves for speaking turns: examine how, at line 2, a pupil who has selected himself to speak is silenced by the teacher's intervention of 'Hands up, hands up'. When a number of students follow this instruction, the teacher exercises her right to select a particular student for a speaking turn (line 5). Finally, notice how, at line 7, the teacher quickly redistributes the allocated turn when the selected student fails to give an answer within the allotted time.

As well as managing the organization of talking turns in classroom interaction, teachers may exert control over the content of each turn. In the 1970s, the linguists John Sinclair and Malcolm Coulthard identified the following three-part routine of turns as being particularly prevalent in traditional classroom interaction. Note that it is strikingly similar to the 'essential speaking exchange' of doctor–patient interaction (which is perhaps rather curious, given that doctors typically speak to one patient at a time, while teachers have to deal with a whole classroom).

1 Teacher initiation

2 Student response

3 Teacher follow-up (sometimes also referred to as 'teacher evaluation').

This *initiation, response, follow-up* (or IRF) structure is realized in classroom discourse in speech exchanges such as the following:

(1) Amy, what do we call words that describe? (I)

(2) Adjectives. (R)

(3) Adjectives, good. (F)

While more recent research on classroom interaction has identified somewhat different communicative routines, which we will look at later, the IRF discourse structure is arguably still the most common form of teacher–pupil speech exchange at all levels of schooling (Cazden 2001). The following extract is from a 2002 junior science lesson.

(1) Teacher: Okay, let me start, hands up but don't shout out, what's electricity?

(2) Pupil 1: Energy.

(3) Teacher: Energy, err, not strictly, electricity will move energy. So when electricity is moving about, we could say it's a flow of energy. But what is electricity itself?

(4) Pupil 2: A source of energy, electrons.

(5) Teacher: Okay, okay, good answer.

Look at how the teacher **initiates** the discussion by the use of the question, 'what's electricity?' The first pupil **responds** with an answer – 'energy' – that does not quite meet the teacher's approval. As a result, at line 3, the teacher presents a somewhat negative **follow-up** utterance, 'not strictly', and, at the same time, rephrases the original question to provide a further **initiation**, 'but what is electricity itself?' The second pupil provides a more accurate **response**, 'a source of energy, electrons', and receives positive **evaluation** from the teacher, 'Okay, okay, good answer'.

As in medical consultations, the 'essential' IRF structure may be realized in more complex exchanges than the typical tripartite routine discussed above. Elicitations and responses may be divided by prompts and clues from the teacher: in exercise 5a the teacher *prompts* a hesitant pupil at line 7 with the expression, 'Come on now', and the following extract includes the embedding of a clue into an initiation-response routine.

(1) Teacher initiation: Who was the first wife of Henry VIII?

(2) Students: [no response]

(3) Teacher clue: Okay, not Anne Boleyn.

(4) Student response: Is it Catherine of Aragon?

Other examples of extensions to IRF exchanges include teachers' repetition of instructions, rephrasing of questions and correcting of pupils' misunderstandings. Furthermore, because exchanges between teachers and pupils take place within 'topically relevant' sets of talk, teachers may not always need to make explicit initiations or provide overt evaluations (Mehan 1979). Rather, teachers rely on shared knowledge about the topic and other contextual cues to give their utterances meaning. When the teacher asks, 'What happens in Lent?' in the earlier extract, for example, he is able to use pupils' names as an initiation strategy: at lines 5 and 7 he nominates students to answer, 'Yes, Jenny', 'No, Amy?'. The teacher's calling of the students' names performs the function of repeating the initial question in this topically bound speech exchange.

If we look back for a moment to the junior science lesson we can highlight many other features typical of teacher–student exchanges. We pause here only to identify the relevant discourse strategies, ready for further discussion later:

- Teachers frame discourse in a manner which sets out both the topics to be discussed and the communicative routines to be followed. This is illustrated at line 1: the teacher's statement, 'Okay, we've been looking at electricity', establishes the topic to be discussed in the ensuing discourse, and her directive, 'so let me start, hands up but don't shout out...' defines the organizational structure of the interaction in which the topic is to be discussed.

- Teachers ask questions and pupils are expected to answer. The teacher asks questions at lines 1 and 3 and students provide responses at lines 2 and 4.

- Teachers phrase their questions in particular ways and often repeat and rephrase their enquiries. At line 1, the teacher asks a 'wh-' question, 'what's electricity?' and this is reformulated at line 3, 'what is electricity itself?'

- Pupils' responses are typically shorter than teachers' questions: compare the teacher's enquiries in lines 1 and 3 with the students' responses in lines 2 and 4.

- Teachers are as likely to provide follow-up utterances that criticize or praise students as they evaluate the content of what students say. At line 5, the teacher's assessment of the second pupil's answer offers praise ('good answer'), but no explanation of why she considers the response to be correct.

Evidence of the maintenance of IRF routines can be seen in research on both sides of the Atlantic. For example, substantial research in British schoolrooms reveals a predominance of 'transmission' teaching in which IRF structures remain prevalent (Galton et al. 1999). Examining primary schooling in particular, Henrietta Dombey (2003) observes a trend of domination of teacher talk in which teachers position themselves as 'kindly' interrogators and place pupils in the position of being the subjects of interrogation. Research in the USA shows that secondary school students do not fare much better. Analysis of the structure of 'interactive' classroom talk shows that, despite the pedagogical commitment to student participation, the practice of the discourse hardly differs from traditional educational settings: teachers were found to propose all topics, initiate all exchanges and seldom took the opportunity to expand on students' responses (Nystrand et al. 1997).

This brings us to a consideration of the consequences of IRF exchanges on teaching and learning. Mercer (1992) points to the benefits of the discourse composed in IRF, commenting that the structure is an effective means by which teachers can both monitor students' knowledge and guide students' learning in ways that are educationally valuable and worthwhile. However, few share this opinion and, more generally, the IRF structure is perceived as a routine that restricts and constrains students' learning.[7]

IRF routines are criticized for restricting the space needed for students to engage in speculative talk, to 'think aloud' or to use exploratory talk to develop understanding. Instead, IRF exchanges compose discourse that leads to brief interactions in which students are cast primarily into the role of listeners and are confined in their verbal contributions to minimally filling the second slot of IRF interactions.

By comparison, when interactive teaching styles are used in which more evenly balanced 'textured discussion' between teachers and students takes place, very different learning outcomes are observed. In such 'properly' interactive classes, students are encouraged to initiate their own topics, to use language as a means of actively exploring the subject matter and to debate with and respond to one another as well as the teacher (Nystrand et al. 1997). It is perhaps significant that, in literacy tests, students taught with these methods outperformed students who had attended classes where transmission teaching and IRF exchanges were the normal order of classroom interaction. Cazden (2001) also observes that non-IRF speech exchanges promote more student talk and, particularly, talk between students and *students* as well as between students and *teachers*.

Encouraging talk between students in the classroom context may be particularly vital for enabling and enhancing opportunities for learning. In teaching undergraduate classes I have often been struck by the quality of work accomplished when students collaborate in peer groups. Not only do such group discussions appear to encourage usually 'quiet' students to contribute to debates, but the types of issues raised in group discussions are often more extended, elaborate, wide-ranging and far-reaching than those that take place in contexts in which classes are managed in more conventional teacher-to-class (or teacher-to-student) interaction routines. Specifically, peer group discussions appear to facilitate creativity in thinking and to encourage discussions that go usefully beyond what I, as the teacher, might too narrowly construe as the 'boundaries' of a particular subject area, topic or theme.

Notably, the benefits of such student–student discussion is not limited to those who are undertaking advanced levels of study. Analysis of 'group work' in primary level education finds that in discussions in peer groups children are set free from the normal confines of classroom interaction in which, for example, pupils are placed in competitive roles where they vie for the teacher's attention. Instead, in peer groups pupils are found to engage in dialogic interaction in which 'cycles of utterances' are collaboratively constructed, leading to the composition of meaningful discourse and imaginative thinking and learning (Barnes and Todd 1995).

However, while valuable, such discussions can only be one part of the learning experience of pupils. The school day is divided into many different events: apart from out-of-class events such as playtime and assembly, classroom time is itself divided into separate lessons, which, in turn, are made up of a number of different activities that may be further broken down into topically bound sets of actions and talk. One of the primary functions of teacher talk is the verbalization of the events that take place in this hierarchical structure. Teachers have often been observed to present a 'running commentary' that keeps students up to speed on the activities in hand and those that are forthcoming.

Examine the following extract, from a junior level mathematics class.

(1) Teacher: Okay, shapes, Sarah, what would the next shape be on our list?

(2) Sarah: A hexagon.

(3) Teacher: Well, a hexagon's got how many sides?

(4) Sarah: Six.

(5) Teacher: Six. How many sides do we want?

Examine how the first question, 'what would the next shape be on our list?' is framed by overt linguistic signalling that a shift in topic is about to take place: in the above example, by the teacher's use of the term 'Okay'. The use of such **framing** language is highly characteristic of classroom communication and is represented by a class of discourse markers such as *now*, *right* and *well*, as illustrated in the following examples.

Now, who can tell me what the heart does?

Right, let's move on to the surface area.

Well, the spread of English, let's think about New Zealand.

In the extract from the mathematics class, the framing use of 'okay' is followed by the teacher's **focus** on the topic of the forthcoming discourse, that is, 'shapes'. The same discourse technique is used in the third example, above: the framing discourse marker, 'well', is followed by an explicit focus on the curricular content, 'the spread of English'.

The discourse routine of framing followed by focusing is a highly productive pattern in classroom interaction, especially as it provides a context in which teachers can make their first initiations. It is to this initiation stage, the first stage of the 'essential' IRF routine, that we now turn our attention.

Initiating classroom communication

We saw in the extract from the mathematics class, above, that the teacher's initiation takes the form of an **elicitation**: 'what would the next shape be on our list?' Elicitations call for a verbal response from students and we will look at these in more detail in a moment. Other initiations serve different purposes, including **informing**, **directing** and **checking**. Look at the following examples of teacher initiations and try to identify the functions that they fulfil.

(1) Open your books at page 11.

(2) What did I tell you about calling out?

(3) Tell me, what were the major events that led to the American involvement in World War II?

(4) Do we understand the difference between these two shapes?

(5) What are the main functions of advertising discourse?

(6) There are many factors to consider in examining the reasons why this chemical reaction works as it does.

Initiations that serve to inform are used to guide the nature of the following discourse and often accomplish the function of expressing facts and ideas. In contrast to elicitations, informing initiations may not require any response from pupils or may call for only minimal acknowledgement. In this respect, example 6 in the list above may be classed as an **informing** initiation. However, as we have seen, language forms do not map in a simple way on to linguistic functions; and, depending on factors including the context and purpose of the interaction, a single form may perform multiple purposes. Consequently, the meaning of the utterance in example 6 may be shaped differently in the sequencing of situated interaction. For example, note how different interpretations may arise depending on whether the utterance is used to open a discussion and so present *new* information (in which case the utterance may be genuinely informative) or follows a student's previous contribution (e.g. one in which the student has only provided a limited explanation of reasons), in which case the teacher's utterance may be interpreted as a warning to the student not to underestimate the factors involved in explaining chemical reactions.

We face similar difficulties in classifying other examples above. At first sight, example 4 appears to be a **checking** initiation that calls for a minimal 'yes' or 'no' response from students. However, it is worth pausing to consider how likely it is that students would provide any answer to this question and, particularly, whether negative responses are likely reactions to such questions. The need for pupils to preserve 'face' in the classroom context often results in such initiations being met with silence, and in the consequent concealment of pupils' lack of understanding.

Initiations that, in general, may be classified as **directive**, such as that in example 1, are used to induce students to carry out actions. However, like elicitations, they may also be employed to elicit verbal responses, as is revealed in example 3. Finally, examples 2 and 5 take the syntactic form of 'wh-' interrogatives and, on the surface, appear to be further instances of **eliciting** initiations. Indeed, we have seen that open-ended 'wh-' questions often encourage extended and elaborated answers. However, while example 5 may be a genuine elicitation, example 2 is more ambiguous. Recall our brief examination of speech act theory earlier in the book and consider the nature of the *illocutionary force* of the teacher's question: 'What did I tell you about calling out?' Is this a request for a verbal response or is it, in fact, a demand for silence? Consider how utterances such as this and other similar examples – 'who's talking?' 'what's going on over there?' – may function as commands in the classroom context, that is, 'stop talking' and 'stop misbehaving', respectively. In this respect, example 2 is as likely (and perhaps more so) to perform a **directive** purpose in the classroom context as it is to fulfil the function of an eliciting initiation.

We have already seen that the opportunity to use talk to formulate ideas and express thoughts is fundamental to the learning process. Consequently, the way in which teachers elicit verbal contributions from students is crucial. What type of questions do teachers ask? Research at all levels of education, from the analysis of primary school lessons to the examination of university seminars, has found that teachers do not typically ask questions to request information, but rather as a means of checking on the students' level of knowledge or understanding. It is generally accepted that much of teacher–class talk is conducted not to explore ideas, but to test, rhetorically, whether the students have learned and can reproduce the information that the teacher has presented to them.

As a result, in many lessons, teachers' questions imply that all that is required of students is the production of the 'right answer'; such forms are described as, for example, 'check', 'display' and 'pseudo' questions. Look at the following two extracts of data and consider the question forms and their functions. Extract A is from a junior mathematics lesson and extract B is from an undergraduate linguistics seminar.

A

(1) Teacher: Now, are we all happy that the angles in a triangle add up to 180? That's 180. You use a formula to find that total. Now, John, can you substitute the next one?

(2) Student: Umm... [pause].

(3) Teacher: The form which we need is precisely working out what's x.

(4) Student: Is x 4 take away 2?

(5) Teacher: In brackets?

(6) Student: Yeah, in brackets.

(7) Teacher: Go on.

(8) Student: Times 180.

(9) Teacher: Good, what's that going to come to?

B

(1) Teacher: Do you think that we can identify someone's social class from their speech patterns alone?

(2) Student: Can we do it from the dialect features?

(3) Teacher: Yes, for sure this is useful, but what if the regional dialects are not familiar to you?

[silence]

(4) Student: What do we do then?

(5) Teacher: Well, it's a genuine question.

Analysis of the construction of discourse in extract A clearly reveals that the teacher asks questions to which she already knows the answers. After using the framing discourse marker, 'now', followed by the (unanswered) first question, 'are we all happy that the angles in a triangle add up to 180?', the teacher pursues discourse strategies aimed at leading pupils to the mathematical explanation she has in mind. At line 1 she provides clues to the answer required by informing students that they need to use a formula. Such clues are typically used to pre-plan questions in the classroom context and provide students with pointers and hints as to forthcoming enquiries. At line 3, after her first elicitation fails to get a response, the teacher swiftly reformulates the question in an attempt to make it more understandable: 'the form which we need is precisely working out what's x'. At line 5 she provides a further verbal clue – 'in brackets?' – and finally, at line 9, the teacher presents positive feedback to encourage pupils to make their way towards the correct explanation.

While it is possible that lessons in mathematics may require analysis leading to a single correct answer, other areas of study and learning can be hindered by such expectations. Extract B illustrates this point. At line 1 the tutor asks a question which, if not constructed for the elicitation of information per se, is at least expressed with the desire for students to voice their own opinions on a debatable topic. However, as the undergraduate's questions at lines 2 and 4 show, the conventional customs of classroom interaction create an assumption on the part of students that teachers know all the answers. In the discussion presented, this was a mistaken assumption and, as a consequence, the tutor has to state explicitly that her question was 'genuine', indicating that she does not have a single 'correct' answer to provide.

The use of pseudo-questions, while not unique to classroom discourse, is particularly characteristic of this context: where else are we expected to answer a barrage of questions in the full knowledge that the questioner already has possession of the relevant answers?

The preceding extracts also illustrate other typical question-asking techniques. Look again at the question in line 1 of extract A, where the teacher asks, 'are we all happy that the angles in a triangle add up to 180?' Does this question call for an answer or does it function purely as a rhetorical device? The rapidity with which the teacher continues, leaving no gap for pupils to respond, indicates that the question is serving the stylistic purpose of revising and summarizing the lessons learnt in order to *focus* on related new material (note that the closely following use of the framing discourse marker, 'now', supports this analysis). The absence of a pause after the question also suggests that, as we discussed above, the teacher does not expect to hear a (negative) response from pupils.

In addition to fulfilling the function of revising, summarizing and focusing, rhetorical questions may also be used to accentuate and emphasize particular points or to serve the stylistic function of simplifying problems for students to solve. Teachers often use such questions to direct students' attention to certain aspects of relevant topics and, specifically, as a way to eliminate absurdities.

> Teacher: Whereabouts is Sweden?
>
> Pupils: [no answer]
>
> Teacher: Is it in America?
>
> (Cited in Sinclair and Brazil 1982: 80)

As well as the frequent use of such rhetorical forms, teachers have also been observed to ask closed-ended questions; just as in the courtroom or medical consultation, classroom discourse is characterized by the prolific use of *yes/no* questions: 'Is Paris the capital of France?' Interrogatives that take a disjunctive form and call for a simple *either/or* response are abundant: 'Is Paris the capital of Germany or France?'; as are questions that ask students to 'fill the gap': 'Paris is the capital of…?'

A recent study of classroom interaction in Hong Kong reveals that such questions are a particular feature of classroom discourse in a variety of cultures. Amy Tsui and her colleagues examine how teachers' questions function to open or close students' 'space for learning' and how the phrasing of questions may increasingly narrow what is considered to be a relevant object of attention.

> (1) Teacher: Oh then surely, now girls, can you explain to me why, why doesn't the motor work?
>
> (2) Students: [Silent]
>
> (3) Teacher: Why doesn't this motor work? Just because motors must use…?
>
> (4) Students: [Silent]
>
> (5) Teacher: The current that is…large or small?
>
> (6) Students: Large.
>
> (7) Teacher: Large.
>
> (Adapted from Tsui et al. 2004: 129)

Examine how, when the teacher's first open-ended question – 'why doesn't the motor work?' – fails to elicit a response from students, it is swiftly rephrased in a 'fill the gap' enquiry: 'Just because motors must use…? Further silence leads the teacher to funnel the discussion into a disjunctive request for an either/or response: 'The current that is…large or small?' Tsui et al. conclude that the space which students have for thinking, exploring ideas and taking an active role in their learning is thereby closed down by the increasingly restrictive questioning techniques of the teacher.

However, in the classroom, questions which appear to ask for a minimal response may actually require more extended answers. A teacher who asks, 'Can you explain the factors that led to the end of the cold war?' requires far more than a simple answer of 'yes' or 'no'. By contrast, 'wh-' questions that seemingly encourage extensive or elaborated responses may, in practice, elicit only minimal replies.

Exercise 5c

Examine the following data taken from a junior level science class and look particularly at the teacher's use of questions.

(1) Teacher: Now, what else do we need for electricity?

(2) Pupil: Wires.

(3) Teacher: Yes, wires, why do you think that they are important?

(4) Pupil: To keep the circuit so that it can keep the current flowing around the circle.

(5) Teacher: Oh, well done, and now why is it called the circuit, can anyone remember? Jane?

(6) Jane: Because it looks a bit like a circle.

(7) Teacher: Because it looks a bit like a circle, yes. And what happens when something keeps going round and round in the circle, George?

(8) George: Um, I, I don't know.

(9) Teacher: You can't remember. Okay, James?

(10) James: It is a circuit.

(11) Teacher: Yes, circuit actually comes from the word circle. It keeps going round and round. So we get the circuit, right?

- What form do the teacher's questions take?
- Why do you think the teacher phrases her questions in the way she does?
- How do the teacher's questions function in her interaction with pupils?

First of all, note how the vast majority of the teacher's questions take 'wh-' form (lines 1, 3, 5, 7). However, despite the predominance of such open-ended enquiries, pupils' responses are relatively minimal (examine students' replies at lines 2, 6 and 10). Why are such short answers given to questions which, in other contexts, might encourage extended responses? Part of the answer is in the question, of course: we have consistently seen that context is crucial for interpreting linguistic functions. It is important to understand that, just as certain linguistic forms may be selected to accomplish particular purposes in specific contexts (for example, lawyers may use yes/no questions in order to restrict witnesses' testimony), the nature of the context in which language is used shapes the construction of meanings that linguistic forms convey.

In the case of the classroom discourse in the exercise above, the function of questions depends particularly on the informational *content* that the teacher is aiming to elicit from students. In seminal research carried out in the 1970s and 1980s, Douglas Barnes observed that the majority of questions asked by teachers requested factual information rather than encouraging 'reasoning' responses. Early twenty-first-century analysis of literacy lessons in UK primary schools, in which a predominance of questions requesting the statement of 'facts' was observed, shows that things have not changed much over the years (Hardman et al. 2003).

Bearing this in mind, look back and observe how the vast majority of the teacher's questions in the exercise call for purely **factual** information (lines 1, 5, and 7), and, as a result, single-word answers or minimally worded responses are all that is required. In some cases, 'wh-' questions do not encourage extended responses, but rather, in the words of Douglas Barnes, function as 'pseudo-open' enquiries. These are to be contrasted with genuinely candid questions (line 3 includes an enquiry which may be described in this way) which are used to encourage children to reflect upon the processes of their own language, learning and understanding: *What do you mean? How did you do that? Why do you say that? How did you arrive at that conclusion?*

Furthermore, as we saw above, it is not just the way in which questions are phrased, but also the context that is important for interpretation. This is equally true for the explanation and interpretation of the questions asked by students. In fact, students appear to pose remarkably few enquiries in classroom interaction. Statistical evidence reveals a striking level of disparity in the number of questions asked by teachers and students: in a survey of 27 lessons on subjects in humanities, teachers were observed to ask an average of 80 questions per hour compared to an average of only 2 questions per hour for *all* students combined (Dillon 1988).

The significance of this vastly asymmetrical distribution of question-asking among classroom participants should not be underestimated; it is paradoxical that those who are learning and seeking knowledge ask fewer questions than those who are teaching and in possession of relevant facts and information. Furthermore, when students do ask questions they tend to be requests relating to matters of organization rather than to the content of lessons. For example, primary school pupils frequently ask questions relating to points of procedure: *Can I start now? What page are we on? Which group am I in?* (Alexander 2003). And while more sophisticated students do engage in enquiries relating to subject content, it is nevertheless true that a great deal of questioning time is still taken up with matters of administration and organization: *When is the coursework due? What is the word limit? How many questions do I need to answer? How long does the presentation have to be?*

A further interesting and revealing use of questions is discussed by Henrietta Dombey (2003), who observes that primary school children frequently respond to teachers' elicitations in question form. Several such communicative routines are included in examples of classroom interaction that we have already discussed: for example, in exercise 5a, a student responds to a teacher's question on right angles with the reply, 'is it like a square corner?' (line 7). And when the teacher poses a question on the meaning of Lent in the extract from a primary school religious education class explored earlier in this chapter, a pupil replies, 'is it when Jesus went into the wilderness?' (line 8). As shown in the extract from an undergraduate linguistics seminar, this habit is not restricted to young pupils: in responding to a tutor's enquiry of whether a speaker's social class can be identified by reference to language use, a student replies, 'Can we do it from the dialect features?'

In these examples the verbal contributions of pupils and students take interrogative form but have the function of *responding* to the teacher's question. Such communicative practice reveals that students' questions are not always used proactively to initiate their own topics, but can also function as reactions to issues instigated by teachers. Why do pupils and students phrase their responses in this way? Henrietta Dombey discusses this question and makes the important observation that presenting responses in question form shields pupils from committing themselves to the correctness of the information they present verbally – a strategy somewhat similar to the use of certain modal verbs and hedging discourse devices in student writing. In other words, pupils may use this strategy as a 'face-saving' device to protect themselves from the implications of giving an inaccurate response.

While it may appear incongruous for students to use questions as a tool for self-protection and face-preservation, this practice continues, in one form or another, throughout educational life. Indeed, it is interesting to observe that, as students acquire the etiquette of classroom interaction, they begin to use questions according to the model provided by their tutors: specifically, students may shy away from asking information-seeking questions, since such enquiries may be considered to show inadequacy or lack of understanding. Students frequently report on the fear of asking 'stupid questions', whatever these may be. So, for much the same reason that teachers' questions are often answered in interrogative form, information-seeking questions are avoided for fear of loss of face. Instead, students frequently ask questions for other, more veiled, purposes: for example, they learn to come up with analytical and judicious questions that are constructed to display their knowledge and to present a positive face to their teachers and peers.

In our years of schooling, therefore, we become highly proficient in the intricate art of question-asking: from making simple enquiries about classroom organization and procedure, to protecting ourselves by answering teachers' questions in interrogative form, and acquiring competence in presenting questions which we hope will be perceived as critical or clever. It is ironic that the one function absent here is the use of questions to request information or to seek knowledge. The type of question that might genuinely facilitate the development of learning and understanding is neglected.

Reacting, replying and responding

Exercise 5d

The following dialogue took place between an adult and a young male child in a New York school. The aim of the interview was to test the child's linguistic abilities. The child has just entered the room and the adult has put a wooden block down in front of him and invited the child to 'tell me everything you can about this'. Examine the data and consider the likely assessment made of the child.

[12 seconds of silence]

Adult: What would you say it looks like?

[8 seconds of silence]

Child: *A space ship.*

Adult: Hmmm.

[13 seconds of silence]

Child: Like a je-et.

[12 seconds of silence]

Like a plane.

[20 seconds of silence]

Adult: What colour is it?

Child: Orange. [2 seconds of silence] An' wh-ite. [2 seconds of silence] An' green.

[6 seconds of silence]

Adult: An' what could you use it for?

[8 seconds of silence]

Child: A je-et.

[6 seconds of silence]

Adult: If you had two of them, what would you do with them?

[6 seconds of silence]

Child: Give one to somebody.

Adult: Hmmm. Who do you think would like to have it?

[10 seconds of silence]

Child: Cla-rence.

➡

Adult: Mm. Where do you think we could get another one of these?

Child: At the store.

Adult: Oh ka-ay!

(Cited in Labov 1972: 206)

- How are the 'wh-' questions functioning in this discourse?
- Why are the child's responses so minimal?
- Do you think that the organization of this speech exchange provides the child with a fair opportunity to display his linguistic abilities?

If you were asked to describe a block, to say what you would do if you had two of them and to consider which of your friends might like one (remember, we are talking about a wooden block), what type of responses do you think you would provide? Would you be able to manage much more than the awkward silences and hesitant, monosyllabic responses produced by the child in the above interaction?

In America in the 1960s there was increasing concern that African American children were failing in education (at that time, it was not considered that the education system might be failing the children). In trying to find out the reasons why, educational psychologists conducted a series of interviews in schools, of which the above is a typical example. Children's performance in the interviews, and particularly their lack of responses and long stretches of silence, led psychologists to an assumption of the linguistic 'deficiency' of children, and in some cases to African American children being classed as having no language at all. The perceived 'lack of language' was held responsible for children's poor educational performance, and the reasons for and roots of the 'deficit' were considered to be in the home: African American families were criticized for not providing the type of 'verbal stimulation' that children require for language development and learning.

The linguist William Labov firmly opposed these conclusions and argued against the claim that African American families failed to provide adequate linguistic sustenance for their children. While language support was not of the type typical of white, middle-class families – for example, oral narratives (including sounding, singing and 'rifting') were preferred to the bedtime book – Labov warned of the dangers of perceiving this difference as a deficit. Indeed, Labov found African American children to be 'bathed in verbal stimulation from morning to night' (1972: 212).

What the American psychologists had ignored was that every culture and society has its own norms for language use and communicative behaviour. Larry Trask (1999) provides the example of how, in traditional Basque households, the master of the house may indicate his desire for a refill of wine by banging his glass on the table, without saying a word. Imagine the reaction in another cultural context.

While the relationship between culture and language has long been recognized by anthropological linguists, it was not until the 1960s that Dell Hymes argued for particular attention to the culture–language interface, in an approach called the *ethnography of speaking* (also referred to as *ethnography of communication*). As we discussed in the introduction to this book, those who take an ethnographic approach to language and discourse focus on the cultural values and social roles that operate in particular communities. Being particularly concerned not to impose their own cultural presuppositions on other societies, they use intricate methods of participant observation to study the language habits and customs of different communities. Such methods are seen to be vital if proper descriptions and explanations of the language patterns of a culture and community are to be made accurately and with due care and attention.

The interviews conducted by American psychologists in the 1960s were at the opposite end of the spectrum to ethnographic study: as we have seen, African American children were interviewed by strangers from another culture. The interviewers imposed their own cultural definition of the interview situation and the definition was one in which children quickly learnt that anything they said could be held against them and so their best bet was to avoid saying anything at all. Indeed Labov argues that it was not 'linguistic deficiency' that had led to children's minimal verbal contributions in interviews, but rather the asymmetry of the situation in which children were placed. Evidence for this argument was later provided by setting up interviews in which African American interviewers conducted informal consultations with children. In these more symmetrical speech encounters children were better able to show their true (linguistic) abilities.

There are a number of important lessons to be learned from the American experience of the 1960s. Clearly the recognition and respect of cultural differences in classrooms is most important. Also, as Labov concludes, it is imperative to recognize that teachers can best facilitate learning through language by creating and sustaining *symmetrical* social relationships in the classroom context. He concludes, however, that 'this is just what many teachers cannot do' (1972: 212). In fact, this seems rather unfair since it is not only teachers who are responsible for constructing classroom conventions. However, teachers do have a considerable amount of control over the type of verbal contributions that students are able to provide.

As we have already discussed, the majority of communicative contributions provided by pupils and students take the form of responses. Statistical evidence for this claim is provided in an analysis of literacy hours in British primary schools, where it was found that 86 per cent of pupils' speaking time was spent in reacting to teacher elicitations (Hardman et al. 2003). Invariably, when constructing replies to teacher enquiries, students concentrate on identifying and presenting responses that they hope will elicit positive evaluations and assessments from teachers. Rather than drawing on their own personal experience, students are therefore placed in the position of having to read the teacher's mind in order to provide 'accurate' answers. Again, the issue of saving face is an important concern: pupils attempt to maintain a positive face by searching for the 'right' answer to teachers' questions, and, as a consequence, enter into the game of 'guess what the teacher is thinking'. Students soon learn that if they are successful at this game, positive evaluation from teachers is likely to follow. In this respect, placing pupils in 'response mode' leads to competition rather than to the type of collaborative discourse that has been found to facilitate creative thinking and learning.

Furthermore, as well as providing answers with the right *content*, pupils also have to structure and present their responses in the correct *form*: prescribed requirements may include the use of particular phrasing (e.g. answering in 'full sentences'); the employment of appropriate or exact language (e.g. technical vocabulary rather than colloquial terms); and the submission of contributions in a certain sequence. Several researchers have discussed how the *timing* of students' responses is crucial in this respect (see, for example, Mehan 1979 and Erickson 1982). Correct answers that are called out or which do not fit neatly into the teacher's strict schedule of class-room discourse may be discounted or denied. What is more, the manner of bidding and competing for turns has to be fine-tuned by students: bidding which is too fervent may antagonize and so alienate teachers, while over-modest bidding is likely to be ignored (Edwards and Westgate 1994).

Students' responses to teachers' elicitations therefore tend to be short, restricted to a semantic content that is pre-defined and highly constrained in the chronology of classroom communication. In the following and final section we examine how teachers react to students' responses, and we take a closer look at the manner in which teachers shape lessons by providing follow-up utterances to student contributions to classroom discussions.

Follow-up, feedback and evaluation

We have already commented on some aspects of what teachers are likely to say and do in their follow-up utterances: for example, we have seen that teachers tend to provide evaluative remarks rather than give instructional guidance. A recent study of primary classroom interaction sub-classified teachers' follow-up turns into four types and noted their numerical distribution: *acceptance* (e.g. 'yes, that's right') was found to be the most frequent form of feedback, occurring in 57 per cent of cases; followed by *praise* (e.g. 'yes, well done') at 21 per cent; *probing of pupil's response* (e.g. 'tell me more about that') was used 14 per cent of the time; *criticism* (e.g. 'no, haven't you been paying attention?') was found to be a relatively rare form of teacher evaluation, occurring in only 7 per cent of teachers' reactions (Hardman et al. 2003). These statistical results are reflected in more qualitative research which shows that, in both the UK and the USA, teachers use follow-up turns primarily as a method by which to build pupils' confidence: in America, expressions such as *Neat! Wow! Nice job! Beautiful sharing! Way to go!* are particularly prolific (Alexander 2003).

While such discourse strategies may be valuable for developing students' self-esteem, they do little to aid the progress of cognitive growth. Indeed in contrast to the invariable praise of 'right' answers, teachers have been found to 'gloss over' pupils' incorrect responses and so close down possible avenues of developing more accurate and advanced understanding (Alexander 2003). Similarly, teachers may use follow-up turns to reject answers which they perceive as incorrect, irrelevant or insufficient and use their turns to reallocate the question for someone else to answer. Examples of such reallocations can be found in several extracts of data included in this chapter ('No, okay, no. Does anyone know what a right angle is? Has anybody heard of it?' in exercise 5a; 'No, Amy?' in the primary school religious education extract; and 'Oh, well done, and now why is it called the circuit, can anyone remember? Jane?' in exercise 5c). Indeed, even when students' responses are broadly correct, the teacher's reaction to student contributions is often to modify and amend them in line with their own predetermined ideas of the semantic content and organizational schedule of lessons (Edwards and Westgate 1994).

However, while a teacher's follow-up turn can be used to constrain and close down speech exchanges, it may also be used more subtly to extend, broaden and develop students' responses. Based on research in the USA, recommendations have been made for sophisticated evaluation that incorporates pupils' answers into subsequent questions, thereby weaving students' contributions into the pattern of classroom interaction (Nystrand et al. 1997). Similarly, in the UK, research has revealed that when follow-up turns are used to elaborate on pupils' responses, and particularly when teachers make their verbal contributions similar in kind to those constructed by pupils, classroom interaction begins to build into a more equally balanced discussion in which collaborative learning is facilitated (Dombey 2003).

Exercise 5e

Study the following interaction. Four early years children (Martin, Helen, Joe and Katy) are engaged with their teacher in a task involving measuring and cutting wallpaper. They need three pieces of wallpaper 1.55 m long, and one piece 1.20 m long. They are using two 1 m rulers.

(1) Martin: It's one metre fifty-five centimetres, isn't it?

(2) Teacher: That's right. How many pieces do you think we'll need for this wall?

(3) Helen: Two.

(4) Joe: Um, three.

(5) Teacher: Yes, three I think, you'll need the same piece of paper how many times?

(6) Joe and Helen: Three... [the children try to measure the 1.20 m piece using the second 1 m ruler]

(7) Teacher: Do you think we need to measure the next bit with the metre ruler? We've got one metre, we need our paper to be how much longer?

(8) Katy: One metre twenty centimetres we said...um...

(9) Joe: Twenty more.

(10) Teacher: Yes, we only need twenty centimetres more. Would it be easier to use a smaller ruler? [pause] It has centimetres, the same as the metre ruler.

(11) Helen: [doubtfully] They'd be the same, wouldn't they?　➡

(12) Teacher: Let's try. [Helen checks the smaller ruler against the metre ruler]

(13) Joe: It will be the same, Helen.

(14) Teacher: It's always a good idea to check if you're not sure.

(Adapted from Wood and Attfield 1996: 108)

- Examine the teacher's follow-up turns. How would you describe their structure?
- How do the teacher's follow-up turns relate to the pupils' preceding turns?
- Examine the form and function of the teacher's follow-up questions. Would you describe them as rhetorical?
- Why do you think the children who are taking part in this interaction feel able to collaborate with each other rather than just with the teacher?

While the above interaction follows a broad IRF structure (as indeed do many interactions of all sorts), the structure is followed more flexibly than in other teacher–pupil speech exchanges that we have studied. This is largely due to the nature and structure of how the teacher responds to pupil contributions. Indeed, if the teacher's follow-up turn is used in a valuable and careful way, then the IRF structure can be positive and productive, rather than rhetorical and restrictive. According to Wells, when the teacher uses the 'third move' of the IRF to *extend* students' contributions (rather than just to provide a narrow evaluation), the follow-up turn may serve as an opportunity to 'make connections with other parts of the student's total experience' (1993: 30).

To a certain extent we have already seen instances of follow-up turns where teachers repeat pupils' answers and use them to elaborate on discussion of relevant topics and themes – though none of them seem to have been handled very convincingly or collaboratively. In exercise 5c, where the topic of electricity is being explored, a pupil's response of 'wires' is followed up by the teacher's utterance, 'yes, wires, why do you think wires are important?', but actually the pupil had not really said that wires were important in the first place; it is the teacher who thinks they are. In a similar way, the extract from a junior science lesson explored earlier in this chapter illustrates a follow-up turn when a pupil has provided an inaccurate response to the question regarding the nature of electricity: the teacher replies, 'Energy, err, not strictly, electricity will move energy. So when electricity is moving about, we could say it's a flow of energy. But what is electricity itself?' I don't know about you, but I cannot help feeling that the teacher's nice distinction here will have been largely lost on the audience, if only because she does not do anything further about it in her follow-up turn, but simply proceeds with targeting more questions at the class.

In the exercise above, however, we see the IRF structure in an interactive and more symmetrical setting. At line 2, for example, the teacher evaluates Martin's answer as correct, 'Yes that's right', and then looks to extend the learning by asking a further question: 'How many pieces do you think we'll need?' Similarly, at line 5, the teacher evaluates Joe's answer, 'Three', as agreeing with her own, 'Yes, three I think', and uses the follow-up turn to ask a question again – though this time the function of the question is to check that the children understand why the answer was correct in the first place. Her question is phrased oddly, by everyday standards, although all teachers will recognize its structure: 'You'll need the same piece of paper how many times?' Structurally, it is a combination of a statement, 'you'll need the same piece of paper', with an appended question, 'how many times?' It is noticeable that Helen, who first answered 'two', now answers 'three' in unison with Joe. (It is also noticeable that the teacher did not immediately correct Helen's first answer, but waited to see what Joe would say.)

At line 7, the teacher self-selects to ask a further question when the children are struggling with the large ruler. Her question again takes the structure just mentioned: 'we need our paper to be how much longer?' This time the question serves to focus, rather than to check, and again it is noticeable that two children are involved in formulating the answer. The teacher again evaluates the answer as correct at line 10, but in so doing she rephrases the answer into the form, 'Yes, we only need twenty centimetres more', that focuses the children on the smallness of the extra measurement and prepares them for her next question, 'Would it be easier to use a smaller ruler?'

Interestingly, the teacher spots that Helen is concerned about whether centimetres will be the same on a small ruler as on a large one, and although she reassures her, Helen is still doubtful, responding with a question at line 11, 'They'd be the same, wouldn't they?' Rather than answer 'yes', the teacher says, 'Let's try' (line 12), encouraging Helen to find the answer for herself. And even though Joe collaborates to assure Helen that the centimetres will be the same, the teacher uses her follow-up turn at line 14 to maintain the heuristics and, incidentally, to offer further advice for pupils to find out and act for themselves, 'It's always a good idea to check if you're not sure'.

Much of the quality of the teaching here depends on how the teacher uses her follow-up turns, and on the refreshing lack of rhetoric that they contain. There is also a distinct matching between the teacher and pupil roles, evidenced in the symmetrical use of inclusive 'we' and the verb 'think': the teacher asks the pupils what they think – 'How many pieces do you think we'll need?' 'Do you think we need to measure the next bit?' – and couches her evaluation of Joe's 'correct' answer at line 5 in the same terms: 'Yes, three I think'. There is little indication here of a teacher who already knows all the right answers. No doubt this type of interaction is made easier by the nature and content of the task being attempted: it is a collaborative, hands-on exercise to solve a practical problem with young children who are not yet subject to examination pressures; but this in turn begs many further questions – not least, whether the nature of electricity is genuinely best learnt and understood in the context of a competitive quiz-and-bid session.

The follow-up utterances provided by teachers are of vital importance to classroom communication and to the quality of the context provided for learning. Phrased in sophisticated ways, follow-up utterances can facilitate collaboration in the construction of extended dialogue between both teachers and students and between students themselves. By contrast, follow-up utterances that are not co-ordinated with pupils' responses and do not develop student contributions may bring discussion to a swift and summary end, and serve to close down opportunities for in-depth dialogue and discussion.

In this chapter we have seen that the discourse of education is characterized by conventions and customs that control both what is considered legitimate knowledge and the way in which this knowledge is expressed. Academic written discourse promotes the use of a particular style of Standard English in which, for example, students are also required to justify their personal views by reference to externally sanctioned sources, and to use an impersonal and remote voice that detaches the writer from what is written. Academic writing conventions thus leave little room for the expression of personal or lifeworld experience or for exhibiting commitment to opinions, beliefs and values. To reiterate the words of Ivanič and Simpson (1992: 166), student writers are often led to believe that 'it's as if it's better if it doesn't matter'.

Spoken classroom interaction is also characterized by a unique set of rules and regulations in which teachers and pupils engage in speech exchanges according to distinctive communicative customs. Rights over the structure of discourse (*who* may speak and *when* they may do so), as well as the semantic content of communication (*what* may be spoken about), tend to be controlled by teachers. From strategies of framing subject boundaries and focusing on topically relevant sets of talk, teachers continue to guide interaction towards a pre-defined end by the use of questions, often rhetorical in nature, and evaluations that are frequently couched in terms of the teacher's own predetermined target outcome. As the established experts in the classroom context, teachers control knowledge by means of restricted routines of question-asking and specific strategies of evaluating and shaping students' responses. Teachers may discard or ignore student contributions that are considered irrelevant or redundant, and reformulate or recontextualize students' contributions to fit their own frame of reference. As with academic conventions for writing, the customs of spoken discourse in the classroom may serve to restrict students' opportunities to draw on their own experience or to build on this experience in order to further their knowledge and understanding.

Recent research shows that, even in classes where interactive and discourse-intensive styles are practised, teachers continue to construct communicative routines in a way that constrains the opportunities for students to initiate and control their own communicative contributions and paths of learning. In research spanning more than 30 years, instances of teachers using more evenly balanced, open and dialogic discussion are still rare. As we have seen, this is at least partly a consequence of the pressures placed on teachers by the imposition of ever-changing and often conflicting government objectives, demands and targets. Where teachers do manage to construct classroom interaction in a cooperative and interactive way, they tend to be identified for their good practice, and students are found to benefit from such pedagogic methods: as we have seen, teaching is dependent on talking, but learning is also reliant on verbally rehearsing knowledge, linguistically drafting ideas and developing new areas of understanding through the construction of meaningful discourse. Our analysis of educational discourse at this level suggests that learning is made far more difficult by institutional use of formal structures and conventions that contrive to deny opportunities for such rehearsal, drafting and construction.

Further exercises

1   As always, go back over the chapter and examine all the data again, including the extracts used in the exercises. Look for examples of all the aspects of educational discourse that we have considered. In particular, look for any evidence of teacher control that appears to you to be closing off opportunities for pupils and students to articulate their own experiences, to verbally rehearse knowledge or to develop new understanding.

2   Consider the following two extracts of classroom interaction. Both involve new teachers who are joining in with early years children's play with the intention of developing learning opportunities. Examine particularly their use of questions. What do you think the first teacher could learn from the second?

A

(1)   Mari: You come on my bus. I'm the driver, you're the Mummy. [pretends to drive]

(2)   Teacher: Where shall we go?

(3)   Mari: Shall we go to Portland?

(4)   Teacher: Is that a long way?

(5)   Mari: Not very far. I've been there, we go to the zoo.

(6)   Teacher: That would be good. I'd love to go to the zoo. How long will it take to get there?

(7)   Mari: I don't know, it's not very far.

(8)   Teacher: Will it take a few minutes or half an hour?

(9)   Mari: What time is it? You look at your watch.

(10)   Teacher: Ten o'clock.

(11)   Mari: It's not very far... Oh, we're there, it didn't take very long. You can come in as well.

(12)   Teacher: Do I have to pay any money to get in?

(13)   Mari: Yes.

(14)   Teacher: How much does it cost?

(15)   Mari: [crossly] I don't know, you've got the watch. [Mari then turned away and lost interest]

(Wood and Attfield 1996: 98)

B

(1)   Teacher: Ow, ow, my poor ankle, what shall I do nurse?

(2)   Jenny: I think that you should stay in for two days and calm yourself down and stop rubbing it.

(3) Teacher: Is it broken nurse? Can I sit down? Ow, ow.

(4) Jenny: Yes, you'd better sit here. I'll go and get the X-ray…no you have sprained it. I'm going to bandage it before I water it.

(5) Teacher: You're going to water my ankle? Why are you going to water my ankle, nurse, it's not a flower?

(6) Jenny: No, I'm going to dab it and then I'll put this bandage on. [begins to bandage over the teacher's shoe]

(7) Teacher: Ow, ow. Do you think I should take my shoe off?

(8) Jenny: Oh yes. Nurse come and help me [to another child]…you hold the safety pin and give it to me when I've done this.

(9) Teacher: Can I walk on it or should I rest it?

(10) Jenny: I'll give you some crutches and when you get home you've got to put it on a stool or table or something soft.

(11) Teacher: Do I have to take any tablets for the pain?

(12) Jenny: I'll give you a 'scription. [asks for help with writing]

(p. 109)

3   If possible, arrange access to (and record) a range of school lessons, or college or university seminars. Make sure that you have full permission from all concerned before you make any recordings. What evidence do you find of the IRF structure in the interactions? Focus particularly on the third part of any IRF structures you note. How much opportunity is afforded to the pupils or students to rehearse learning linguistically? How much control does the teacher exert over the lifeworld experiences of the pupils or students? Try to record a broad enough range to allow you to examine the interactions comparatively. (Alternatively or additionally, you may also be interested to assemble a small corpus of teachers' or tutors' comments on written work and examine this in a similarly critical light.)

Conclusion

From the cradle to the grave we construct ourselves though the social rehearsal of language as we negotiate our place in the world and make our way through life; and the discourse we engage in shapes the way we construct ourselves. Indeed, we are to some extent influenced by this discourse before we are born. Even as we are in the womb, medical discourse, for example, will be determining whether our mothers should be receiving supplements of folic acid or undergoing amniocentesis tests. Such discourse may be in written or spoken form, constructed by doctors, health educators or professional advertising agencies; it may be subject to government guidelines or recommendations; it will certainly be regulated by legal restrictions and safeguards.

Our early life will be shaped and constructed by the way we negotiate our discourse with our carers and our educators: it will be subjected to the constant seductive discourse of advertisers, the paternalistic discourse of our health care providers and, unless we are very careful, the forbidding discourse of the law. Our later lives will be punctuated by momentous occasions: by illnesses, perhaps, legal disputes, examinations, crimes, marriages, divorces, births and deaths, as well as by the highlights and lowlights of the professional careers or commercial endeavours we choose to engage in: jobs may be found, promotions gained, contracts lost, resignations accepted, companies founded, bankruptcies filed, lawsuits endured. We may be dealing with (or actively participating in) growth or recession, prosperity or instability, strife and even war. In all these moments of our social construction, as we develop and express our own individual identities and negotiate our relationships with the society we are born into, our interactions are more or less bound by cultural conventions and customs that contrive to locate us in particular positions and roles.

In examining the discourse that circumscribes these interactions, we have noted how powerful and pervasive are the pressures put on us to conform to custom and convention. We have seen, for example, how advertisers seek to construct us as consumers; to persuade us of the value of commercial products and possessions, and to engage us in the profitable cycle of consumerism that underpins the society we inhabit. Political discourse itself aims to be equally compelling and convincing, leading us to a particular view of political reality and endeavouring to attract our support for, or at least acceptance of, the maintenance and development of power structures that determine how we are governed. We have seen how the laws and regulations of our democracies are elevated to a position of reverence and mystery, and how undemocratic and coercive can be the experience of coming into conflict with them: we may be equal under the law, but fair access to it is denied to all but the most resourceful. We have seen too how illness cannot only deprive us of our health and well-being, but can also – as we are relegated to 'battlegrounds' on which the medical profession fights its wars with disease – rob us of our individuality and our personhood: doctors hold both our lives and our lifeworlds in their hands. Finally, we have seen how educational contexts – precisely the places in which we learn to develop our identities and rehearse the knowledge and understanding that will shape our negotiations with the world – contrive or connive to impose a model of learning that favours and requires a voice that is detached, impersonal or uninvolved.

The professional discourses that we have looked at simultaneously order our society and define our place within it, and there are significant similarities between them. Just as it is almost impossible, in a description of 'real language in real use', to separate out linguistic levels of analysis, so too it is difficult to distinguish definitively between different discourses. Reflecting the interdependent complexity of the society we live in, the professional genres draw on each other's resources: advertisers may look to educate us as well as to convince us to buy the goods or services they are promoting; medical treatment is governed by political as well as legal guidelines, and its discourse may variably be legalistic, educational or persuasive. Political discourse draws heavily on public relations, just as educational discourse draws on the impersonal scientific models that are so characteristic of medical writing. Texts have histories, but their annals are not necessarily of the same genre: a legal action may have its roots in the discourse of a medical issue; a political speech may be dealing with education; and medical information may be an advertisement in disguise.

At a general level, all the discourses studied here can be described, in one sense or another, as asymmetrical, and all share a resulting imbalance in power relations. Equally important, though, is the tension we have identified in the various discourses between the professional voice of institutions and the personal voice of lifeworld. Often this is a consequence of the representation of knowledge: be it legal, medical, educational, political or even commercial. From our earliest days at school to the last days leading to our death we are involved in conventionalized discourses which sanction particular views of knowledge (while rejecting and ignoring others) and authorize the way it is expressed.

Of course, our discussion has been limited to a few examples of discourse taken from a single culture. Clearly there is much more to examine. Nevertheless, I hope that what has been presented here – some practical advice for describing the data – will help you to study further discourses, be they other examples of the types discussed in this book (professional-public discourses such as those which take place in religious contexts or in areas of social policy, for example), those of more everyday writing practices or speech encounters (in which more symmetrical communicative exchanges may be enacted) or those constructed in different cultures. Indeed, it may be particularly interesting to examine cultural differences in discourse construction, as such analyses make visible the variability of expectations and assumptions that we bring with us to the enactment of discourse, and the diversity of conventions characteristic of different, culturally defined texts.

At the outset of this book, I emphasized the importance of context, which I defined loosely as the context we bring with us when we use language, the context that includes our social and cultural experience and expectations and the context which changes as we construct our relationships with others. And change is possible – not in the pseudo-political sense of 'change' as something that happens to us, and with which we have to somehow 'keep up'; but rather, as Norman Fairclough has said, as something in our own hands and under our own control – the way we can challenge and alter dominant discourses, and the roles they prescribe, by our engagement with them in particular social and cultural contexts. By noting, criticizing and resisting discourses that predetermine, classify and label us and the things that are important to us, we can challenge the professional orders that position us as credulous consumers, unsuspecting citizens, unwitting suspects, passive patients and silent students.

Notes

Chapter 1

1. Because of the popularity of the catchphrase, 'jubbly' may be on its way to acquiring a new meaning in Britain. A trawl on the Google search engine in February 2006 achieved almost 60,000 hits, with a considerable number featuring it as a slang term for 'money', along the lines of 'wonga' and 'dosh'.
2. *Life on the Home Front*, Reader's Digest Association (1993: 51–4).
3. The Nescafé adverts of the 1990s are a good example of how one discourse (advertising) may draw upon another (soap opera) for particular effect.
4. I am indebted to Larry Trask (1997) for this and for several other lucid definitions and examples.
5. Acronyms are another widely used form of abbreviation, but they differ from initialisms in tending to be pronounced as a single word – PIN (personal identification number) and ASBO (antisocial behaviour order) are well-known examples in Britain at the time of writing.
6. F = Feature headline, A = Advertisement slogan, AF = Advertorial headline
   Get balance in your crazy life (F)
   Your shape, your way (F)
   Less is more (F) & (A)
   Relax on the perfect sofa (F)
   Big, bold and beautiful (F)
   Small is beautiful (F)
   Entertaining ideas (A)
   Get into the groove (AF)
   Great hair, no effort (F)
   Real stock, real simple (A)
   The personal touch (AF)
   Stay perfect (A)
   What's your favourite way to dance? (A)
   Everything you need for the great outdoors (A)
   The secret of youthful looks (A)
   Want to colour away the years? (A)
   Curiously, 'less is more' appeared both as the headline of a fashion feature and as the slogan for a moisturizing cream.
7. Norman Fairclough defines synthetic personalization as 'a compensatory tendency to give the impression of treating each of the people "handled" en masse as an individual. Examples would be air travel (have a nice day!), restaurants (welcome to Wimpy!), and the simulated conversation (e.g. chat shows) and bonhomie which litter the media' (2001: 52).
8. For an exposition of the corporate use of 'we', see Fairclough (2001).
9. Presupposition is defined somewhat differently in various branches of linguistics (not to mention other disciplines). Here we are most interested in the analysis of presupposition as it relates to assumptions and propositions whose truth must be accepted in order for discourse to make sense.

10. Furthermore, as Fairclough (2001) and other critical discourse analysts note, presupposition serves as an ideological function which is pivotal to the creation of synthetic personalization. We will return to this theme and to the critical discourse approach in the next chapter.

Chapter 2

1. Throughout this chapter we will make frequent reference to Professor Norman Fairclough's highly acclaimed critical analysis of the discourse of the Labour Party in power in Britain at the time of writing: *New Labour New Language?* (2000).
2. See Chilton (2003) for further discussion of this example.
3. See Fairclough for an incisive account of Blair's use of 'Estuary English' (2000: 101).
4. See Wilson's (2001) review of his collaborative research with B. Gunn.
5. See Atkinson (1984) for a full discussion of the manner in which Margaret Thatcher changed her voice and other personal characteristics on becoming prime minister.
6. Geis (1987) notes that 'many studies of political discourse and language reveal their own political bias. This is inescapable. There is no such thing as value free analysis.'
7. Collocation refers to the tendency for certain words to occur together – for example, 'surgery' is highly likely to follow 'cosmetic'. Many words have such associations of which we are not consciously aware. See Fairclough (2000) for a full discussion of the adjective 'new' and its collocations in the discourse of New Labour.
8. 'Collateral damage' is defined by the USAF Intelligence Guide as 'unintentional damage or incidental damage affecting facilities, equipment or personnel occurring as a result of military actions', and the following example is provided: 'During Linebacker operations over North Vietnam…some incidental damage occurred from bombs falling outside target areas'. It is therefore a euphemism describing the killing of innocent civilians, not necessarily accidentally. 'Friendly fire' is, of course, just an oxymoron.
9. Reported in the *Sunday Times* (1 February 2004). Campbell's article originally appeared in *Today* (now defunct) in 1994.
10. Chilton explains that metaphor is not simply a linguistic expression that characterizes oratory and literature, but rather is a fundamental part of human conceptualization and communication (2003: 51).
11. See Charteris-Black (2005).
12. There is applause at this point on the video I have seen of the speech, but I am aware that it had been edited. Fairclough (2000: 105) drew my attention to this possibility.
13. Discourse analysts distinguish between *inclusive we* (me, you and, perhaps, others too) and *exclusive we* which excludes the addressee (me and the people I represent, but not you).
14. We shall be looking in more detail at the conversation analysis approach to turn-taking in the discussion of courtroom interaction in the next chapter; and we will consider topic management when we discuss doctor–patient consultations in chapter 4.

Chapter 3

1. Conley and O'Barr (2005) succinctly note that while the law exists to resolve human problems and regulate human behaviour, legal discourse is about neutral principles whose application transcends the variability of human life.
2. The exact origins of the principle are not apparent, but examples of prerogative writs frequently have wordings such as *Praecipimus tibi quod corpus in custodia vostra detentum, una cum causa detentionis suae, habeas coram nobis ad subjiciendum,* or 'we demand that you produce in our court, for examination, the person in your custody, along with

the reason for his detention'. It would appear that this form of words has been abbreviated down to 'habeas corpus'; or, more precisely in legal terms, *habeas corpus ad subjiciendum*, since other types of habeas corpus writs exist.

3. Anna Trosburg (1997) examines a corpus from UK contract law (including statutes, judgements, rules and regulations) and finds that almost half the documents included feature statements of obligation, mostly introduced by 'shall'. Notably, prohibitions also showed *shall...not* as the preferred form of proscription.

4. See the review by Bhatia (1993).

5. Discussed by Judge Mark Painter, *Ohio Lawyers Weekly*, 12 April 2004.

6. Speech to launch Labour Party general election manifesto, 13 April 2005.

7. Questions are notoriously difficult to define. While some look to syntactic structure for a definition, it is clear that not all utterances that function as questions take interrogative form: an example might be 'you're not from round here, then'. Conversely, if we confine ourselves just to the examination of intention or function, and define questions as (for example) utterances that seek and/or receive a response, then we would have to say that rhetorical questions are not questions at all. In fact, many discourse analysts do work with precisely this functional definition. In the rest of this book we will examine the functions of many different forms of questions.

8. The notion of *adjacency pair* has been criticized by some discourse analysts. For example, and as we shall see later, first pair parts and second pair parts are often separated in real language use and so adjacency pairs are not always adjoining in discourse structures.

9. Researchers in conversation analysis have spent considerable time and effort trying to provide an adequate definition of 'interruption', and particularly to distinguish interruption from 'overlapping' speech. However, a fully adequate description has proved elusive. Traditional definitions which concentrated solely on the extent to which a speaker's turn was cut short by another's intrusion (e.g. by three, four or five words) are certainly inadequate, since our sense of being interrupted is related to the extent to which we feel that the topic of our turn has been violated. In other words, we are more likely to feel that we have been interrupted if our topics are cut short (if the interruption is used to change the theme of the conversation) than if the intrusion into our speaking turn engages with our chosen topic. For an interesting analysis of the forms and functions of interruptions in context, see James and Clarke (1993).

10. See for example, *Queensland Sun-Herald*, 12 July 1992, in which demands were persistently made for an independent public inquiry.

11. See Coulthard (1996) for a substantive analysis of the manner in which police scribes may 're-invent' spoken interviews with suspects.

12. See Brenda Danet, who concludes that, in the courtroom, 'one cannot separate what happened from the language that is used to describe or explain what happened. When the meaning of the act is ambiguous, the words we use to talk about it become critical' (1980: 189).

13. See Conley and O'Barr, who note that 'even if the witness answers in the negative, the denial may be lost in the flow of the lawyer's polemic' (2005: 26). Interestingly, in other contexts, tag questions have been classified as examples of 'powerless' language: in traditional approaches to describing women's language, for example, it was claimed that tag questions represent female speakers' tentativeness, hesitancy and unwillingness to state anything as conclusive (see for example, Lakoff 1975). We will return to the form and function of tag questions in our discussion of medical discourse in the next chapter.

14. For a full discussion of conversational turn-taking, see Sacks, Schegloff and Jefferson (1974).

Chapter 4

1. This term, which sounds archaic, was actually coined in 1957 by Tom Paterson, a specialist in military and business leadership. Paterson's research into the medical profession was conducted as a private favour for a friend, and although his findings were widely acclaimed at the time, his paper 'Aesculapian authority and the doctor–patient relationship' remained unpublished until 2000.
2. Note that the combination of technical vocabulary and vague wording found in medical discourse mirrors the amalgamation of similar types of vocabulary in legal writing. In both discourses, the mixture of specialized and ambiguous language appears to be a recipe for confusion and misunderstanding.
3. This figure of speech, incidentally, is known to linguists as synecdoche, where a part is used to represent a whole: 'we have three new faces on the staff' is a typical example, where *faces* represent *people*. The term also applies when a whole is used to represent a part: for example, 'England won by three runs', where *England* represents the national cricket *team.*
4. See Wakefield et al. (1998).
5. BBC News Online, 2 December 2001.
6. See, for example, BBC News Online, 13 March 2002.
7. See the report by Sarah Ramsey (2001).
8. *NHS Magazine*, March 2001.
9. Perhaps it is just a personal interpretation, but I cannot help feeling that the graphic representation of the 'i' in *immunization* is very reminiscent of the internationally recognized symbol for *information*. It reinforces the question, I feel, of whether the discourse in the documents is merely seeking to inform or, rather more subtly, to convince and persuade.
10. You will find the yes/no question, 'does drinking make it worse?' and a question calling for an either/or response: 'is the pain sharp or is it more of a dull ache?' In exercise 4c, we see a question that calls for a simple confirmation: 'feeling squeamish?'
11. We return to a discussion of the flexible relationship between the form and function of 'wh-' questions in the following chapter.
12. See, for example, Henzl (1990) and West (1984), but also Ainsworth-Vaughn (1998) for counter-evidence.

Chapter 5

1. See Galton et al. (1999).
2. Note that this is a shift which mirrors the trend away from doctor-directed to more patient-centred medical practice and discourse.
3. See Fairclough (2001) for an authoritative discussion of the role of 'common sense' in sustaining existing social orders and discourse practices.
4. Reported in *The Observer*, 15 September 2002.
5. Reported at BBC News Online, 22 February 2006.
6. For an interesting selection of papers on *critical language awareness*, see Fairclough (1992).
7. Wells (1993) claims that the triadic discourse structure composed in IRF is 'neither good or bad'. We return to discuss his arguments in more detail later.

Bibliography

Ainsworth-Vaughn, N., 1998, *Claiming Power in Doctor–Patient Talk*, Oxford: Oxford University Press.

——, 2001, 'The Discourse of Medical Encounters', in D. Schiffrin, D. Tannen and H. Hamilton (eds), *The Handbook of Discourse Analysis*, Oxford: Blackwell, 453–69.

Alexander, R., 2003, 'Oracy, Literacy and Pedagogy: International Perspectives', in E. Bearne, H. Dombey and T. Grainger (eds), *Classroom Interactions in Literacy*, Maidenhead: Open University Press, 23–35.

Anspach, R., 1988, 'Notes on the Sociology of Medical Discourse: the Language of Case Presentation', *Journal of Health and Social Behaviour* 29, 357–75.

Atkinson, J. and Drew, P., 1979, *Order in Court: the Organisation of Verbal Interaction in Judicial Settings*, London: Macmillan.

Atkinson, M., 1984, *Our Masters' Voices: the Language and Body Language of Politics*, London: Methuen.

Austin, J. L., 1962, *How to Do Things With Words*, Oxford: Clarendon Press.

Bakhtin, M., 1981, *The Dialogic Imagination: Four Essays*, ed. M. Holquist, trans. V. McGee, Austin: University of Texas Press.

Bakhtin, M., 1986, *Speech Genres and Other Late Essays*, Austin: University of Texas Press.

Barnes, D., 1976, *From Communication to Curriculum*, London: Penguin.

Barnes, D. and Todd, F., 1995, *Communication and Learning Revisited: Making Meaning Through Talk*, Portsmouth, NH: Heinemann.

Barry, C., Stevenson, F., Britten, N., Barber, N. and Bradley, C., 2001, 'Giving Voice to the Lifeworld. More Humane, More Effective Medical Care? A Qualitative Study of Doctor–Patient Communication in General Practice', *Social Science and Medicine* 53, 487–505.

Bax, M., 1986, 'Feelings for Feelings: Expressive Information and its Role in Doctor–Patient Communication', in T. Ensink, A. van Essen and T. van der Geest (eds), *Discourse Analysis and Public Life. Papers of the Groningen Conference on Medical and Political Discourse*, Dordrecht, Holland: Foris Publications, 101–22.

Bell, A., 1991, *The Language of News Media*, Oxford: Basil Blackwell.

Benkendorf, J., Prince, M., Rose, M., De Fina, A. and Hamilton, H., 2001, 'Does Indirect Speech Promote Nondirective Genetic Counseling? Results of a Sociolinguistic Investigation', *American Journal of Medical Genetics* 106, 99–207.

Bhatia, V. K., 1993, *Analysing Genre: Language Use in Professional Settings*, London: Longman.

Blanchard, C., Ruckdeschel, J., Blanchard, E., Arena, J., Saunders, N. and Malloy, D., 1983, 'Interactions Between Oncologists and Patients During Rounds', *Annals of Internal Medicine* 99, 694–9.

Blanchard, C., Labrecque, M., Ruckdeschel, J. and Blanchard, E., 1986, 'Information and Decision-Making Preferences of Hospitalized Adult Cancer Patients', *Social Science and Medicine* 27 (11), 1139–45.

Bogartz, H., 1997, *The Advanced Reader's Collocation Searcher* (ARCS), www.geocities.com/Athens/Acropolis/7033 (accessed 9 April 2006).

Bolinger, D., 1980, *Language: The Loaded Weapon*, London: Longman.

Brierley, S., 2002, *The Advertising Handbook*, 2nd edn, London: Routledge.

Brown, P. and Levinson, S. C., 1987, *Politeness: Some Universals in Language Usage*, Cambridge: Cambridge University Press.

Campbell, J., Smith, D., Boulton-Lewis, G., Brownlee, J., Burnett, P., Carrington, S. and Purdie, N., 2001, 'Students' Perceptions of Teaching and Learning: the Influence of Students' Approaches to Learning and Teachers' Approaches to Teaching', *Teachers and Teaching: Theory and Practice* 7 (2), 175–87.

Carroll, L., 1876, *The Hunting of the Snark: An Agony in Eight Fits*, New York: Macmillan and Company.

Cazden, C., 2001, *Classroom Discourse: the Language of Teaching and Learning*, Portsmouth, NH: Heinemann.

Charon, R., 1992, 'To Build a Case: Medical Histories as Traditions in Conflict', *Literature and Medicine* 11 (1), 115–32.

Charteris-Black, J., 2005, 'Britain as a Container: Immigration Metaphors in the 2005 Election Campaign', paper presented at *New Directions in Cognitive Linguistics, First UK Cognitive Linguistics Conference*, University of Sussex, 23–25 October 2005, Brighton, UK.

Chilton, P., 2003, *Analysing Political Discourse: Theory and Practice*, London: Routledge.

Clark, R., 1992, 'Principles and Practice of CLA in the Classroom', in N. Fairclough (ed.), *Critical Language Awareness*, London and New York: Longman, 141–73.

Coates, L., Beavin Bavelas, J. and Gibson, J., 1994, 'Anomalous Language in Sexual Assault Trial Judgements', *Discourse and Society* 5 (2), 189–206.

Conley, J. and O'Barr, W., 2005, *Just Words*, 2nd edn, Chicago: Chicago University Press.

Cordella, M., 2004, *The Dynamic Consultation: A Discourse Analytical Study of Doctor–Patient Communication*, Amsterdam: John Benjamin.

Cotterill, J., 1998, '"If it Doesn't Fit, You Must Acquit": Metaphor and the O. J. Simpson Criminal Trial', *Forensic Linguistics* 5 (2), 141–58.

——, 2002, '"Just One More Time..." Aspects of Intertextuality in the Trials of O. J. Simpson', in J. Cotterill (ed.), *Language in the Legal Process*, New York: Palgrave Macmillan, 35–53.

Coulmas, F., 1989, *The Writing Systems of the World*, Oxford: Basil Blackwell.

Coulthard, R. M., 1996, 'The Official Version: Audience Manipulation in Police Reports of Interviews with Suspects', in C. R. Caldas-Coulthard and R. M. Coulthard (eds), *Texts and Practices: Readings in Critical Discourse Analysis*, London: Routledge, 164–76.

——, 2002, 'Whose Voice Is It? Invented and Concealed Dialogue in Written Records of Verbal Evidence Produced by the Police', in J. Cotterill (ed.), *Language in the Legal Process*, New York: Palgrave Macmillan, 19–34.

Coyle, J., 1999, 'Exploring the Meaning of "Dissatisfaction" with Health Care: the Importance of "Personal Identity Threat"', *Sociology of Health and Illness* 21 (1), 95–123.

Crystal, D. and Davy, D., 1969, *Investigating English Style*, London: Longman.

Danet, B., 1980, '"Baby" or "Fetus"? Language and the Construction of Reality in a Manslaughter Trial', *Semiotica* 32, 187–219.

Davis, K., 1988, *Power Under the Microscope*, Dordrecht, Holland: Foris Publications.

Dillon, J. T., 1988, *Questioning and Teaching: a Manual of Practice*, New York: Teachers' College Press.

Disbrow, E. A., Bennett, H. L. and Owings, J. T., 1993, 'Preoperative Suggestion and Postoperative Recovery', *Western Journal of Medicine* 158, 488–92.

Dixon, A., 1983, 'Family Medicine – at a Loss for Words?', *Journal of the Royal College of General Practitioners* 33, 358–63.

Dombey, H., 2003, 'Moving forward together', in E. Bearne, H. Dombey and T. Grainger (eds), *Classroom Interactions in Literacy*, Maidenhead: Open University Press, 36–48.

Donnelly, W., 1986, 'Medical Language as Symptom: Doctor Talk in Teaching Hospitals', *Perspectives in Biology and Medicine* 30 (1), 81–94.

——, 1997, 'The Language of Medical Case Histories', *Annals of Internal Medicine* 127 (11), 1045–8.

Douglas, G. N., 1917, *South Wind*, London: Secker & Warburg.

Dunn, E. and Wolfe, J., 2001, 'Let go of Latin!', *Veterinary and Human Toxicology* 43 (4), 235–6.

Dyer, G., 1982, *Advertising as Communication*, London: Routledge.

Edwards, A. D. and Westgate, D. P., 1994, *Investigating Classroom Talk*, 2nd edn, London: Falmer Press.

English, E., Hargreaves, L. and Hislam, J., 2002, 'Pedagogical dilemmas in the National Literacy Strategy: Primary Teachers' Perceptions, Reflections and Classroom Behaviour', *Cambridge Journal of Education* 32 (1), 9–26.

Ensink, T., 1997, 'The Footing of a Royal Address: An Analysis of Representativeness in Political Speech, Exemplified in Queen Beatrix' Address to the Knesset on March 28, 1995', in C. Schäffner (ed.), *Analysing Political Speeches*, Clevedon: Multilingual Matters, 5–32.

Erickson, F. E., 1982, 'Classroom Discourse as Improvisation: Relationships between Academic Task Structure and Social Participation Structures in Lessons', in L. Wilkinson (ed.), *Communicating in the Classroom*, New York and London: Academic Press, 153–82.

Evans, K., 1998, *The Language of Advocacy*, London: Blackstone.

Fairclough, N. (ed.), 1992, *Critical Language Awareness*, London and New York: Longman.

Fairclough, N., 1995, *Critical Discourse Analysis. The Critical Study of Language*, London: Longman.

——, 2000, *New Labour, New Language?*, London: Routledge.

——, 2001, *Language and Power*, 2nd edn, London: Longman.

——, 2003, *Analysing Discourse: Textual Analysis for Social Research*, London and New York: Routledge.

Fairclough, N. and Wodak, R., 1997, 'Critical Discourse Analysis', in T. van Dijk (ed.), *Discourse as Social Interaction*, London: Sage, vol. 2, 258–85.

Fleischman, S., 2001, 'Language and Medicine', in D. Schiffrin, D. Tannen and H. Hamilton (eds), *The Handbook of Discourse Analysis*, Oxford: Blackwell, 470–502.

Foster, M., 1995, 'Talking That Talk: The Language of Control, Curriculum and Critique', *Linguistics and Education* 7, 129–50.

Frankel, R., 2002, 'The (Socio)linguistic Turn in Physician–Patient Communication Research', in J. Alatis, H. Hamilton and A. Tan (eds), *Round Table on Languages and Linguistics 2000. Linguistics, Language and the Professions: Education, Journalism, Law, Medicine, and Technology*, Washington, DC: Georgetown University Press, 81–103.

Galton, M., Hargreaves, L., Comber, C. and Wall, D., with Pell, A., 1999, *Inside the Primary Classroom: 20 Years On*, London: Routledge.

Geis, M., 1987, *The Language of Politics*, New York: Springer Verlag.

Gibbons, J., 1994, 'Introduction: Language Constructing Law', in J. Gibbons (ed.), *Language and the Law*, London: Longman, 3–10.

Goddard, A., 1998, *The Language of Advertising*, London: Routledge.

Goffman, E., 1967, 'On Face-Work: An Analysis of Ritual Elements in Social Interaction', reprinted in A. Jaworski and N. Coupland (eds), 1999, *The Discourse Reader*, London: Routledge, 306–20.

Goodrich, P., 1987, *Legal Discourse: Studies in Linguistics, Rhetoric and Legal Analysis*, Basingstoke: Macmillan Press.

Grice, P., 1975, 'Logic and Conversation', reprinted in A. Jaworski and N. Coupland (eds), 1999, *The Discourse Reader*, London: Routledge, 76–88.

Hadlow, J. and Pitts, M., 1991, 'The Understanding of Common Health Terms by Doctors, Nurses and Patients', *Social Science and Medicine* 32 (2), 193–6.

Haidet, P., Hamel, M., Davis, R., Wenger, N., Reding, D., Kussin, P., Connors, A., Lynn, J., Weeks, J., Phillips, R. and other support investigators, 1998, 'Outcomes, Preferences for Resuscitation, and Physician–Patient Communication among Patients with Metastatic Colorectal Cancer', *The American Journal of Medicine* 105 (3), 222–9.

Halliday, M. and Hasan, R., 1976, *Cohesion in English*, London: Longman.

Hardman, F., Smith, F. and Wall, K., 2003, 'Interactive Whole Class Teaching in the National Literacy Strategy', *Cambridge Journal of Education* 33 (2), 197–215.

Harres, A., 1998, '"But Basically You're Feeling Well, Are You?": Tag Questions in Medical Consultations', *Health Communication* 10 (2), 111–23.

Harris, S., 2001, 'Fragmented Narratives and Multiple Tellers: Witness and Defendant Accounts in Trials', *Discourse Studies* 3 (1), 53–74.

Henzl, V., 1990, 'Linguistic Means of Social Distancing in Physician–Patient Communication', in W. von Raffler-Engel (ed.), *Doctor–Patient Interaction*, Amsterdam: John Benjamin, 77–91.

Heydon, G., 2005, *The Language of Police Interviewing*, New York: Palgrave Macmillan.

Holland, J., Geary, N., Marchini, A. and Tross, S., 1987, 'An International Survey of Physician Attitudes and Practice in Regard to Revealing the Diagnosis of Cancer', *Cancer Investigation* 5 (2), 151–4.

Holmes, J., 1984, 'Hedging your Bets and Sitting on the Fence: Some Evidence for Hedges as Support Structures', *Te Reo* 27, 47–62.

Hunter, K., 1991, *Doctor's Stories: The Narrative Structure of Medical Knowledge*, Princeton, NJ: Princeton University Press.

Hymes, D., 1964, 'Introduction: Towards Ethnographies of Communication', in J. Gumperz and D. Hymes (eds), 'The Ethnography of Communication', *American Anthropologist* 66 (6), 1–34.

Hymes, D., 1971, 'Sociolinguistics and the Ethnography of Speaking', in E. Ardener (ed.), *Social Anthropology and Linguistics*, Association of Social Anthropologists, Monograph 10, London: Tavistock, 47–93.

Hymes, D., 1972, 'On Communicative Competence', in J. Pride and J. Holmes (eds), *Sociolinguistics*, Harmondsworth: Penguin, 269–85.

Ivanič, R. and Simpson, J., 1992, 'Who's Who in Academic Writing?', in N. Fairclough (ed.), *Critical Language Awareness*, London and New York: Longman, 141–73.

James, D. and Clarke, S., 1993, 'Women, Men and Interruptions: a Critical Review', in D. Tannen (ed.), *Gender and Conversational Interaction*, Oxford: Oxford University Press, 231–80.

Johnson, D. and Murray, J., 1985, 'Do Doctors Mean What they Say?', in D. Enright (ed.), *Fair of Speech: The Uses of Euphemism*, Oxford: Oxford University Press, 151–8.

Johnstone, B., 2002, *Discourse Analysis*, Oxford: Blackwell Publishing.

Kai, J., 1996, 'Parents' Difficulties and Information Needs in Coping with Acute Illness in Preschool Children: a Qualitative Study', *British Medical Journal* 313, 987–90.

Kiralfy, A. K. (ed.), 1958, *Potter's Historical Introduction to English Law*, 4th edn, London: Sweet & Maxwell.

Klinck, D., 1992, *The Word of the Law*, Ottawa: Carleton University Press.

Labov, W., 1972, *Language in the Inner City: Studies in the Black English Vernacular*, Philadelphia, PA: University of Pennsylvania Press.

Lakoff, R., 1975, *Language and a Woman's Place*, New York: Harper & Row.

Leacock, S., 1924, *Garden of Folly*, Toronto: S. B. Grundy.

Leith, D., 1983, *A Social History of English*, London: Routledge.

Ley, P., 1979, 'Memory for Medical Information', *British Journal of Social and Clinical Psychology* 18, 318–24.

Linell, P. and Jonsson, L., 1991, 'Suspect Stories: On Perspective Setting in an Asymmetrical

Situation', in I. Markova and K. Foppa (eds), *Asymmetries in Dialogue*, Hemel Hempstead: Harvester Wheatsheaf, 75–100.

Maley, Y., 1994, 'The Language of Law', in J. Gibbons (ed.), *Language and the Law*, London: Longman, 11–50.

Matoesian, G. M., 1993, *Reproducing Rape: Domination Talk in the Courtroom*, Cambridge: Polity Press.

McKinstry, B., 2000, 'Do Patients Wish to be Involved in Decision Making in the Consultation? A Cross-Sectional Survey with Video Vignettes', *British Medical Journal* 321, 867–71.

Mehan, H., 1979, *Learning Lessons*, Cambridge, MA: Harvard University Press.

Mellinkoff, D., 1963, *The Language of the Law*, Boston: Little, Brown.

Mercer, N., 1992, 'Talk for Teaching and Learning', in K. Norman (ed.), *Thinking Voices: The Work of the National Literacy Project*, London: Hodder & Stoughton (for the National Curriculum Council), 215–23.

Mishler, E., 1984, *The Discourse of Medicine: Dialectics of Medical Interviews*, Norwood, NJ: Ablex Publishing Corporation.

Mitchum, P., 1990, 'Verbal and Nonverbal Communication in a Family Practice Consultation: A Focus on the Physician–Patient Relationship', in W. von Raffler-Engel (ed.), *Doctor–Patient Interaction*, Amsterdam: John Benjamin, 109–57.

Myhill, D. and Warren, P., 2005, 'Scaffolds or Straitjackets? Critical Moments in Classroom Discourse', *Educational Review* 57 (1), 55–69.

Navasky, V., 1982, *Naming Names*, Boston: John Calder.

Nystrand, M., Gamoran, A., Kachur, R. and Prendergast, C., 1997, *Opening Dialogue: Understanding the Dynamics of Language and Learning in the English Classroom*, New York: Teachers' College Press.

Ong, L., De Haes, J., Hoos, A. and Lammes, F., 1995, 'Doctor–Patient Communication: a Review of the Literature', *Social Science and Medicine* 40 (7), 903–18.

Orwell, G., 1936, *Keep the Aspidistra Flying*, London: Victor Gollancz Ltd.

——, 1946, 'Politics and the English Language', in W. F. Bolton and D. Crystal (eds), 1969, *The English Language. Vol. 2: Essays by Linguistics and Men of Letters, 1858–1964*, Cambridge: Cambridge University Press, 217–19.

——, 1954 (first published 1949), *Nineteen Eighty-Four*, Harmondsworth: Penguin Books in association with Martin Secker & Warburg.

Paterson, T., 2000, 'Aesculapian Authority and the Doctor–Patient Relationship', *Journal of Orthomolecular Medicine* 15, 82–8.

Pinker, S., 2002, *The Blank Slate: the Modern Denial of Human Nature*, London: Allen Lane.

Pliskin, K., 1997, 'Verbal Intercourse and Sexual Communication: Impediments to STD Prevention', *Medical Anthropology Quarterly* 11 (1), 89–109.

Priestley, J. B., 1966, *The Moments and Other Pieces*, London: Heinemann.

Ramsey, S., 2001, 'UK Starts Campaign to Reassure Parents about MMR-Vaccine Safety', *The Lancet* 357: 290.

Reiser, S., 1980, 'Words as Scalpels: Transmitting Evidence in the Clinical Dialogue', *Annals of Internal Medicine* 92 (6), 837–42.

Russell, S., 2002, '"Three's a Crowd": Shifting Dynamics in the Interpreted Interview', in J. Cotterill (ed.), *Language in the Legal Process*, New York: Palgrave Macmillan, 111–26.

Sacks, H., Schegloff, E. and Jefferson, G., 1974, 'A Simplest Systematics for the Organisation of Turn-Taking for Conversation', *Language* 50 (4), 696–735.

Sauer, C., 1997, 'Echoes from Abroad – Speeches for the Domestic Audience: Queen Beatrix' Address to the Israeli Parliament', in C. Schäffner (ed.), *Analysing Political Speeches*, Clevedon: Multilingual Matters, 33–67.

Searle, J. R., 1965, 'What is a Speech Act?', in M. Black (ed.), *Philosophy in America*, Ithaca, NY: Cornell University Press, 221–39.

Sinclair, J. and Brazil, D., 1982, *Teacher Talk*, Oxford: Oxford University Press.

Sinclair, J. and Coulthard, R. M., 1975, *Towards an Analysis of Discourse: the English used by Teachers and Pupils*, Oxford: Oxford University Press.

Shuy, R. W., 1993, *Language Crimes: The Use and Abuse of Language Evidence in the Courtroom*, Oxford: Blackwell.

Smeeth, L., Cook, C., Fombonne, E., Heavey, L., Rodrigues, L., Smith, P. and Hall, A., 2004, 'MMR Vaccination and Pervasive Developmental Disorders: a Case-Control Study', *The Lancet* 34, 963–9.

Stubbs, M., 1983, *Discourse Analysis: The Sociolinguistic Analysis of Natural Language*, Oxford: Blackwell.

Stygall, G., 2002, 'Textual Barriers to U.S. Immigration', in J. Cotterill (ed.), *Language in the Legal Process*, London and New York: Palgrave, 35–53.

Tate, P., 2003, *The Doctor's Handbook*, 3rd edn, Abingdon: Radcliffe Medical Press.

ten Have, P., 1989, 'The Consultation as Genre', in B. Torode (ed.), *Text and Talk as Social Practice*, Dordrecht, Holland: Foris Publications, 115–135.

The, A.-M., Hak, T., Koëter, G. and van der Wal, G., 2000, 'Collusion in Doctor–Patient Communication about Imminent Death: an Ethnographic Study', *British Medical Journal* 321, 1376–81.

Trask, L., 1997, *A Student's Dictionary of Language and Linguistics*, London: Arnold.

——, 1999, *Key Concepts in Language and Linguistics*, London and New York: Routledge.

Trosburg, A., 1997, 'Contracts as social action', in B. Gunnarsson, P. Linell and B. Nordberg (eds), *The Construction of Professional Discourse*, London: Longman Pearson Educational, 54–75.

Tsui, A., Marton, F., Mok, I. and Ng, D., 2004, 'Questions and the Space for Learning', in F. Marton and A. Tsui (eds), *Classroom Discourse and the Space for Learning*, Mahwah, NJ: Lawrence Erlbaum Associates, 113–37.

van Dijk, T., 2001, 'Critical Discourse Analysis', in D. Schiffrin, D. Tannen and H. Hamilton (eds), *The Handbook of Discourse Analysis*, Oxford: Blackwell, 352–71.

Vestergaard, T. and Schrøder, K., 1985, *The Language of Advertising*, Oxford: Blackwell.

Wakefield, A., Murch, S., Anthony, A., Linnell, J., Casson, D., Malik, M., Berelowitz, M., Dhillon, A., Thomson, M., Harvey, P., Valentine, A., Davies, S. and Walker-Smith, J., 1998, 'Ileal-Lymphoid-Nodular Hyperplasia, Non-Specific Colitis, and Pervasive Developmental Disorder in Children', *The Lancet* 351, 637–41.

Wells, G., 1993, 'Reevaluating the IRF Sequence: a Proposal for the Articulation of Theories of Activity and Discourse for the Analysis of Teaching and Learning in the Classroom', *Linguistics and Education* 5, 1–37.

West, C., 1984, '"Ask Me No Questions…" An Analysis of Queries and Replies in Physician–Patient Dialogs', in A. T. Fisher (ed.), *The Social Organisation of Doctor–Patient Communication*, Washington, DC: Centre for Applied Linguistics, 55–75.

Widdowson, H., *Teaching Language as Communication*, Oxford: Oxford University Press.

Wilson, J., 1990, *Politically Speaking*, Oxford: Blackwell.

——, 2001, 'Political Discourse', in D. Schiffrin, D. Tannen and H. Hamilton (eds), *The Handbook of Discourse Analysis*, Oxford: Blackwell, 399–415.

Wood, E. and Attfield, J., 1996, *Play, Learning and the Early Childhood Curriculum*, London: Paul Chapman.

Index

Lightning Source UK Ltd.
Milton Keynes UK
01 March 2011

168430UK00004B/32/P